UNEQUAL BRITAIN

Unequal Britain

Equalities in Britain since 1945

Pat Thane ed.

Contributors:

Liza Filby, Nick Kimber, Helen McCarthy,
Simon Millar, Mel Porter, Becky Taylor

Centre for Contemporary British History,
Institute of Historical Research, University of London

continuum

Continuum UK, The Tower Building, 11 York Road, London SE1 7NX
Continuum US, 80 Maiden Lane, Suite 704, New York, NY 10038

www.continuumbooks.com

Collection and Introduction © Pat Thane 2010
Foreword © Julia Neuberger
The copyright of each essay resides with the author

The material in this book was originally commissioned for the Equalities Review.
All material has been reworked for this publication.

First published 2010

British Library Cataloguing-in-Publication Data
A catalogue record for this book is available from the British Library.

ISBN 978 1 84706 298 7

Typeset by Pindar NZ, Auckland, New Zealand
Printed and bound by MPG Books Ltd, Cornwall, Great Britain

Contents

Illustrations

Figures

Foreword

Julia Neuberger

This is a book that should make its readers very angry. It details the changes in how various minority, and majority, groups, hitherto and often still disadvantaged, have fared since the end of the Second World War. It's not that things have not got better. Of course they have. Women do not have to put up with the stereotypes of the willing housewife of the post war period, and the various expectations made of them back in 1945, even though they had been massively engaged in the war effort and were more professionalised than they had ever been. Older people have pensions and an entitlement to free health care in the NHS. Homosexuals are 'out' these days, and most people under 60 simply do not turn a hair at the idea that someone is gay or straight, or somewhere in between, except within some of our religious institutions, where sex and sexuality appear to cause more upset than what many of us would describe as 'real' moral issues, such as the ignoring of isolated older people. Disabled people, if physically disabled, have made huge strides in being able to get about, now that there are widespread rules and regulations that force public access buildings to provide wheelchair friendly access. People with enduring mental health issues are increasingly campaigning for better treatment, as well as represented by a variety of organisations, and the idea that they would be incarcerated in a long stay institution for life is seen as shocking, and is long behind us. People with learning disabilities increasingly live in the community, in small group homes, and are visible, out and about, whilst 'racist' is truly a word of abuse, even though we are seeing a slight growth in the electability of the far right racist BNP.

So, in a way, one could argue that this book should not be necessary. Or that it should make us feel pleased with ourselves and our efforts. We have improved things. It's better for most disadvantaged, formerly discriminated against, groups. Except that that is not true, in two important respects. First, racism is undeniably there, though different, and is to be perceived particularly in the growing hostility towards Muslims, and the capacity that many otherwise sensible and tolerant people seem to have to misunderstand Islam as a religion. They see it as a faith in which there are no disagreements and different shades and movements, unlike, say Christianity, where everyone knows there are High and Low churches, Protestant and Catholic, orthodox and free, where there are as many opinions as church members Or, if you take Judaism, the spectrum ranges from the ultra orthodox who

wear eighteenth century dress as their normal clothes and live an entirely
separate life from the rest of the community, to the most liberal of Liberal
Jews, and many stops on the way. Yet Islam is lambasted as if there are no
shades of opinion, as if it is theologically designed to destroy the west. It
is a dangerous and perverted criticism, yet it is also widespread, and one
might argue that it is the new form of racism, as Liza Filby argues to some
extent in her chapter.

Then, although older people are now not suffering from the abject poverty
to be found all too often in the late 1940s and 1950s, they are still surprisingly
discriminated against in all sorts of areas. They are caricatured, described
as 'wrinklies', shown bent over on sticks on road signs, and excluded from
paid work in all too many circumstances. More importantly even than that,
the very health services which have relieved so many of the worries older
people used to express before the NHS existed, also discriminates against
them. Older women (over 70) are not called for routine breast screening,
even though the incidence of breast cancer increases with age. It is as if the
NHS itself has deemed the life of older women to be worthless. Similarly,
older people with mental illness, a double whammy, as it were, are often not
offered the same support or even the same drugs as younger people. It is
only recently (October 2009) that the Royal College of Psychiatrists, which
itself had perpetuated the organisation of services for older people with
mental illness as a separate specialty, have started campaigning for equal
treatment and equal regard for people with mental illness at whatever age.
Add into that the evidence about the abuse of the use of drugs commonly
used for schizophrenia being given to older people with dementia to keep
them quiet, and you have a very worrying view of older people emerging.
Meanwhile, specialist geriatricians seem to describe older people's quality
of life in quite different terms from those older people themselves use, as
if being old somehow disables you from being able to tell what matters
to you, and what makes your life worth living. And, if you then examine
the training, pay and conditions for the care workers who look after older
people in care homes, you might well argue wonder whether we as a society
value our older people at all. That is all the more worrying as we are ageing
significantly as a society.

But, of all the categories of discrimination discussed in this volume,
the one that is the most heart rending is about Gypsies and Travellers, for
whom the picture has barely brightened since 1945, and for whom tolerance is little greater than it was, and local authority provision arguably even
worse. Gypsies still have problems locating school places for their children
(especially in schools where places are much in demand), authorised sites
are still often in places where people do not want to be, and, from the 1990s
onwards, if the sites are not 'official', the rate of eviction from land Gypsies
have occupied over long periods has been increasing considerably. The
effigy of a Traveller van burned at a bonfire night in a Sussex village in 2003
did not lead to prosecution after the organisers claimed there had been
problems with Travellers camping on local farm land. And government has

done little to restore the old 'official' sites, presumably believing that, if the problem is ignored long enough, it will simply disappear. In 2005, a MORI poll conducted for Stonewall found that Gypsies and Travellers were the group people were most likely to be prejudiced against. The story from 1945 to the present day suggests this is not just the population's view, but that of the government and the wider social leadership.

Things do not change without concerted effort. This book tells us where and how it happened that things improved for Jews and Afro-Caribbeans, for gays and transsexuals. But it is what is *not* said, the history *not* written here, which really begs the question. Who is really campaigning seriously for the rights of older people? And who is really concerned about Travellers, Gypsies, and their children? Inequality still exists. Health inequalities are widening in society, and child poverty is ever present. This is a book to read to set the record straight, but it begs many further questions of us all – the greatest of which is the obvious one. Why, in the last sixty years and more, have we not achieved more?

Julia Neuberger
November 2009

Introduction

Pat Thane

Since the end of World War II in 1945, there have been greater changes in relation to equalities than at any period of similar length in British history. In 1945, most forms of inequality – relating to age, race and ethnicity, religion, gender, sexual orientation or disability – were deep-rooted, taken-for-granted facts of British culture, rarely discussed openly and even less openly challenged by most of those who experienced inequality. Since then, there has been a remarkable growth in recognition of the dimensions of most of these inequalities, and some social groups have acquired legal rights, entitlements, social respect and cultural recognition to a degree that was unimaginable at the end of World War II. But not all groups have gained equally:

1. In 1945, older people were recognized as victims of poverty and beginning to speak up against it. It was hardly at all recognized that they were treated inequitably in the workplace, the health care system and other services, and unjustly undervalued in society in general. Only in recent years, as the number of articulate older people has grown and they have demanded equal treatment, and as their importance to the economy has become more obvious – with more of them staying fit to later ages and the number of younger workers declining – have they begun to gain some legal protection against unequal treatment. Nevertheless, age discrimination remains embedded in British culture and is only recently and slowly beginning to shift.

2. After World War II, awareness of the persecution of Jews in Europe increased public sensitivity to open expressions of anti-Semitic racism, but it did not eliminate prejudice against Jews as a race and Judaism as a religion. At that time, there were no legal barriers to discriminatory language or treatment directed at any racial or religious group, apart from the century-old Blasphemy Act, which protected only Christians against abuse. With increasing immigration of people from a broader range of cultures from the late 1940s, inequalities were increasingly pervasive and damaging to social cohesion and economic success. Inequalities that were initially identified with race were seen also to apply to religious groups; in the case of Muslims, this occurred very openly after the events of September 11th, 2001 (9/11, as it is popularly known) but in reality it was in place long before. A combination of

pressure from representatives of those experiencing inequality, with support from sympathetic others and goodwill from governments (more from some than others), has led to a situation where everyone, in principle, has the right to legal protection against abuse and unequal treatment based on race or religion. Legal change has probably moved faster than cultural change in this as in other dimensions of inequality, but now, in contrast to 1945, legal rights exist, to be invoked by those who experience inequality.

3. Still, all minority ethnic groups do not have equal life chances. Gypsies and Travellers fare worst on most key indicators, including health, educational attainment and employment, and they experience much overt prejudice. They have found it hardest of all to gain recognition of the inequalities they experience, partly because their migratory culture and relatively small numbers have made it difficult for them to connect with potential supporters in the wider community and to make their case known. Only very recently have their inequalities been clearly acknowledged officially, although they are far from being resolved.

4. Women are not a small minority but a majority of the population, many of them well connected to the wider community and to political groupings. By 1945, after more than 100 years of campaigning, women had the vote and improved access to public life, the law, education and the workplace, although massive gender inequalities remained in all spheres of their lives. Up to the present, continual campaigning, combined with gradual cultural shifts, has brought changes in the law, granting women legal protection against unequal treatment in most spheres, as well as greater cultural acceptance of the principle of gender equality. But substantial inequalities in opportunities and outcomes remain between males and females among all social and economic groups in all spheres, including the workplace. However, in some otherwise particularly disadvantaged groups, such as Pakistani and Bangladeshi communities, women are closer than men to the educational attainment of the rest of the population.

5. If inequalities of race and gender were at least publicly acknowledged in 1945, 'homosexuals' were social outcasts, deemed to deserve punishment rather than equal rights. Theirs was indeed 'the love that dare not speak its name'. The notion that they might be regarded as being as 'Good As You' – as activists began to propose in the 1970s – was unimaginable to most people 25 years earlier. Despite continuing instances of homophobia, the shift towards cultural acceptance and legal equality since the 1960s, when lesbians and gay men began to demand equality, has been dramatic – from imprisonment to civil partnerships.

6. Also dramatic, in a quieter way, has been the transformed experience of the smaller number of transsexual and transgender people. In 1945, most people hardly acknowledged, or probably even knew about, their situation. They now have formal legal rights to live equally with people of their lived gender, although these have been very recently acquired

and serious problems of implementing them remain. Again, these changes have been achieved as a result of campaigning by articulate, highly educated trans people, directed at politicians in Britain and the European Union, and by action in the law courts. The potential for increased equality has been assisted by developments in medical expertise and gradual changes in attitudes in the medical profession, enabling those who desire and need it to receive appropriate treatment.

7. In contrast, many forms of physical and mental disability have been publicly well known for centuries. Some disabilities – generally, physical disabilities such as being blind, deaf or dumb – have always been more sympathetically treated than others, such as mental disabilities. For centuries there have been efforts, within the limits of available resources, to enable physically disabled people to live their lives as fully as possible in the community, while large-scale institutionalization even of the seriously mentally ill dates only from the eighteenth century. Nevertheless, in 1945, there were low expectations of what most disabled people could achieve. Since then, scientific development in various forms has changed the definitions and experiences of disability. The range of conditions defined as 'disabilities' has grown, largely driven by developments in medical treatment and diagnosis. For example, depression and attention deficit disorder were long regarded as essentially 'social' conditions: people 'feeling a bit low', children 'being naughty'. Now they can be medically defined and treated. At the same time, technological change has expanded the capacity of society to enable some disabled people to live like everyone else, aided by smart wheelchairs, adapted motor vehicles, computer technology and other innovations that were unimaginable to most people in 1945. And, as in all other areas of inequality, the increasingly articulate demands of disabled people themselves has increased access to support and achieved legal and cultural changes. These, at least in principle, protect them against previously accepted attitudes that anyone with a 'disability' was inferior to everyone else.

'Good As You' could have been the campaign slogan for any of the groups whose experience in the recent past is surveyed in this report. This is what they have all aspired to, in different ways, on different timescales and with different outcomes (although all, to some degree, positive). None has yet achieved the degree of cultural and legal equality they aspire to. But since 1945, they have come closer, as a result of political leadership at local, British and European Union levels, broad social, economic and cultural trends and, above all, by making their own voices heard as never before, using media opportunities that were unthinkable at the end of World War II. This legacy of successfully speaking up is perhaps their best guide for the future.

The chapters that follow should be read in the context of key aspects of change in Britain since 1945:

- **Population**
  - 1945 to early 1970s: high birth rate compared with the periods immediately before and after; falling death rate; high marriage rate and low divorce and 'illegitimacy' rates; rising immigration, first from Europe then from the Commonwealth
  - early 1970s to the present: falling birth rate; falling marriage rate; rising divorce and 'illegitimacy' rates; increasing life and health expectancy; substantial immigration from the Commonwealth, then increasingly from other European countries and from crisis-hit countries worldwide.
- **Work**
  - 1945 to 1970s: full employment (for men); high but falling levels of industrial employment; increasing female employment, a large proportion of it part-time
  - mid-1970s to present: decline of heavy industry; increased service employment, on a spectrum ranging from low-paid (such as fast-food and call-centre industries) to high-paid work (such as financial services)
  - early 1980s to mid-1990s: high unemployment, particularly among men, older workers and some minority ethnic groups
  - 1980s to present: increased hours of work and of reported stress at work, but not the extreme shift away from the 'job for life' towards short-term contracts often assumed, except in a few sectors;[1] steadily expanding range of employment open to women (although much of it still part-time) and members of some minority ethnic groups, but still with inadequate pay, promotion and training opportunities; unemployment rising again in 2008–9.
- **Education**
  - 1945 to present: increasing length of stay in formal education following the minimum leaving age rising to 15 in 1947 and 16 in 1973; steadily increasing numbers staying on in education and entering university, and increased numbers passing national examinations, particularly girls and members of some minority ethnic groups.
- **Social class**
  - Since 1945: increased numbers identifying as 'middle class', but a substantial, low-paid 'underclass' remains. Persistent differences relating to economic situation remain among males and females and within all ethnic groups, including White British people, in educational achievement, income, health and life expectancy.
- **Poverty**
  - 1945 to early 1970s: narrowing of the gap between richest and poorest
  - 1980s to present: widening of the gap between richest and poorest, with slight narrowing in early 2000s, particularly between lowest and middle incomes.

- **Culture**
  - 1960s to present: a less deferential culture, more critical of government and knowledge elites (such as the medical profession), evidenced in a less deferential, more intrusive and critical media and more assertive activist groups; increased access to a widening range of mass media.
- **Travel**
  - 1946 to present: greater ease of movement around the world for pleasure and for work (both legal and illegal economic migration); increasing awareness of and contact with other cultures.

Chapter 1

Older people and equality

Pat Thane

TIMELINE

1908	Means-tested state Old Age Pensions introduced in the United Kingdom at age 70.
1925	National Insurance pension introduced for insured manual workers at age 65.
1935	National Spinsters' Pensions Association campaigns for lower pension age for women.
1938	Pensioners form National Federation of Retirement Pensions Associations to fight for higher pensions.
1939	Report of Select Committee on Pensions for Unmarried Women.
1930s–50s	Concern about ageing of the population.
1940	Pension age for women reduced to 60; supplementary pension introduced for poorest pensioners. Foundation of campaigning group that became Age Concern.
1942	Beveridge Report.
1946	National Insurance Act introduced universal pensions from 1948.
1947	Foundation of National Corporation for the Care of Old People, later the Centre for Policy on Ageing.
1948	National Health Service and National Assistance Board established.
1950s–60s	Spread of retirement at 60–5. 'Rediscovery' of poverty among older people.
1952–3	National Advisory Committee on the Employment of Older Men and Women.
1954	Committee on the Economic and Financial Problems of Old Age.
1961	Formation of Help the Aged.
1965	State pensions increased.
1975	Social Security Pensions Act introduces State Earnings-Related Pension Scheme.

1979	Trades Union Congress forms National Pensions' Convention.
	Increased militancy of older people about continuing low level of pensions.
1980s–90s	Spread of early retirement.
	Fall in real value of state pension.
	Deregulation of private pensions.
	Increased concern about ageing of the population.
	Pensioners campaign about inadequate pensions and discrimination against older workers.
1988	Formation by retired people of Campaign against Age Discrimination in Employment.
1990	Equalization of male and female pension ages at 65 to be implemented gradually, following European Union ruling.
1992	Maxwell scandal.
1992	Scottish Pensioners Forum set up.
1998	Third Age Employment Network set up.
2000s	Closure and cutback of many public and private sector employer pension schemes.
2006	Employment Equality (Age) Regulations introduced in response to European Union initiative to end age discrimination in the workplace.
2007	Pensions Act, 2007.
	Equality and Human Rights Commission opens, with responsibility to age equality (October).
2008	Pensions Act, 2008.

INTRODUCTION: BEFORE 1945

It is often thought that, until recently it was rare to grow old. In fact, throughout British history older people have been a substantial presence in society. Even in the eighteenth century, people aged over 60 constituted about 10 per cent of the English population. This was not exceptional.[1] Also throughout history, many older people, especially women, have experienced significant inequality, as one of the largest groups in poverty. Some also experienced severe discrimination – at the most extreme, the persecution of older women as witches in England and Scotland in the seventeenth century.

Modern campaigning by and on behalf of older people in Britain against various forms of inequality began in the late nineteenth century, when the Trades Union Congress (TUC), individual trade unions and working class activist groups campaigned, first for state pensions and then, through World War I and the 1920s and 1930s, for better pensions.[2] The pension, introduced in 1908, was very low, means-tested, not intended to provide a living income and not paid until the late age of 70. It was financed wholly from taxation and primarily designed to meet the needs of older women, due to their relatively high level of poverty. Of the 490,000 people who qualified for the first pensions on 1 January 1909, almost two-thirds were women.[3] The pension age was reduced to 65 in 1925, but only for (mainly male) workers in the national insurance scheme, which had been set up in 1911, and their widows. The pension remained very low, but it was felt to be less stigmatizing than the ancient Poor Law, previously the only public provision for impoverished people of all ages.

The campaigns of the 1920s and 1930s took place amid economic depression and high unemployment and, like today, concern at the rising numbers of older people and shrinking numbers of younger people. This was because, just as now, the birth rate had fallen while life expectancy was rising. Just as now, damaging social and economic effects were predicted. Publications by William Beveridge, often described as the architect of the modern welfare state, and the economist John Maynard Keynes, as well as government reports, stressed the challenges for society and the economy that were expected to result.[4]

Campaigning for improved pensions continued. In 1935, Florence White formed the National Spinsters' Pensions Association (NPSA) in Bradford, Yorkshire, to fight for a lower pension age for unmarried women – 55 instead of 65 – on the grounds that older women who needed to work for their living found it more difficult than men of comparable ages to enter or re-enter employment if, for example, they became unemployed or took time off to care for an older relative. They also claimed that they were likely to be dismissed at younger ages, due to age and gender prejudice. There is strong evidence that both claims were well founded. Many employers dismissed, or would not employ, women who were over a certain age because they were thought not 'decorative' enough, or due to ill-founded assumptions about their capabilities and rates of sickness. The NPSA consisted mainly of unmarried working and lower middle class women, including many textile workers. About 15 per cent of all women (and about 9 per cent of men) never married at this time, so they represented a substantial section of the population. Their lobbying led to the appointment of the Select Committee on Pensions for Unmarried Women, which reported in 1939.[5] It found that older women workers did have somewhat higher rates of absence due to sickness than men, but there was no evidence of their lesser capability for work. It led to the lowering of the pension age for all women to 60 in 1940, although the government did not admit that older women suffered discrimination in the workplace.

In 1938, the National Federation of Retirement Pensions Associations (NFRPA and, later, the National Federation of Old Age Pensions Associations, NFOAPA) was founded. It was formed by pensioners in Manchester who were concerned about poverty among older people, including those struggling to live on the very low state pension, and about the fact that unemployed older people found it harder to re-enter work than younger people. They gained press publicity and made contact with similar organizations being formed in London, mainly by working and lower middle class people, with support from the churches.

In 1939, these activists from Manchester and London demonstrated, lobbying the government for the pension to be doubled from 10s (50p) per week to £1. The Prime Minister, Neville Chamberlain's refusal on the grounds that all government expenditure should focus on the coming war was widely criticized in the press. Within six weeks, more than five million signatures were collected for a petition to double the pension. NFRPA members kept up pressure on their local members of parliament.

Perhaps as a result, a means-tested supplementary pension was introduced for the poorest pensioners in 1940. When first introduced, 1,275,000 pensioners received it. Not all who were eligible applied – a problem with means-tested or targeted benefits that has never been overcome – leaving many still in poverty. Nevertheless, the number of claimants far exceeded the 400,000 the government had estimated. *The Times* commented on 'a remarkable discovery of secret need'.[6] The new benefit was uprated in line with inflation throughout World War II, but still met only the most basic of pensioners' needs. Government investigations into the living conditions of the new supplementary pensioners revealed their serious poverty.[7] The very active local branches of NFRPA kept demanding higher basic pensions.

A meeting of civil servants and voluntary organizations that were concerned about old age poverty led to the formation in 1940 of the Committee for the Welfare of the Aged (CWA, soon changed to the Old People's Welfare Committee and, in the 1970s, to Age Concern, England). Its first chair was Eleanor Rathbone, the feminist Independent MP and campaigner for family allowances.[8] In close association with the National Council of Social Services, the CWA developed voluntary services, especially residential homes for older people, that were subsidized by the government. Its mission was to work *for* improvement in the health, welfare and pensions of the most deprived older people, rather than to encourage action *by* them.

In 1942, the Beveridge Report, *Social Insurance and Allied Services*, the foundation document of the modern welfare state, recommended the introduction of adequate, subsistence-level pensions for all. Because of the high cost, Beveridge proposed their introduction should be gradual, over a 20-year period. Due to his concern about the ageing of the population and in the light of evidence that many people were fit to work beyond age 65, Beveridge also recommended a flexible pension age, to discourage early retirement by providing higher pensions in return for later retirement. But on health service reform, the report stated that 'it is *dangerous* to be in any way lavish to old age until adequate provision has been assured for all other vital needs, such as the prevention of disease and the adequate nutrition of the young'(our emphasis).[9] This iconic social policy document took for granted discrimination against older people in health care, reflecting contemporary cultural assumptions that have not wholly disappeared.

These assumptions were challenged in evidence to the Beveridge committee, for instance by the National Council of Social Services, which pointed out how poorly older people were served by medical services already, compared with other groups, and demanded equal care with younger age groups. NFRPA was very critical of Beveridge's proposal for the gradual introduction of subsistence-level pensions, which, if adopted by the government, would have left many to die in poverty during the 20-year transition period.

1945 TO THE 1970s

The Labour government elected in 1945 introduced a path-breaking package of health and welfare reforms that came to be described as having created a 'welfare state'. This included the 1946 National Insurance Act, which was based on the Beveridge Report but differed in important respects from his recommendations. It introduced higher, universal pensions from 1948, but rejected Beveridge's proposal for a gradual transition to subsistence benefits. The new pensions were higher than previously, but still too low to live on without supplementation of some kind. Retirement from work was a condition of receiving the pension, but there was no serious attempt to offer incentives to delay retirement. Trade unions had long argued that, after years of labour, workers deserved retirement and a period of rest. In the eyes of the Labour government, this outweighed Beveridge's argument that the ageing of the population required later retirement.

Almost immediately, one million pensioners had to apply to the new National Assistance Board (formed in 1948) for a means-tested supplement because the pension was too low. Many more who were in need and would have qualified did not apply, for a variety of reasons that are imperfectly understood – perhaps due to people's pride and unwillingness to reveal their poverty, or simply because they did not know about their rights. This has been the situation for millions of pensioners ever since, most of them women. Men were more likely to receive occupational pensions through their workplace to supplement the state pension. These pensions were generally fixed according to income and years of work, and were often small. In 1953, 34 per cent of employed men and 18 per cent of employed women were eligible for an occupational pension; in 1991, there were 57 per cent and 37 per cent respectively.[10] Women, then and now, had unequal access to occupational or private pensions. Their employment records were shorter because of their caring responsibilities, they received relatively low pay when in work, and occupational pensions were simply not available to women in some occupations.[11] Similar problems of poverty in old age due to incomplete work and contribution records, low incomes and concentration in non-pensionable employment have been, and are, experienced by immigrants, Gypsies and Travellers, and people suffering from long-term disabilities.[12]

The failure of successive British governments to provide adequate basic pensions for all, comparable with those in most West European countries since the 1940s and 1950s, has been a major cause of pensioner poverty.[13] Through the 1950s and early 1960s, as already low pensions failed to keep up with inflation, further increasing pensioner poverty, the NFOAPA continued protesting to MPs and Ministers through large local meetings throughout the country and petitions to government, and in the press.[14] In 1953, 4,000 old age pensioners took part in a rally in Central Hall, Westminster. In 1955, the NFOAPA had 350,000 subscribers, overwhelmingly pensioners.

The inauguration of the National Health Service (NHS) in 1948 did much to help older people, including providing optical, dental and chiropody services. These were free of charge for the first time, to remedy often minor but seriously disabling conditions that were common among older people. One older woman in Glasgow was bedridden, apparently deaf and thought to be suffering from mild dementia. When her severe corns were treated, the impacted wax removed from her ears and her severe constipation dealt with, she was active again.[15] Many older people could not see well because they could not afford spectacles or were wearing those they had inherited from relatives or bought second hand from market stalls, until the NHS provided them free of charge. The NHS transformed the lives of many older people, but inadequate community care facilities for older patients who could have managed at home with support meant that 'blocked beds' full of older people willing and able to leave hospital was already an issue, on which the NFOAPA campaigned.[16]

In refusing to adopt Beveridge's proposal for flexible retirement, the Ministry of Pensions responded to pressure from trade unions and to the Labour Party's long-term commitment to give workers a time of rest after their long working lives. This was understandable at a time when most work-ers in their 60s, male and female, would have started work aged about 12 or 13 and led lives of hard labour on low incomes. At the same time, through the late 1940s and 1950s, another government department, the Ministry of Labour, tried to keep older people at work. It was concerned about the unprecedented labour shortage after the war, together with the ageing labour force and declining numbers of younger workers. The Ministry, the Nuffield Foundation and other organizations funded research that revealed just how skilled and effective older workers could be in most jobs (even involving heavy labour) and that, contrary to popular belief, workers in their 60s could learn new skills. A study of miners in a Scottish pit showed that men in their 50s and 60s could perform as well as younger men at cutting coal; what caused them most strain was the walk through the pit to the coalface, where the pace was set by younger, faster-moving men.[17] Research showed that that whatever older workers lost in terms of speed, adaptability and capacity to learn new techniques (which was much less than was often asserted), was compensated in most occupations by skill, experience and reliability. Through public and private meetings, the press, leaflets and films, the Ministry tried to persuade employers to retain workers past the pension age, offering advice on how to employ older workers most effectively.

This approach continued when Churchill's Conservative government succeeded Labour in 1951. It appointed the National Advisory Committee on the Employment of Older Men and Women (1952–5) to investigate and advise on how workers might be encouraged to delay retirement. It found that despite evidence to the contrary, most employers refused to believe that older men and women were effective workers. Also in the 1950s, increasing numbers of immigrant and female workers were filling the demand for workers, often more cheaply than experienced male workers. Employers felt no need to change their attitudes to older people. This committee and the later Committee on the Economic and Financial Problems of Old Age (1954) recommended more flexible and later retirement ages to overcome what they still believed was a problem of long-term population ageing and discrimination against older workers. However, this serious attempt by successive governments, supported by the NFOAPA, to reduce ageism in the labour market, failed.

This was partly because the attitudes of older people themselves were mixed. Some were eager to retire, even on inadequate pensions, but contemporary surveys showed that others were not. They still felt fit and active at the ages of 60 to 65, were reluctant to face a life of poverty on a pension, and preferred a flexible retirement age. After lives of hard work, some, especially men, could not imagine life without it. There was more continuity in the lives of most women: domestic duties carried on, even when they were working outside the home. For men, retirement meant an abrupt and sometimes frightening change in their lives for which the older men of the 1940s and 1950s, unlike later generations, were not prepared.

Nevertheless, by the 1950s retirement at the state pension age became the norm for manual workers. Of men aged over 65, 48 per cent were in paid work in 1931, falling to 31 per cent in 1951 and 19 per cent in 1971. This created a more rigid barrier than ever before between 'old age pensioners', most of whom were retired, and younger people still in the labour market. They came to be seen as very distinct social groups, whereas previously the boundary had been more fluid, because working class people in particular worked for as long as they were able, from financial necessity.[18]

In the 1950s, concern about the ageing population and shrinking workforce declined, as it became apparent that the birth rate had continued to rise since the war. Growing immigration (see Chapter 2) and the increasing participation of women in the labour market (see Chapter 5) expanded the workforce. Government efforts to diminish ageism in employment vanished. The confident projections of the 1930s and 1940s of a future of continuously low birth rates and an ageing population appeared to be wrong, at least in the short term.

In the 1950s and early 1960s, research revealed continuing high levels of poverty among older people, especially for women, who were the majority of over 65s.[19] Appalling conditions were also exposed in some residential homes.[20] In popular discourse, 'old age pensioner' was equated with retirement and poverty, although the term 'elderly' came increasingly into use to indicate greater respect than 'old'.

Campaigns *for* relieving the inequalities suffered by older people were more prominent than action *by* them at this time. In 1961, Help the Aged was formed out of earlier charities for older people by the Christian philan-thropists who had formed OXFAM a few years earlier. NFOAPA continued to campaign, lobbying very actively in the 1964 general election that brought Labour back to power.

In 1965, the Labour government raised the state pension to about 21 per cent of the average earnings of male manual workers, its highest level ever, although it was still not a living income and did not rescue hundreds of thousands of older people, mostly female, from poverty and means-testing. Labour had been committed to improving the pension system for some years, although the 1965 change fell short of the radical proposals in its 1957 policy document, 'National Superannuation'. These recommended linking pensions and contributions to earnings, to guarantee the 'average wage earner' a pension equivalent to half pay at age 65, protected against inflation by linking to the cost of living – similar to the pension systems being developed elsewhere in Western Europe.[21] In 1965, after gaining a very narrow victory in 1964, Labour was bidding for votes in a difficult economic situation. It knew the number and voting power of pensioners and the sympathy they attracted among other voters. Since the mid-1950s, Labour had also been under pressure from the academic advisers behind 'National Superannuation' (who were also advisers to the post-1964 govern-ment), Richard Titmuss, Peter Townsend and Brian Abel-Smith, from the London School of Economics. Their research, published in the mid-1960s, described at the time as 'the rediscovery of poverty',[22] revealed high levels of poverty, particularly among older people and children, and showed that the post-war welfare state had not abolished poverty after all. Labour planned further pension improvements, but lost the 1970 election and could do noth-ing until 1975, following its re-election in 1974. The 1975 Social Security Pensions Act introduced earnings-related state pensions and established a mechanism for them to gradually increase, over 20 years, linked to aver-age earnings. While this failed to satisfy many campaigners, including the NFOAPA, it was an improvement on previous pension levels.

In the late 1960s and 1970s, many new activist groups were formed in the social policy and inequality arenas. They were more outspoken, more media savvy, and had more memorable, media-friendly names than older-style voluntary organizations. They included the Child Poverty Action Group (CPAG), Shelter, and the Disablement Income Group (DIG, see Chapter 7).[23] They employed professionally trained workers, many of them products of an expansion of training in social work and social policy in the universities, influenced by the 'rediscovery of poverty' research and committed, in the spirit of post-1968 radicalism, to working with, rather than for, excluded groups. Older organizations changed along similar lines, often adopting snappier names. The National Old People's Welfare Committee became Age Concern in the early 1970s and devoted more time to helping older people with social security claims and encouraging research into their conditions, along with lobbying and charitable help. It became increasingly active in supporting older people from minority ethnic groups, who were becoming visible following increased Commonwealth immigration. Help the Aged also shifted from essentially philanthropic activity to lobbying government for improved pensions and services and supporting older people's activism. Activists in the United States, such as the Grey Panthers and the American Association of Retired Persons, who were highly visible in the 1960s and 1970s, inspired British organizations.[24] Post-1968 feminists in the United States also campaigned against age discrimination, unlike youthful British feminists, who did not.[25] The focus of activism in Britain at this time was on reducing material inequalities and pensioner poverty and on improving services – for which there was urgent need and, unlike in the United States, a welfare state that was potentially able to respond – rather than on cultural inequalities such as age discrimination in the workplace, health and other services, and in other areas of life.

Longer-established activist groups of older people, such as NFOAPA, weakened partly because they were supplanted by these better-resourced groups. NFOAPA was funded mainly by subscriptions from pensioners with limited resources, but in 1970 it played an important role in the founding of the All-Party Parliamentary Group on Old Age Pensions (now the APPG on Ageing and Older People). Some supporters of NFOAPA thought it too moderate at a time of increasingly outspoken campaigning by all age groups,[26] but in the 1970s, it increasingly worked to demand improved pensions.

At the same time, after a long gap, trade unions, which were generally more militant than before, revived their interest in pensions. In 1979, this led to the TUC forming the National Pensioners' Convention (NPC), committed to pensions of not less than half average gross earnings, inflation-proofed by being linked to national average earnings. This was the target for state pensions set by the European Union, of which Britain was a member from 1973. The NPC's 'Pensioners' Charter' also called for:

- free health care, community care and services to assist independent living
- free nationwide travel on public transport (introduced in 2007)
- free education and access to leisure and cultural services
- 'good services and benefits without age discrimination'
- active engagement and consultation on national and local issues
- 'advocacy, dignity, respect and fair treatment in all aspects of their lives'.

Most of these requests are still contentious.

The NPC was led by Jack Jones, the recently retired general secretary of the Transport and General Workers Union. It was formed largely because people in their 50s were losing their jobs faster than younger workers and, as in the 1930s, finding it harder to return to the workforce during the economic recession of the later 1970s.[27]

1980s TO NOW

The NPC was active and vocal throughout the 1980s, holding annual rallies in London and lobbying government. But it had little influence at a time of declining trade union power and membership. The Conservative government de-linked the state pension from earnings in 1982, reducing its real value. Since then, it has steadily fallen to its lowest rate as a percentage of average earnings since 1945, of 15.9 per cent in 2008.[28] At the same time, the Conservatives encouraged private pension savings in an increasingly deregulated market. The 1980s also saw cuts in spending on health care for older people relative to younger people, and reduced expenditure on the local services that enabled many older people to live independently.

At the same time, there was a revival in political and public concern about the ageing of the population of Britain and other high-income countries.[29] Earlier panic about this issue, from the 1920s to 1950s, and the research it had prompted into the positive aspects of an ageing population, was forgotten. Also in the 1980s and 1990s, high unemployment, economic recession and 'downsizing' (by companies that believed they had most to gain from dismissing older, often more expensive, workers) increased the number of people who had effectively retired from work in their 50s. This was sometimes presented as the unavoidable outcome of technological change, due to the incapacity of older workers to adapt and retrain. 'Older' workers, even those in their 40s, often were not offered training opportunities.[30] This ignored research showing that smart 60-year-olds could out-perform average 25-year-olds at most mental activities, due to their greater experience, and that older people could learn new skills.[31] Research also showed that older workers tended to be absent less often due to sickness or other reasons, and to be more highly motivated and productive than younger workers.

By the early 1990s, one-third of workers in Britain and elsewhere in Western Europe had retired before their 60th birthday, sometimes on comfortable company or private pensions, but often not.[32] Women, members of minority ethnic groups, the long-term disabled, Gypsies and Travellers were particularly likely to retire on low incomes. At the same time, people could expect to live longer, on average, although there were differences among regions and socio-economic groups, and between the sexes. Women tended to live longer than men and people in poorer areas of Scotland, in particular, tended to have shorter lives than elsewhere. On average, in the United Kingdom in 1950–1, a 65-year-old man could expect to live another 11 years and a 65-year-old woman 13; by 1995, this had risen to almost 15 years for men and 18 for women, and in 2001 to 16 and 19 years respectively. On average, Scotland had a lower life expectancy than most West European countries. In 2005–7, a Scottish man of 65 could expect, on average, to live for another 16 years (compared with 17.3 in England), and a woman for 18.7 years (compared with 20).[33] In inner-city Glasgow, a 65-year-old man could expect to live only 13.8 more years, and a woman 17.4.[34] In general, the years of dependency on a pension were growing. And people not only lived longer on average, but remained healthy until later ages, suggesting that many were fit to work to later in life at the very time that they were retiring younger.

In 1992, the Maxwell scandal highlighted the insecurity of employer pensions, at a time when more people than ever were dependent upon them and state pensions were falling in value. After the body of the media tycoon Robert Maxwell was found floating in the Atlantic in 1991, the Serious Fraud Office found that about £400 million had been diverted from the pension fund of Maxwell's Mirror Group as unauthorized loans to his foundering private companies. Large numbers of Maxwell employees, past and present, lost their pensions. There were also revelations in the 1990s, following deregulation of the financial sector by the Thatcher governments, of the extent to which private finance companies had persuaded people with secure public sector pensions to transfer to more expensive and less favourable private pensions to their serious disadvantage.[35]

These experiences further stimulated activist groups of older people, angry at their inability to work for their living, even when they were highly skilled, experienced and active, and at the prospect of insecurity after retirement, even when they believed they had saved for a secure pension. They were, on average, better educated and physically fitter than older people of previous generations and so all the more willing and able to be assertive. In 1988, the Campaign Against Age Discrimination in Employment (CAADE, still active) was formed and, in 1992 the Scottish Pensioners Forum, initiated by the Scottish TUC with support from Help the Aged, Age Concern and the Scottish Old Age Pensions Association (OAPA), 'to allow pensioners to speak on behalf of pensioners'. In 1998, the Third Age Employment Network (now the Age and Employment Network) was formed, with support from Help the Aged, to advise older people on opportunities for work and training and to lobby for greater opportunities. These organizations, and individual older people, have done much to increase the involvement of older people in voluntary and community action, in which they are a vital force. In 2001, 27 per cent of people in the United Kingdom aged 65 and over participated in community and voluntary activities.[36] There is no sign that the numbers have fallen since then. In 2008, 28 per cent of volunteers with Voluntary Service Overseas (VSO) were aged 50 or over, compared with about 3 per cent 20 years earlier. VSO's British director commented:

> The needs of the developing countries have changed . . . They now require volunteers that have got more experience and higher levels of professional skills and experience . . . This has coincided with an increase in the number of retirees that don't want to put their feet up . . . when they retire and are looking for something quite different . . .[37]

The skills and energy of many of the early retired, lost to the paid workforce, were redirected into the voluntary sector. Yet older volunteers are not always welcome. While being commendably anti-discriminatory in their

anxiety to recruit more volunteers from minority ethnic groups, some organizations, in their anxiety to attract younger volunteers, were unaware they
were practising age discrimination – a symptom of how taken-for-granted
this was in society at large.

In 1990, male and female state pension ages were equalized, following a
ruling in the European Court on a sex discrimination action, brought by a
man. It was a rare example of discrimination against males. The government
responded by gradually raising the age of eligibility for the female pension
from 60 to 65 between 2010 and 2020. There was no evident public protest,
compared with protests against later proposals to raise pension ages for
men and women.

Since the mid-1990s, activist groups have increasingly focused on, and
raised public awareness of, discrimination against older people in employment and other areas of life. Previously, the concept of 'age discrimination'
was almost unknown. There have been increasing complaints about age
discrimination in the delivery of health care, probably as a result of older
people and their relatives being less willing to tolerate practices that had long
been taken for granted, rather than an increase in such discrimination.

The numbers of people who have retired before the age of 60 has since
declined. In 2000, the mean retirement age of men in Britain was 63, and
of women, 60.[38] This probably owes most to employers recognizing the loss
to their businesses from over-enthusiastic dismissal of older people in the
1990s, and to government (as in the 1940s and 1950s) wanting to keep older
people at work to compensate for the declining number of younger workers
and to cut the cost of pensions. The Pensions Act 2007 sets out plans to very
gradually raise the state pension age to 68 for men and women between 2024
and 2046. The government has moved cautiously, in view of resistance by
many people to the prospect of losing a period of leisure they look forward to
in later life. Popular opinion is divided and, of course, not everyone is fit and
active in their mid sixties. Activists argue that individuals should be judged
by their capabilities, rather than crudely by age, and that flexible pension and
retirement ages are preferable, as Beveridge once recommended.

In 2006, the Employment Equality (Age) Regulations were introduced in
Britain, as part of a European-wide initiative against age discrimination in
the workplace.[39] The regulations apply to discrimination against people at all
ages. They may reinforce other efforts to encourage more flexible attitudes
towards the capabilities of older people in society as a whole, but it is too
soon to tell, and the British government has been less than wholehearted
in banning discrimination against older people at work. Although workers
may now request the right to stay at work beyond the age of 65, employers
have the right to refuse, without giving reasons. In September 2008, this was
unsuccessfully challenged in the European Court by older people, backed
by Age Concern, but the challenge is unlikely to go away.

Activist groups have also sought to change cultural attitudes toward older
people, challenging what they see as commonplace denigration and offensive language that is no longer acceptable in respect of other social groups.

The use in recent years of the term 'older people', in place of 'old' or 'elderly', is intended to diminish stereotyping of all people past a certain age – since everyone, from shortly after birth, is older than someone else.

Such efforts have had only limited success, judging, for example, by the media discourse around the introduction of 2006 Regulations. Among all-too-many examples, a speaker on BBC Radio Four's *Today* show on 28 October 2006 described 'younger' workers as generally 'more enthusiastic and energetic' than 'older' ones, despite much evidence to the contrary. Comedians such as Russell Brand and Jonathan Ross can 'joke' at the expense of older people as they no longer can, acceptably, against other minorities. When rock stars such as Mick Jagger, or actors such as Helen Mirren, aged in their mid-60s, are active, successful and not evidently conforming to any stereotype of 'old age', this is cause for surprise, rather than recognition that the same is true of many of their age group.

A national sample survey conducted by Age Concern in late 2005 reported that more people (29 per cent) reported experiencing age discrimination than any other form of discrimination. Those aged over 55 were nearly twice as likely to have experienced age prejudice than any other form of discrimination. One-third of people surveyed viewed people aged over 70 as 'incompetent and incapable'. Nearly 30 per cent believed that age discrimination was more serious than it had been five years before.[40] However, these findings should be interpreted with care. They show that growing numbers of people are aware that treating everyone over a certain age as incompetent constitutes discrimination rather than a statement of obvious fact. Awareness of age discrimination is more recent than that of other forms of discrimination. Greater awareness may be the first step to abolition.

CONCLUSION

Over the past 60 years, there has been unprecedented change in the physical condition of most older people. More are healthy and active for longer, due to improved living standards and health care. There have been great changes in the lifestyles of many older people, with many, although not all, leading more varied and active lives than older people in the past. The physical state and cultural experiences of older people have changed more rapidly than attitudes to them. Popular attitudes have not kept pace with the emergence of a large, active, assertive group of people aged over 60 – although change may be beginning. Nor is there recognition of the diversity among the very large group of people popularly defined as 'old' and aged from about 60 to over 100. This 'age group' contains some of the fittest and the most frail (from the growing number of marathon runners in their 80s to growing numbers of sufferers from Alzheimer's), some of the wealthiest (including Queen Elizabeth and Mick Jagger) and some of the very poorest members of the population, from increasingly diverse cultural backgrounds. It makes no sense to stereotype them as a single group. We need to distinguish between the very different contributions and needs of fit and active and of frail older people. More radically, people at all ages (including the very young) should be judged, in the workplace and elsewhere, by their capabilities rather than by their age. This will be challenging but not impossible for employers, while insurance companies, for example, will have to consider defining risk groups by characteristics other than (as they do at present) age and gender.

But not everything has changed. Contrary to popular belief, family support for older people has not been in long-term decline; it remains strong.[41] Older people also perform substantial services for their communities and their families, for instance as grandparents, as they always have.[42] They are not all, or mostly, dependents, despite their access to employment tending to deteriorate over time, triggered by economic conditions and management decisions – although there are slow signs of improvement. And many older people, especially women aged over 75 but other groups as well (see below), continue to experience severe poverty due to institutional failure, especially of the pensions system.

British state pensions have never been adequate for survival. In 2005, the then Pensions Minister, Alan Johnson, described women's pensions as a 'scandal'.[43] The difficulty for women and for others with incomplete records of paid work arises because the levels of state, occupational and private pensions are determined by years of employment. This currently disadvantages those who have not worked and paid national insurance contributions continuously for at least 40 years. It mainly affects women whose years of paid work are interrupted by caring responsibilities, but also many disabled people who have broken work records and therefore qualify only for the minimum state pension, and other groups, including many Gypsies and Travellers and immigrants, who have worked for less than the maximum period and receive commensurately lower pensions.[44]

Under the Pensions Act 2007, from 2007 the number of qualifying years needed to receive a full state pension will fall from 39 for women and 44 for men to 30 for both, which will lessen but not remove the problem; and national insurance credits will be introduced for those with long-term disabilities and caring responsibilities for young children or severely disabled people. The 2007 Act also proposes to proof the state pension against inflation by linking it to average earnings, from 2012, 'subject to affordability and the fiscal position' and at latest 'by the end of the next parliament' (possibly 2015). Since 2003, Pension Credit has raised the incomes of the poorest pensioners to the level of a liveable income, but the problem remains that two-fifths of eligible and very poor older people do not claim it. The Pensions Act 2008 aims to enable and encourage people to build up safe private pensions to supplement their state pensions. From 2012, it is planned to automatically enrol all eligible workers who are not already in a good workplace scheme into either an employers' scheme or into a new, low-cost personal savings account. The scheme will be subsidized by employers and by the tax system. How beneficial this will be, especially to lower-paid workers, remains to be seen.

Members of minority ethnic groups who have lived in Britain through-out their lives also tend to have lower incomes after retirement, and are less likely than White British people to belong to private or occupational pension schemes, although there is considerable diversity among and within all ethnic groups.[45] At present, minority ethnic groups generally have a younger age structure than the White population. In 2001, 5.1 per cent of the minority ethnic population was aged 65 or over, compared with 16.9 per cent of the White population. Inequalities in income at later ages arise, above all, from the labour market position of the various ethnic groups. Unemployment rates are higher for non-White groups, both male and female, and higher for Black Africans and Pakistanis than for Indians. Self-employment rates are also higher, especially among Pakistani and Chinese populations. These patterns reduce access to employer-provided pensions. The lower incomes of many in minority ethnic groups reduce their opportunities for pension saving – for instance, two-thirds of Bangladeshi and half of all Chinese men in employment work in the distribution, hotel and catering trades, which pay low wages and have low rates of participation in private and occupational pensions.[46] It is not clear whether recent changes in pension laws will substantially help these disadvantaged groups.

Discrimination against older people continues in the health service. For instance, women aged over 65 are not routinely called for breast scans, despite breast cancer being more common in women over 65; and certain medical procedures are refused purely on age-based criteria.

Although there has been a reduction since 1945 in retirement income and employment inequality between older and younger people (and any such reduction has been slight), it was driven by the campaigning of activist groups leading to European Union, government and employer action and, on the part of employers, by labour and skill shortages, rather than by increased awareness of the capabilities of older people and the extent of age discrimination. The increased extent and effectiveness of older people's activism has been fuelled by their growing physical fitness, education and confidence in recent decades, and growing awareness of the discrimination they experience.

It is sometimes argued that the current generation of retirees is exceptionally privileged, enjoying at its leisure the benefits of having bought homes cheaply in the past, of free university education and good pensions financed by a younger generation that is crippled by the costs of university loans and mortgages, and that this may cause serious tension between generations. Such fears overlook the great inequalities *within* generations documented in this and other chapters, as well as the extent to which many of the privileged older generation (only 7 per cent of whom attended university, even in the 1970s) support their children and grandchildren, both through their studies, now that 40 per cent of young people attend university and are required to pay fees, as they were not in the past, and in the housing market. The generations do not live in isolation from one another.

The main drivers of change towards greater age equality over the past 60 years have been:

- campaigning by older people – this was most active in the 1930s and 1940s and since the 1980s, both times at which public concern about the economic consequences of an ageing population increased their clout. In the 1930s and 1940s, the chief concern was poor pensions and services. Recently, these continue to be major concerns, accompanied by resistance to age discrimination in the workplace and elsewhere
- increased physical and mental fitness and levels of education, training and self-confidence among older people, which have increased their campaigning effectiveness
- campaigns by voluntary organizations on behalf of older people since the 1940s, increasingly since the 1970s in partnership with older people themselves, focused on poverty and poor services and, since the 1980s, on age discrimination. Voluntary organizations have been increasingly professional and media-savvy since the 1960s
- Labour governments, which have done more than Conservative governments to advance age equality, in response to campaigns, the voting power of older people and, recently, to concern about the economic consequences of age discrimination, especially at work
- the European Union, which has prompted government action, responding to campaigns across Europe and concern about the economic consequences of an ageing population
- role models of active older people in a wide variety of spheres of life, from the stage and rock music to high finance and the monarchy
- the very slow cultural shift towards awareness of age discrimination.

Inhibitors of change include:
- the continuing poverty of very many older people
- cultural conservatism – the continuing belief that it is 'common sense' to expect inequality past a certain age
- attitudes reinforced by the mass media presenting stereotyped, negative images of older people.

In 2007, the Equality and Human Rights Commission was appointed by the British government to take over the roles of existing statutory bodies charged to prevent inequalities involving race, gender and disability. It also took on responsibility for other forms of inequality, including that arising from age, and to account for these not being discrete categories, since many individuals experience multiple inequalities.[47] Its impact cannot yet be assessed.

THE CHANGED EXPERIENCE OF OLDER PEOPLE SINCE 1950

Age 65 in 1950:
- Born 1885, a time of high levels of poverty when most of the population was working class
- Left school aged 12, at most 13, probably to do heavy manual work or, if female, domestic service
- Lived through two world wars and high inter-war unemployment. If male, fought in World War I, possibly followed by long period of unemployment. If female, a succession of pregnancies, childbirth, miscarriage, sometimes alongside paid work. Ready for retirement at 65 after long, hard lives
- Rented home, often in poor condition
- Average life expectancy: men c. 76 years, women c. 78 years – but that is average for whole population of England and Wales, including the wealthy; actual life expectancy was more closely related to a person's socio-economic situation and lowest for the poorest people.

Age 65 in 1970:
- Born 1905, when there were still high levels of poverty
- Left school aged 12–14, in the midst of the Depression
- University attended by 1.8 per cent of age group, but this opportunity was 80 per cent lower if female
- If male, probably fought in World War II; if female, fewer pregnancies than for previous generations and a falling birth rate
- Gained in later life from post-war full employment, NHS, improved housing (probably rented), pensions, better opportunities for children, more leisure, perhaps first holidays abroad
- Average life expectancy at age 65: men 77 years, women, 81 years.

Age 65 in 2000:
- Born 1935
- Early years dominated by economic Depression and war then, post-war, full employment, improved education and health
- Left school aged 15 or older; 5.4 per cent attended university (female opportunity to attend university still 75 per cent lower)
- Married and had children in early 20s; increased risk of divorce, triggering poverty for women
- Increased opportunity for home ownership
- More likely than previous generations to be in service industry than heavy industrial employment; possibly unemployed during 1980s
- Average life expectancy at age 65: men 81 years, women 84 years.

Age 65 in 2040:
- Born 1975
- Possibly experienced family unemployment in early years
- Left full-time education aged 16–21; 40 per cent attended university, 50 per cent of students female
- Married/partnered/and had children (if any) in 30s
- High mortgage, student debt, unlike previous generations
- Probably skilled white-collar job. Heavy manual labour now a minority experience, but many of the less educated in low-paid, long hours, service employment. Longer hours and higher stress in most occupations than in previous generations
- Projected average life expectancy at age 65: men and women, 85–95, assuming that average standards of health over the lifetime continue to improve.

STATISTICS

All of the following figures are drawn from *Pensions: Challenges and Choices. The First Report of the Pensions Commission.* (2004).

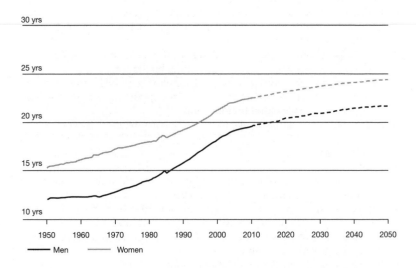

Figure 1.1 Cohort life expectancy for men and women at 65 in England and Wales: Historic and Government Actuary's Department projection

Source: Pensions Commission analysis, based on Government Actuary's Department (GAD) historical data to 2002 for England and Wales, and GAD population projection, from 2003 onwards, *Pensions: Challenges and Choices*, p. 3.

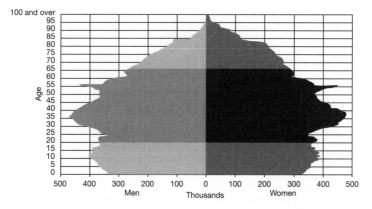

Figure 1.2 Distribution of population by age: 2002a

Note:
(a) A smoothing assumption for the population groups aged 90–4 and 95–9 years has been made by applying the distribution of the 85–9 year cohorts five and ten years previously. The darker area highlights those aged 20–64.

Source: GAD. 2002 based population projection, Pensions Commission analysis, *Pensions: Challenges and Choices*, p. 6.

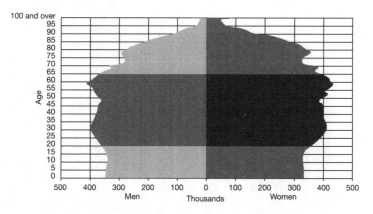

Figure 1.3 Projected distribution of population by age: 2050a

Note:
(a) A smoothing assumption for the population groups aged 90–4 and 95–9 years has been made by applying the distribution of the 85–9 year cohorts five and ten years previously. The darker area highlights those aged 20–64.

Source: GAD 2002 based population projection, Pensions Commission analysis, *Pensions: Challenges and Choices*, p. 6.

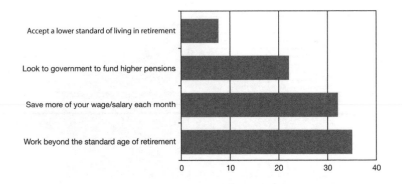

Figure 1.4 Preferred responses to the demographic challenge

Source: Pensions and Savings Index, Survey 1 (Sep. 2003) by YouGov for the Association of British Insurers, *Pensions: Challenges and Choices*, p. 23.

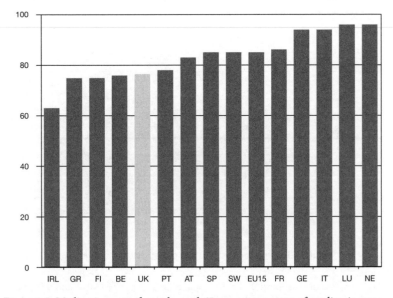

Figure 1.5 Median income of people aged 65+ as a percentage of median income of people aged less than 65: 2001

Source: Eurostat, European Community Household Panel Users Survey Database (ECHP-UDB), July 2003, *Pensions: Challenges and Choices*, p. 23.

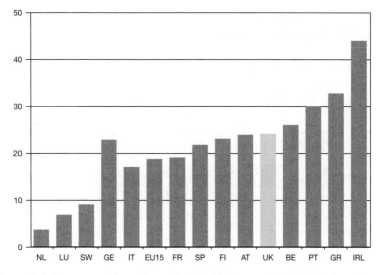

Figure 1.6 Percentage of people aged 65+ with income below 60% of median employment

Source: Eurostat, ECHP-UDB, version July 2003, *Pensions: Challenges and Choices*, p. 69.

Figure 1.7 Employment rates for men and women aged 50 to state pension age: 1973–95

Source: General Household Survey, GB, *Pensions: Challenges and Choices*, p. 36.

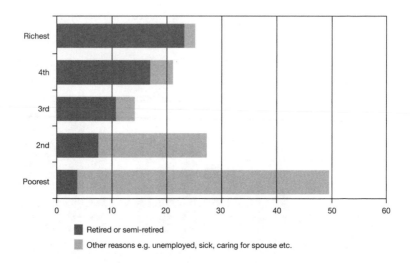

Figure 1.8 Inactivity by wealth quintile: Men aged 55–9

Source: English Longitudinal Study of Ageing, 2002, *Pensions: Challenges and Choices*, p. 36.

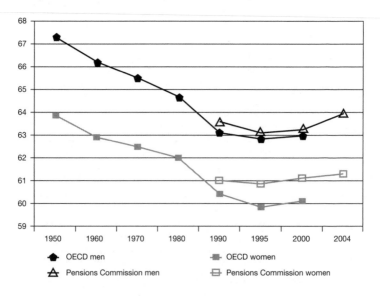

Figure 1.9 Trends in mean age of retirement

Source: Blondel and Scarpetta (1999), Pension Commission estimates, World Economic Forum, *Pensions: Challenges and Choices*, p. 55.

Chapter 2

Race and equality

Nick Kimber

TIMELINE

1290	Jews expelled from England until late seventeenth century.
1905	Aliens Act, first restriction on immigration of people not born in Britain or the Empire, designed to restrict Jewish immigration.
1931	Foundation of the League of Coloured Peoples, the first activist group of Black people after centuries of presence in Britain.
1948	British Nationality Act confirms right of all British and Commonwealth citizens to enter the United Kingdom. *Empire Windrush* docks at Tilbury: symbolic beginning of post-war immigration.
1950	Reg Sorenson introduces unsuccessful Private Member's Bill to outlaw racial discrimination.
1958	Riots against West Indians in Nottingham and London. Claudia Jones publishes *West Indian Gazette*. West Indian Standing Conference and Indian Workers' Association founded.
1959	Murder of Kelso Cochrane, first known instance of racially motivated murder in the United Kingdom.
1962	Commonwealth Immigrants Act limits right of entry and imposes employment voucher system (citizens of Republic of Ireland excluded from control).
1964	Campaign Against Racial Discrimination founded. MP for Smethwick, Patrick Gordon Walker, defeated by racist campaign.
1965	Race Relations Act sets up Race Relations Board to receive and investigate complaints of unlawful discrimination.
1968	Enoch Powell's 'Rivers of Blood' speech. Commonwealth Immigrants Act restricts immigration by United Kingdom-issued passport holders. Race Relations Act enlarges and extends scope of Race Relations Board and establishes Community Relations Commission.

1969	Death of David Oluwale first recorded death of a minority ethnic individual in police custody.
	Learie Constantine becomes first (Life) Peer of African descent.
1971	Immigration Act replaces Aliens Restriction Act 1914 and Commonwealth Immigrants Acts of 1961 and 1968.
1972	Expulsion of Ugandan Asians; 27,000 accepted by Britain.
1976	Race Relations Act makes discrimination unlawful in employment, training and education; makes an offence of inciting racial hatred; establishes Commission for Racial Equality.
	Notting Hill Carnival ends in rioting.
1977	Rock Against Racism and Anti-Nazi League formed.
1979	Campaigner Blair Peach dies at demonstration in Southall as Anti-Nazi League protestors clash with Metropolitan Police.
1981	British Nationality Act revises definition of British nationality, introducing three classes of citizenship.
	Inner-city riots; Scarman Report into causes.
	Election of Labour-led Greater London Council; introduces anti-racist policies imitated in many borough councils.
1985	Riots in Handsworth and Tottenham, clashes on the Broadwater Farm Estate lead to death of a policeman.
1987	Four minority ethnic MPs – including Bernie Grant – returned to Parliament.
1991	Bill Morris becomes first Black general secretary of a trades union, the Transport and General Workers Union.
1993	British National Party wins local council seats on the Isle of Dogs.
	Murder of Black teenager Stephen Lawrence.
1995	Riots in Brixton after a death in police custody.
1997	Nine Black and Asian MPs returned at general election.
1999	Macpherson Report criticizes Metropolitan Police handling of investigation into Stephen Lawrence murder.
2000	Race Relations Amendment Act fulfils recommendations of Macpherson Report, extending RRA 1976 to include the police and all public authorities and outlawing direct and indirect discrimination.
2001	Riots in Burnley, Oldham and Bradford, followed by Cantle Report.
2005	Suicide bombings in London by four British Muslims intensify debates about the merits of British multiculturalism.
2007	Equality and Human Rights Commission takes over responsibilities of Commission for Racial Equality.

INTRODUCTION

Diverse minority ethnic groups, and the issues of equality and inequality they have experienced, have been a significant presence in Britain for many centuries. The Jewish minority was expelled from England in 1290, following a century of persecution. A Jewish community was not re-established until the late seventeenth century, when, like Black, Asian and other small communities that continued to live in Britain, their numbers began to grow with the expansion of Britain's Empire and role in world trade (including the slave trade).

In the twentieth century between World Wars 1 and 2, a substantial population of African and Asian seamen, recruited from the Empire to the merchant navy during World War I, settled in Britain, especially in port cities such as Liverpool and Cardiff. They experienced discrimination in the labour market and the benefits system when they sought to exercise their rights as British citizens.[1] Historically, anyone born within the vast British Empire was a British subject of the British monarch and entitled to the same rights as those who were born in Britain.[2] However, registration of births was not complete throughout the Empire, and immigrants from poorer backgrounds often could not provide evidence of their place of birth, which could disqualify them from claiming their rights.

Throughout the nineteenth and much of the twentieth centuries, especially following the famine of the 1840s, there was substantial immigration to England, Scotland and Wales from Ireland due to poverty. Ireland at this time was part of the United Kingdom and movement between the two was relatively easy. And between the 1880s and World War I, perhaps 100,000 Jews fled to Britain to escape brutal persecution in the Russian Empire. Like later immigrant groups, both the Irish and Jewish communities tended to live in geographically concentrated clusters and to experience hostility from the indigenous population, which influenced government action.[3] For example, the 1905 Aliens Act, the first major restriction on immigration to Britain, was a response to popular hostility to Jewish immigrants. It required immigrants to show an immigration officer that they were able to support themselves and their dependants 'decently'. Criminals, the insane and anyone deemed likely to become a charge on the relief system were excluded. Asylum was given to immigrants who could prove, as the 1905 Act put it, that they were escaping from 'persecution involving danger of imprisonment or danger to life or limb on account of religious belief'.

Following further hostility as war approached, especially to German Jews, the British Nationality and Status of Aliens Act 1914, altered the terms under which British naturalization could be granted, excluding those who could not 'speak, read or write English reasonably well'. Previously, it had been sufficient for the applicant to pay taxes, obey the law and pay a fee. The Home Secretary explained that:

> ... every applicant for British nationality in this country shall show that he or

she has the intention to associate himself or herself with British institutions, and we say that as a first evidence of that intention a man or women who comes to live here must learn the English language.[4]

Members of minority ethnic groups have a long history of participation in British political life. William Davidson, Jamaican by birth, was one of the Cato Street conspirators executed for allegedly plotting to blow up parliament in 1820. William Cuffay, of African descent, was one of the leaders of the Chartist movement in the 1840s, and three MPs of Indian origin sat in the House of Commons between 1892 and 1929.[5] Through the nineteenth and early twentieth centuries, Jews with British nationality by birth or naturalization campaigned for equal civil rights with other Britons, from which they had been excluded by reason of their non-Christian faith (see Chapter 3).[6]

Before and after World War II, Britain served as a base for colonial intellectuals and politicians who were active in nationalist movements across the Empire. They included the writer C. L. R. James and the cricketer Sir Learie Constantine, both of Caribbean origin, who had a considerable impact on Britain's cultural and political life. The League of Coloured Peoples was established in 1931 by Harold Moody, modelled on the National Association for the Advancement of Coloured People, an American lobby group. It fought against racial discrimination in the 1930s and 1940s. In particular, it acted as an advocate for nurses and seamen from minority ethic backgrounds whose employment opportunities were becoming increasingly limited; in a period of high unemployment, they, like others such as women and older people (see Chapter 1), suffered discrimination in the workplace. In 1943, the League persuaded the Colonial Office to open up a limited number of junior positions in the imperial civil service that had previously been closed to 'colonials'. Similarly, the Indian Workers' Association (in Hindustani, Mazdoor Sabha) was founded in Coventry in 1938, then formed branches in London and elsewhere. It existed to promote the cause of Indian independence, and to fight for the rights of Indian workers in Britain and against all forms of discrimination.

POST-WAR IMMIGRATION

The British Nationality Act 1948 confirmed the right of 800 million colonial citizens to enter the United Kingdom. It was designed to reinforce the long-established principle that everyone born within the British Empire had equal rights of citizenship throughout Britain and the colonies. However, few expected that non-White colonial citizens would take up their rights in large numbers, since they had not done so in the past. Even the relatively small number of immigrants who arrived from the Caribbean on the SS *Windrush* in 1948 provoked some panic.[7] West Indians began to migrate to Britain in large numbers in the 1950s. The decreasing cost and increasing availability of transatlantic travel made the journey easier than before, and the greater employment opportunities in booming post-war Britain and the closure of traditional migration routes to the southern United States made Britain attractive.

In the late 1940s, the British government had focused on attracting Irish workers and Europeans displaced by wartime upheaval, in particular from Poland and the Baltic countries, to fill the country's labour shortage. When this source of supply dried up, it appealed for immigrants from the former enemy countries: Germany, Italy and Austria. By 1949, at least 56,000 European immigrants were working in Britain, mainly in manual and public sector jobs. Then the continuing demand for labour led British Rail, London Transport and the National Health Service, among others, to establish recruitment schemes in the West Indies, where there was high unemployment. Despite this, most immigrants travelled independently to Britain.

Many migrants to 1950s Britain, especially those from the Commonwealth, found the experience deeply disappointing. The educational attainment of most newcomers was quite high – probably higher than the average in Britain – drawn as they were from comparatively affluent sections of colonial society. However, most migrants to Britain became concentrated in manual occupations and low-paid shift work.[8] They faced discrimination in the labour market and housing, and were even denied access to leisure venues such as pubs and dance halls.

Left-wing Labour MP Fenner Brockway unsuccessfully proposed a series of private Members' Bills throughout the 1950s to outlaw overt discrimination. Without government backing, or even committed support from the opposition Labour front bench, these had little hope of success. Opponents argued that parliament could not prescribe social attitudes by statute.

Immigration from India and Pakistan grew rapidly at the end of the 1950s. All migrants from South Asia and the Caribbean were designated 'coloured' in public discourse.

MINORITY ETHNIC ORGANIZATION AND GOVERNMENT RESPONSE, 1950s–60s

Few organizations campaigned on behalf of immigrants during the first half of the 1950s and there were even fewer in which immigrants' own voices predominated. The League of Coloured Peoples declined in the early 1950s, after the death of Harold Moody. The Movement for Colonial Freedom (MCF, founded in 1954 and renamed the Movement for Colonial Liberation in 1970) involved a number of Black trade unionists and colonial students, and campaigned for race discrimination legislation as well as for colonial liberation, but was run predominately by White activists who were prominent in the Labour and Communist parties.[9]

Most migrants did not intend to stay in Britain for more than a few years, and many of them were preoccupied with the growing independence struggles in their homelands. Participation in mainstream politics was unusual.

Exceptions included David Pitt, born in Grenada, who came to Britain in 1947 to lobby for West Indian independence. He stayed, becoming a general practitioner in central London and, in 1985–6, president of the British Medical Association. He ran for Parliament as a Labour candidate in the upper-middle class, liberal London seat of Hampstead in 1959, the first of a succession of parliamentary seats in which he was defeated, all too often in contests tainted by racism. In 1961, he was elected as a Labour representative on the London County Council, later Greater London Council (GLC), for working class, multi-ethnic Hackney, later becoming the first Black chair of the council. In 1975, he was made a Life Peer, ironically as Lord Pitt of Hampstead.

Black activism was spurred on by a series of unprovoked attacks by White youths on Black men in Nottingham and London's Notting Hill in the summer of 1958, and the murder of Antiguan carpenter Kelso Cochrane in Leeds a year later. In the winter of 1958, the West Indian Standing Committee (WISC) was formed, and it coordinated the activities of a range of associations based on island origin. The *West Indian Gazette*, a campaigning newspaper seeking to assert West Indians' cultural identity in Britain, was also founded in 1958, selling between 3,000 and 4,000 copies per issue – although during the month-long Notting Hill riots in 1958, it sold 30,000. Its editor, Claudia Jones, was a key figure in the early incarnations of the Notting Hill Carnival. She died in 1965 and the *Gazette* died soon after. Like later attempts to establish a Black press, it suffered from a lack of support from advertisers. Carnival, which had a number of precursors, became an annual event in 1966 and continues to this day, attracting about a million visitors each year. Despite serious disorder in 1976, which prefigured the urban riots of the 1980s, Carnival became an institution with broad appeal, while remaining an important assertion of Caribbean identity.

The Indian Workers' Association (IWA) continued, grew and formed the federal IWA (GB) in 1958, largely in response to increasing Asian immigration. As well as providing help in finding accommodation and with language skills, and organizing cultural activities, it continued to focus on organising Indian workers in trade unions and on anti-racist campaigning. In the 1960s, it allied with other minority ethnic organizations, such as WISC and the Campaign Against Racial Discrimination (CARD), which was formed in 1964 as a broadly based group of Black and White activists focused largely on lobbying for race relations legislation. CARD, in which David Pitt was prominent, had close informal links with the Labour Party and it developed closer ties with government officials, MPs and public bodies than any other race-based group.[10] It became divided between those who wanted to develop a grassroots movement and those who saw its role as that of an insider lobby group, and it fell apart in the late 1960s.

Largely in response to growing evidence of popular racism since 1958, at a time when the economy was flagging, the Conservative government passed the Commonwealth Immigration Act, 1962. This instituted a system of job vouchers that restricted admission of Commonwealth immigrants to those with 'special skills' or guaranteed employment. It imposed no restriction on immigrants from Ireland, who were not members of the Commonwealth but retained full rights of British citizenship following that country's independence in 1921.

The Labour Party leader, Hugh Gaitskell, led passionate opposition to the Bill in parliament, describing it as 'a plain anti-colour measure'.[11] However, given the popularity with voters of restricting immigration, demonstrated in opinion polls, the Labour Party became more circumspect. As the 1964 general election approached, it promised only to review the Act in consultation with Commonwealth governments, although it did commit itself to some form of anti-discrimination legislation if it won the election. Race did not play a prominent role in the election campaign, which Labour narrowly won, but Labour's prospective foreign secretary, Patrick Gordon-Walker, was defeated in an overtly racist campaign, against the national swing, in Smethwick, a Midlands seat he had represented since 1945. In the following year, he stood in a by-election in the normally safe Labour seat of Leyton, East London. Again, he was defeated, in a campaign that featured anti-immigration campaigners dressed as monkeys, bearing placards stating: 'We immigrants are voting for Gordon Walker.' He won Leyton in the 1966 general election.

The Labour government renewed the Commonwealth Immigration Act while, more positively, introducing the 1965 Race Relations Act. For the first time, this declared unlawful discrimination on grounds of colour, race, ethnic or national origin in certain public places and provided for the establishment of a Race Relations Board (RRB), consisting of a chair and two other members appointed by the Home Secretary. It established local conciliation committees tasked with considering complaints of discrimination, securing a settlement or, failing that, reporting to the RRB, which could refer the case to the Attorney-General with a view to court proceedings. The mechanism was unwieldy and, in the statute's lifetime, the Attorney-General failed to bring a single successful prosecution.

The Race Relations Act was considered unsatisfactory by lobby groups because it excluded the areas that most concerned migrants, such as housing, employment, insurance, credit facilities and financial services. However, the Act set up the institutional arrangements that have, broadly, framed British race relations legislation to the present day. Campaigning organizations such as CARD, WISC and IWA combined with influential backbenchers and insider groups like the Society of Labour Lawyers to pressure the government for more comprehensive and effective legislation. The institutions created by the 1965 Act also acted as powerful drivers for further change. During his tenure as Home Secretary (1965–7), Roy Jenkins made a significant contribution to promoting equality in a number of spheres (see Chapters 5 and 6), and gave these groups a sympathetic hearing.

At the same time, pioneering social research demonstrated the depth of prejudice in British society. In 1966, the independent and well-respected think tank Political and Economic Planning (PEP) published a report on

racial discrimination, commissioned by the RRB, particularly examining
the areas not covered in the 1965 Act.[12] Its key findings were:

- widespread discrimination in employment, housing and services on
  the basis of colour rather than status as an immigrant
- discrimination most marked against West Indians, with strong
  prejudice against their employment in clerical and professional
  positions
- colour prejudice as problematic for second-generation minority groups
  as for recent Black Caribbean and Asian immigrants
- employers concerned that if they employed 'coloured' people, they
  would face a competitive disadvantage.

The RRB included in its 1967 annual report a strong appeal for the extension
of the Race Relations Act. The impact of this research, combined with activist
pressure and the liberal tendencies of the Home Office under Roy Jenkins,
paved the way for the Race Relations Act 1968. This broadly retained the
structure of its predecessor, but the RRB was given powers to investigate
discrimination without receiving a prior complaint. A Community Relations
Commission (CRC) was established to promote good community relations
and to advise the home secretary in this area. However, sanctions against
transgressors remained weak and the arrangements for employment discrimination cases were confusing and laborious. Few members of minority
ethnic groups were aware of the Race Relations Board and its functions, and
many who were had little confidence that a complaint would be satisfactorily
investigated.[13] Once again, the main impact of the Act was probably as a
public declaration that discrimination was unacceptable.

However, progressive anti-discrimination legislation was again the flip-
side of restrictive immigration legislation. The Commonwealth Immigrants
Act, 1968, was passed hurriedly in response to the increasing number of
Kenyan Asians coming to Britain to escape persecution. It further restricted
the rights of Commonwealth citizens to migrate to Britain, with opinion
polls suggesting that the measure was popular with the public.[14]

Labour failed to stop race being a political issue. The Conservative
Enoch Powell made a notorious speech in 1968, predicting racial conflict
in inflammatory terms that were subsequently much misquoted: 'As I look
ahead, I am filled with foreboding. Like the Roman, I seem to see "the River
Tiber foaming with much blood"' (Powell, a classical scholar was referring to a passage in Virgil's *Aeneid*, which was, understandably, not widely
recognized.) This, and his subsequent dismissal from the Conservative
front bench, made race a key issue in the 1970 general election and may
have been a reason for Labour's defeat. Responding to these pressures, the
Conservatives passed the Immigration Act 1971. Commonwealth citizens
now had the right of abode in Britain only if they, their husbands (but not
wives), parents or grandparents had British passports. More creditably, the
government accepted more than 20,000 Ugandan Asians who were fleeing
from Idi Amin's Africanization policies in 1973.

THE 1970s AND 1980s: PROGRESS?

By the 1970s, the experiences of minority ethnic groups had become more diverse, but inequalities persisted. Few Black people had managed to move into professional and managerial occupations. There was some penetration into skilled manual work, but members of all minority ethnic groups were disproportionately concentrated in semi-skilled and unskilled manual work.[15] The educational attainment of members of minority ethnic groups did not correlate with employment opportunities. One fifth of all men from minority ethnic backgrounds who had university degrees equivalent to British standards were in manual jobs in 1974.[16] The majority of Asian women and about a third of Asian men could speak English only slightly or not at all, although there were substantial differences among Asian groups: whereas 76 per cent of Bangladeshi women had little or no command of English, this was true of only 42 per cent of Indian women; while for men from these communities, the respective figures were 50 and 15 per cent.[17]

On the whole, minority ethnic groups remained segregated in inner cities, with fewer amenities than the national norm. People of Black Caribbean origin had increasingly become owner–occupiers and council tenants at a rate that brought them up to parity with White people, whereas only 4 per cent of Asian households were council tenants and three-quarters were owner–occupiers. This rate of home ownership was partly a result of their exclusion from decent rented accommodation, and the quality of homes they bought was often poor.

After the 1974 general election, which returned Labour to power, an influential report by the CRC brought the growing importance of the 'Black vote' to the attention of politicians.[18] The increasing politicization of minority ethnic communities during the 1960s, as well as their growing permanency, meant that many more were registered to vote than during the 1950s. The report suggested that 'ethnic marginals' existed, where the size of constituencies' majorities was smaller than that of the Commonwealth-born population. It identified 59 such seats in the two 1974 elections, which was more than enough to swing the result either way. Although this research was questioned on the grounds that it erroneously assumed the minority ethnic population to have similar levels of voter registration and turnout to that of the White population, political parties reacted by making more effort to appeal to minority ethnic voters. Vote-seeking strategies may have played some part in the Labour government bringing forward new anti-discrimination legislation and in the Conservative Party's acquiescence in such proposals, along with pressure from activist groups and from institutions established by the legislation.

The Race Relations Act 1976 made discrimination unlawful in employment, training, education and in the provision of goods and services, and made it an offence to stir up racial hatred. It also extended the definition of discrimination to include indirect discrimination and victimization. It amalgamated the CRC and RRB into the Commission for Racial Equality

(CRE), which was granted proactive powers of investigation. The focus was now on individuals taking complaints directly to the courts, although the commission could assist if called upon. It had shifted from changing the behaviour of individuals to changing that of organizations.

Also in the 1970s, women from minority ethnic groups joined the Women's Liberation Movement (see Chapter 5) to campaign for gender, as well as racial, equality. Organizations founded during the 1970s and later, such as the Organization of Women of Asian and African Descent, Southall Black Sisters, Brixton Black Women, Liverpool Black Sisters, Baheno Women's Organization in Leicester, and other groups throughout Wales, Scotland and England, campaigned in particular against immigration restrictions, virginity tests imposed on women arriving in Britain, police brutality and domestic violence, as well as discrimination in employment and other spheres. These organizations have continued to campaign on a wide range of issues affecting women and their communities.

The late 1970s saw the rise of the National Front (NF) on a platform of opposition to immigration and multiculturalism. It performed relatively well in by-elections in 1972 and 1973, and in local elections in 1977, but did not gain more than 3.6 per cent of the vote in any constituency in the general elections of 1970 and 1974, and in subsequent elections it declined to insignificance. The anti-racist organizations Anti-Nazi League (ANL) and Rock Against Racism (RAR) were formed in response to the rise of the NF.[19] Black people were involved in these campaigns, but did not predominate. Some Black activists argued that the ANL's very name harked back to anti-fascist campaigns of the 1930s rather than dealing directly with Black people's everyday experiences of racism.[20] Nonetheless, by the early 1980s, the ANL's street tactics were important in de-legitimising the National Front and detaching it from all but its most virulently racist supporters. The NF split in 1982 when its leader, John Tyndall, left to form the British National Party (BNP).

The 1970s saw a shift in trade unions to active support for anti-racism. As well as participating in anti-racist campaigns, the TUC put aside the strong reservations that had characterized its approach to the race relations legislation of the 1960s, and welcomed the 1976 Race Relations Act. In 1976, it supported a strike at the Grunwick photo-processing plant in Brent, North London, in which most of the strikers were Asian women. The strike, against an employer supported by right-wing individuals and groups, failed, not least because the unions failed to support it fully. However, it began to break down some trade unionists' prejudices against workers from minority ethic groups, which arose from the unwillingness of some of them to unionise, arising, in turn, from doubts about the attitudes of White trade unionists towards them.[21] As minority ethnic membership grew, unions developed more progressive equal-opportunities policies. By the 1990s, the trade union movement had gone some way to shedding its traditional White, male image, establishing annual conferences for workers from minority ethnic groups from 1993, through the TUC. Bill Morris emerged as one of

Britain's leading trade unionists during the 1980s, becoming the first Black general secretary of a union (the Transport and General Workers Union) in 1991. It was another decade, however, until Beverly Malone became the first Black female leader of a large organization of workers, the Royal College of Nursing.

At the beginning of the 1980s, minority ethnic groups remained concentrated in limited sectors of the economy, in particular the public sector, catering and 'ethnic' business. The contraction of Britain's manufacturing base during the early 1980s disproportionately affected members of minority ethnic groups because of their concentration in manual work. In 1984, members of minority ethnic groups were twice as likely to be unemployed as White people. Asian self-employment grew, possibly due to unemployment, but also to cultural preferences. An increasingly diverse picture of inequality among minority ethnic communities emerged. Regional differences were important, especially among Asians. Pakistanis who had settled in northern textile towns in the 1960s and Bangladeshis who settled in the historically impoverished East End of London in the 1970s faced bleaker prospects than East African Asians who settled in pockets of London and the south-east that were less affected by recession.

An historically poor relationship between the police and Black Caribbean youth was further aggravated by the 'mugging' (street robbery) panic of the 1970s and the Metropolitan Police's increasing use of the so-called 'Sus' law.[22] Using provisions in the Vagrancy Act 1824, the police were empowered to stop and search people who they suspected of having intent to commit a crime. The power was used disproportionately against young Black men. In combination with the increasingly bleak economic prospects of inner-city youths, police tactics contributed to major riots in British cities in the summer of 1981. An investigation Lord Justice Scarman carried out for the government looked into the causes of the riots and recommended government action to alleviate inner-city decline and racial disadvantage. Lord Scarman's report acknowledged widespread discrimination and inequality, but disavowed that 'institutional racism' existed within the police. It recommended making efforts to recruit members of minority ethnic groups into the police force. The report's partial implementation did not prevent further outbreaks of violence during the 1980s, sparked by negative perceptions of police tactics. The most serious occurred in 1985 on the Broadwater Farm Estate in Tottenham, North London, where a policeman was killed. Substantial investment following these disturbances led to the area's regeneration and improved relationships between the local community and the police force that serves it.[23]

In 1981, Margaret Thatcher's Conservative government introduced the British Nationality Act, which further restricted the rights of members of the British Commonwealth to British citizenship. Three classes of citizenship were introduced, with the right to live in Britain largely restricted to those with a British grandparent. From the race riots in Nottingham and Notting Hill in 1958 to the disturbances in Oldham in 2001, breakdowns in public order have been a key driver for change at local and national level, stimulating legislation that both restricted immigration and sought to improve race relations. They also encouraged members of the minority ethnic groups affected and the authorities to negotiate to prevent further clashes. Following the Oldham disturbances, the Labour Home Secretary, David Blunkett, commissioned Ted Cantle, who had long experience of local government, to review Oldham's efforts to achieve racial harmony. The resulting report and subsequent investigations have contributed to an increasing emphasis in government on the concept of community cohesion, which can be seen as a development of the often-misunderstood concept of multiculturalism, counterbalancing the emphasis on cultural difference with encouraging awareness of shared values and commonalities.[24]

The 1970s had seen minority ethnic political activity focused on particularist organizations inspired by the American Black Power movement of the late 1960s. By the end of the 1970s, members of minority ethnic groups began to participate actively in municipal politics, particularly in London where the GLC was at the forefront of anti-racist campaigning. Organizations such as Greater London Action for Racial Equality (GLARE) emerged. Such activities were often linked to, or grew out of, the large and growing range of voluntary and community organizations created by minority ethnic groups throughout Britain, sometimes based on faith or leisure interests, or with more direct political objectives to safeguard and promote participation and greater equality.

Increasingly, a few members of minority ethnic groups moved into positions of influence within the Labour Party. By the mid-1980s, Bernie Grant, Linda Bellos and Merle Amory all led Labour-run London councils. A campaign was launched in 1983 for a separate Black caucus within the Labour Party. It helped secure the selection of more minority ethnic candidates in the 1987 general election, with the result that more (although still only four) minority ethnic MPs were returned in 1987. They formed the Black Parliamentary Caucus with the now-ennobled David Pitt.

Minority ethnic media became more firmly established and more diverse. *The Voice* newspaper, combining populist campaigning with spotlighting Black music and Black celebrities, came to speak for and to many Black people, gaining the advertising from the public sector that was required to satisfy equal opportunities criteria. *Pride*, aimed at Black women, was founded in 1991. An increasingly successful Asian press, including *Eastern Eye* (started in 1989, initially as a popular anti-racist journal), had less difficulty in attracting advertising, despite the continued under-representation of minority ethnic groups in the advertising industry. They continued also to be under-represented in all the mainstream media.

1990s TO NOW

In 1991, the death of Black teenager Stephen Lawrence in a racist attack and the subsequent mishandling of the investigation by the police, with the outcome that, by 2009, no one had yet been brought to justice for the killing, caused outrage in the Black Caribbean community and more widely, and received sustained coverage in the national media. The Macpherson Report, chaired by a former High Court judge, Sir William Macpherson, into the police investigation was not published until 1999, but it was damning. It led to the extension of the 1976 Act to the police and other public authorities in the Race Relations (Amendment) Act, 2000. This placed a new, enforceable, positive duty on public authorities to promote equal opportunities and eliminate discrimination. Macpherson introduced the concept of 'institutional racism' to a wider public.

Social survey evidence from the 1990s pointed to continuing divergence in the experiences of minority ethnic groups. Since the 1980s, growing numbers of economic migrants and political refugees from a growing range of countries have created an increasingly diverse minority ethnic population, with fewer of them originating in Britain's former colonies. Following enlargement of the European Union since 2004 to include former communist countries in Eastern Europe, these countries have grown as sources of economic migration.

At the same time, there was increasingly confident organization within and across minority ethnic groups. For example, the 1990 Trust grew out of Black community and lobby groups that had been founded in the 1970s and 1980s, as a policy research and networking organization to coordinate campaigning on local and national issues and on behalf of individuals who suffer discrimination or other forms of mistreatment. Increasingly, modern technology enabled organizations and individuals to exchange information and to organize effectively. In 1996, the Trust, together with Charter 88 (which campaigns for democratic reform) established Operation Black Vote. This continues to be active, seeking to build political participation and a political voice among Asian, African, Caribbean and other minority ethnic groups by urging people to register and use their votes, to campaign on issues of inequality and promote cultural diversity.

In terms of economic opportunities, by the 1990s, the Chinese and African–Asian populations had reached broad parity with the White population by some measures. African–Asians and White people experienced similar levels of unemployment, on average, with unemployment among Chinese people the lowest of any ethnic group. On average, African–Asian employees were more likely than White people to be earning more than £500 per week. Both Chinese and African–Asian people had higher educational attainment than their White peers.[25] At the other extreme, serious poverty remained in Pakistani and Bangladeshi communities. In 1994, more than four out of five Pakistani and Bangladeshi households had incomes below half the national average – four times as many as White non-pensioners.[26]

Pensioners from ethnic minority groups were likely to be poorer than White pensioners (see Chapter 1). By 1999, the average unemployment rate for all minority ethnic groups was double that of White people.[27] Disadvantage in employment undoubtedly triggered inequality in other key areas such as household income, health, education and housing.

Statistics on differences in the educational experience of population groups have been poor until recently. The Parekh Report, *The Future of Multi-ethnic Britain*, commissioned in 2000 by the Runnymede Trust (founded in 1968 as an independent body seeking to promote improved race relations) and chaired by a distinguished political scientist of Asian origin, found that fewer than one in 200 schools had satisfactory arrangements for monitoring by ethnicity, and few existing statistics on ethnicity and school achievement took account of the key variable of social class. Despite the unsatisfactory statistics, the report reached some broad conclusions:

- Black Caribbean pupils started school at age 5, performing at the national average. By age 10, they had fallen behind, the difference being greater in maths than in English. At age 16, the proportion of Black Caribbean students achieving GCSEs at A*–C was considerably less than half the national average and markedly lower among males than females.
- At Key Stage 2, in English and maths and at GCSE level generally, Indian pupils achieved above the national average. The difference at GCSE was even higher than at Key Stage 2.
- Bangladeshi and Pakistani pupils achieved below the national average, but steadily closed the gap in the course of their education. In some Local Education Authorities, they performed at or above the national average.
- There was substantial polarization within minority ethnic groups, with young Bangladeshis and Pakistanis well represented in terms of entry to university, but over-represented among school pupils with the poorest qualifications.
- The information for A-Level outcomes and entry to higher education was of a higher quality than for school education.
- A-Level participation for all Asian and most Black students was the same or higher than the national average, with Black Caribbean men a significant exception. Participation rates among young Bangladeshi and Pakistani women were higher than among young White women.
- National average levels of attainment on entry to university were exceeded by Indian, Pakistani and Black Caribbean women, and by Indian, Pakistani and Bangladeshi men.
- About 70 per cent of Black Caribbean and 60 per cent of Indian, Pakistani and Bangladeshi students pursued their degrees at post-1992 universities, compared with only 35 per cent of White students.

National statistics for 2003–4 confirmed that these broad patterns had changed little. Most successful in attaining five or more GCSE grades A*–C in England were Chinese students, with 79 per cent of Chinese girls and 70 per cent of Chinese boys attaining this level. Indian students had the next highest attainment levels, of 72 and 62 per cent respectively. The lowest levels of attainment were among Black Caribbean boys (27 per cent), with 44 per cent of Black Caribbean girls gaining the target level. Other Black and mixed White and Black groups had the next lowest levels of attainment. Among White British students, 48 per cent of boys and 57 per cent of girls met the target. In all ethnic groups, girls outperformed boys.[28] These patterns were further confirmed by 2004–5 data for A-Level and university degree performance.[29]

PERCEPTIONS OF MINORITY ETHNIC GROUPS

Polling data from the British Social Attitudes Survey for 1983 to 1991 suggests that less than 5 per cent of British people held strongly prejudiced views. However, one-third reported some prejudice and, when considering the views of others, more than half of respondents suggested that minority ethnic groups experienced serious racism.[30] On one reading, this data suggests that racism was still prevalent in the 1990s; on the other hand, it suggests widespread acknowledgement that members of minority ethnic groups were disadvantaged. It perhaps pointed to a basis of support for further legislation to reduce inequality. Overt racism had become unacceptable in public but, as the 1990s progressed, frequent use of rhetoric that was dismissive of 'political correctness', in the media, for example, came close to assertions, common in the 1950s, that ethnic and other minorities were oversensitive and quick to take offence.

Since the 1950s, when minority ethnic groups had broadly similar socio-economic circumstances, increasingly diverse patterns of work, housing tenure and leisure have emerged[31] and can lead to tensions between communities. This was evidenced in 2005 by clashes between Birmingham's Black Caribbean and Pakistani populations.[32] These tensions, generally concentrated in inner urban areas, can arise as minority groups try to make sense of an increasingly differentiated experience of disadvantage. This suggests that generalized discrimination against minority ethnic groups is not necessarily the cause of all disadvantage. Also, in recent years, very similar forms of hostility and discrimination have been directed against immigrants from Eastern Europe, who are White but differ from the indigenous British community predominantly in language. Following the 9/11 terrorist attacks on the United States and the July 2005 attacks on London, concern about discrimination and disadvantage has increasingly focused on religious rather than ethnic minority groups, especially Muslims. (This is discussed in Chapter 3.)

Change over time in the language used to describe minority ethnic groups is one measure of cultural change. The term 'coloured' as a catch-all term fell into disuse in the 1970s in response to more assertive forms of

Black cultural politics. Terms such as Black, Black British, British Asian and Afro-Caribbean became commonplace in the 1980s, while the trans-ethnic nature of Muslim identity has meant that people of Pakistani and Bangladeshi descent are now more often described as British Muslims. However, racist language has not disappeared, with 'asylum seeker' emerging in recent years as code for an immigrant/member of an ethnic minority.

The growth of commercially successful ethnic minority media in the 1980s and 1990s may have been a factor in the increasing ability of minority communities to influence the language used to describe them. Publications like *The Voice* and *Asian Age* have also provided ethnic minority journalists with a route into the mainstream media, although research suggests that 'low-level racism' still pervades the culture of the newsroom.[33] A heavy reliance on unpaid internships and personal contacts as ways into the media tends to exclude those who are outside the 'old boys' network' and those with fewer financial resources. Television has a better record than newspapers, with the success of pioneers such as Trevor MacDonald and Moira Stewart in the 1970s, replicated by Krishnan Guru-Murthy and Zeinab Badawi since the 1990s, although minority ethnic groups remain under-represented in the mainstream media.

It is difficult to determine whether these trends have had a significant effect on the way in which minority ethnic groups are represented in newspapers and on television or are perceived by viewers and readers. Many people remain dissatisfied with the way the mainstream media portrays minority ethnic people. The hostile response of some popular national newspapers to the Metropolitan Police Commissioner's comments in early 2006 that minority ethnic victims of crime were treated with less concern than White victims, or even overlooked by the media, suggested how difficult it remains to discuss structural racism in public.[34] It also showed how far the Met had come since the early 1980s, although by 2008, protests by senior officers of minority ethnic origin about their experience of racism in the force overshadowed such gains and showed how far there was still to go.[35]

The portrayal of minority ethnic people on television provides one index of cultural change. In the 1960s, the popular sitcom *Till Death Do Us Part* portrayed White working class racism ambiguously, while programmes like *Curry and Chips* and *The Black and White Minstrel Show* relied on simple derogatory stereotyping. The latter was the subject of a petition presented to the BBC in 1967 by CARD, but the programme's demise, as late as 1977, had as much to do with the decline in popularity of the variety genre as with increasing sensitivity to the feelings of minorities. Generally, coverage has become increasingly sensitive since the 1970s, with BBC 2 and Channel Four pioneering programming with specific appeal to minority ethnic audiences in the 1980s and 1990s. Programmes such as the all-Asian sketch show *Goodness Gracious Me* inverted the racial stereotyping characteristic of 1970s staples like *It Ain't Half Hot Mum*. However, some White minority ethnic groups, notably Gypsies and Travellers, continue to be vilified by the media (see Chapter 4).

Research suggests that minority ethnic communities remain distanced from national television culture, showing little interest in programmes with 'strongly White, middle England associations' and preferring shows with an urban context and American and Australian imports.[36] It is now possible to access channels from many parts of the world, and the growth of digital media has seen a proliferation in Britain of broadcasting designed for and produced by minority ethnic groups. For example, there are now almost 40 Asian television channels.

CONCLUSION

The extent of anti-Irish feeling in the nineteenth century and of anti-Semitism at the turn of the century, the inequalities suffered by both groups at the time and the relative decline of these inequalities over the twentieth century is worth noting. In neither case have the inequalities disappeared, but they have diminished in virulence. IRA bomb attacks in Britain in the 1970s and 1980s did not give rise to the equivalent of the anti-Muslim feeling since the terrorist attacks of 9/11 and July 2005, or of the anti-Irish hostility following Fenian attacks in the mid-nineteenth century. Over time, both Jewish and Irish people appear to have become more accepted within the general culture, although hostility sporadically recurs.[37]

Reductions in racial inequality over the past 60 years have been piecemeal and uneven across population groups. The extremely unequal access to goods, services and employment that was characteristic of the 1950s has been replaced by an environment where formal access is guaranteed. However, a survey by the charity Business in the Community of data on senior managers between 2000 and 2007 concludes that management prospects are 'disproportionately bleak' for people from Black and minority ethic backgrounds.[38] Some minorities still face overt discrimination, with the CRE continuing, until its absorption in the Equality and Human Rights Commission in 2007, to receive complaints against pubs with signs saying 'No Travellers' or, to evade race relations legislation, 'No caravan-dwellers'.

Government action and the campaigning of lobby groups and think tanks have been important drivers for change. On the one hand, successive restrictions on immigration and the rights of immigrants have contributed to diminishing hostility. More positively, measures against discrimination have had some effect. Statutory bodies have resulted, which have been powerful advocates for change. However, it may be that the institutional arrangements resulting from race relations legislation have stifled other political and social groupings based more firmly on minority ethnic participation. It is difficult to judge whether these formations would have been better able to secure change. In the aftermath of urban riots in which race has been a factor, minority ethnic groups have exerted a strong, but temporary, voice expressing their concerns. Significant changes, especially in the relationship between minority ethnic groups and the police, have more often than not resulted from conflict and controversy rather than from constructive dialogue.

A major change has been the mainstream attitude to the proper role of law in eliminating discrimination. Legislation has contributed to changing certain forms of behaviour and has played an important role in attempting to eliminate racial prejudice and in establishing belief that the absence of prejudice is an enduring public good. The overt discrimination practised in the 1950s has diminished, but indirect forms stubbornly persist. Legislation has played an important role in de-legitimising certain forms of behaviour, but has not significantly changed material conditions. Inequalities remain in access to jobs, education and training, but their incidence varies across ethnic groups, which suggests that discrimination against ethnic minority groups is not the whole, or necessarily the main, driver of these inequalities, but that socio-economic, institutional, policy and perhaps cultural influences must also be assessed. Members of minority ethnic groups are seriously under-represented in high-profile roles in business, the media and politics. There would need to be a four-fold increase in parliamentarians from minority ethnic backgrounds at Westminster to be genuinely representative of cultural diversity in twenty-first-century Britain.

There is increasing diversity among minority ethnic groups, to the point where some no longer experience serious disadvantage. Although these successes are cause for celebration, there should be no automatic assumption that they will be repeated by other groups over time.

The main drivers towards greater equality over the past 60 years have been:

- cultural change: diminished hostility by sections of the White British community to most minority ethnic groups – such as Irish and Jews over the past 100 years – following increased cultural contact, greater integration into the workforce and greater prosperity of some, but not all minority ethnic groups. However, change has been very slow and is still incomplete
- campaigning, mainly by members of minority ethnic groups, on all the dimensions of equality; increasingly assertive and effective over time, due to greater numbers and confidence
- the effect of government institutions and legislation, mostly put in place following activist campaigns
- Labour governments doing more to promote equality than Conservative governments
- the European Union and European courts prompting British government action and giving minority groups levers to promote greater equality.

Inhibitors of change include:

- the continued poverty and unequal access to education and training of members of some minority ethnic groups
- popular racism, expressed, for example, in voting; somewhat weaker

over time but still prevalent, particularly in relations to specific groups, such as Gypsies and Travellers (see Chapter 4)
- external events, such as the impact of 9/11, July 2005 and subsequent events on experiences of many Muslims and others perceived as Muslim; and of criticism by Israel's government of the attitudes of some towards British Jews
- the media generally, for its poor record of employing people from ethnic minority groups; the popular press, in particular, for reinforcing stereotypes.

In 2007, the Community Relations Commission was replaced by, and its responsibilities absorbed into, the new Equality and Human Rights Commission, chaired by Trevor Phillips, previously head of the CRE. Through its unprecedentedly broad remit, this has the potential to support victims of multiple deprivation, such as older disabled women from minority ethnic backgrounds. Its impact is, as yet, unclear.

STATISTICS

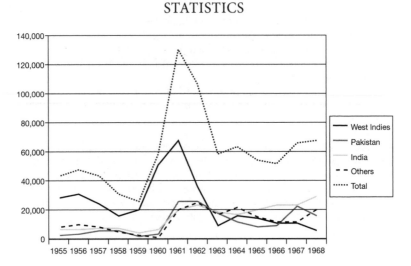

Figure 2.1 Net immigration from the new Commonwealth into Britain: 1955–68

Source: Adapted from Hill, Clifford, *Immigration and Integration: A Study of the Settlement of Coloured Minorities in Britain* (Pergamon Press, 1970).

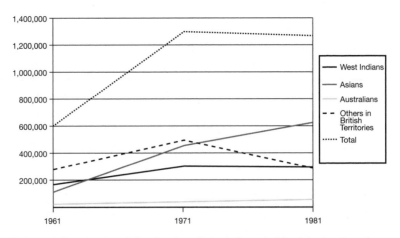

Figure 2.2 Immigration defined as those living in households whose head was born in the relevant area: 1961, 1971 and 1981 censuses

Source: Adapted from David Butler, *Twentieth Century British Political Facts, 1900–2000* (Macmillan, 2000).

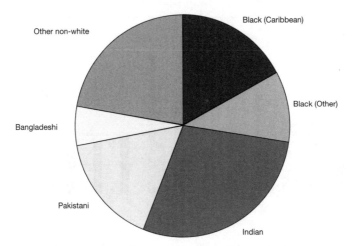

Figure 2.3 1991 Census: non-white self categorisation
Source: Office for National Statistics.

	Total numbers	% of overall population	% of non-White population
White	54,152,898	91.1	–
Mixed	677,117	1.2	14.6
Indian	1,053,411	1.8	22.7
Pakistani	747,285	1.3	16.1
Bangladeshi	283,063	0.5	6.1
Other Asian	247,664	0.4	5.3
All Asian or Asian British	2,331,423	4.0	50.3
Black Caribbean	565,876	1.0	12.2
Black African	485,277	0.8	10.5
Black Other	97,585	0.2	2.1
All Black or Black British	1,148,738	2.0	24.8
Chinese	247,403	0.4	5.3
Other ethnic groups	230,615	0.4	5.0
All minority ethnic population	4,635,296	7.9	100
All population	58,789,194	100	

Figure 2.4 Population of the United Kingdom by ethnic group. 2001 Census
Source: Office for National Statistics.

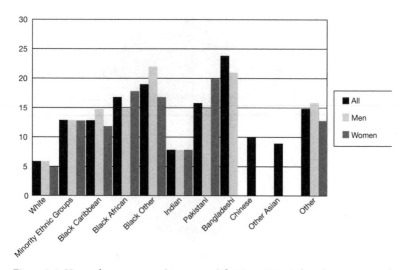

Figure 2.5 Unemployment rates (percentage) for Great Britain by ethnic group and
gender for all persons 16 and over: 1999
Source: Adapted from Pilkington, p. 68.

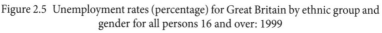

	Number of self-employees	As percentage of employees	As percentage of economically active
Whites	2,766,334	12.3	11.19
Black–Caribbean	13,097	5.79	4.69
Black–African	5,334	7.59	5.54
Black–other	3,796	7.76	6.03
Indian	66,522	19.55	16.99
Pakistani	22,480	22.79	16.24
Bangladeshi	5,019	17.75	12.14
Chinese	17,613	26.63	24.10
Other–Asian	7,744	9.42	8.16
Other–other	11,820	13.24	10.87
Total non-White	153,425	14.61	11.92
All ethnic communities	2,919,759	12.40	11.23

Figure 2.6 Ethnic variation in self-employment rates: 1991 Census
Source: Adapted from Pilkington, p. 144.

	White	Caribbean	Indian	African–Asian	Pakistani	Bangladeshi	Chinese
Average weekly income	£294	£249	£308	£334	£202	£196	£350
Average for non-pensioner households	£343	£259	£317	£338	£203	£196	£354

Figure 2.7 Total household income: 1994

Source: Adapted from Modood, *Ethnic Minorities*, p. 158.

Chapter 3

Religion and belief
Liza Filby

TIMELINE

1829	Catholic Relief Act allows Catholics to enter parliament.
1836	Board of Deputies of British Jews establishes its constitution.
1838	Blasphemy Act; relates only to the Church of England.
1855	Liberty of Religious Worship Act enables all religious groups to establish houses of worship.
1858	Jews allowed to enter parliament; non-Christians able to take parliamentary oath of office.
1880	Atheist Charles Bradlaugh refuses his seat in parliament.
1889	Britain's first mosque built, in Woking.
1905	Aliens Act restricts immigration to Britain.
1911	Britain's first Sikh Gurdwara established in Putney, London.
1922	John William Gott the last man imprisoned for blasphemy.
1936	Battle of Cable Street against fascist anti-Semites.
1940	Jewish Trades Advisory Council established.
1944	Glasgow's first mosque built.
1962	Federation of Students Islamic Societies and UK Islamic Mission established.
1970	Inauguration of the General Synod, the 'parliament' of the Church of England.
	A national network of local organizations, Union of Muslim Organizations, formed.
1976	Race Relations Act prohibits discrimination on racial, but not specifically religious, grounds.
	Commission for Racial Equality set up.
	Sikhs exempted from 1972 law making crash helmets compulsory for motorcyclists.
1977	Mary Whitehouse brings private prosecution under Blasphemy Act against editor of *Gay News*.
	Regent's Park Mosque completed in London.
1984	Imams and Mosques' Council of Great Britain and Council of Mosques in United Kingdom and Eire established.
1985	Law Commission recommends amending Blasphemy Act.

1988	Controversy over *The Satanic Verses*. UK Action Committee on Islamic Affairs formed.
1994	Meeting of Muslim organizations and institutions calls for 'Islamic consensus on national affairs'.
1996	Employment tribunal hears that preventing observance of Islamic festivals amounts to indirect racial discrimination.
1997	Formation of Muslim Council of Britain, umbrella body for Islam in Britain and national voice for British Muslims. First Muslim MP enters parliament.
1998	Human Rights Act guarantees right to freedom of thought, conscience and religion, and to practise one's beliefs within the law.
1999	Prison service appoints its first Muslim adviser.
2000	Feversham College for Girls in Bradford is Britain's first Muslim school to gain state aid.
2001	Home Office report, *Religious Discrimination in England and Wales*. Race/religious riots in Oldham and Bradford, Cantle Report.
2003	Employment Equality (Religion and Belief) Regulations forbid workplace religious discrimination.
2004	Shabina Begum loses High Court battle to wear jilbab at school, but later wins on appeal. West Yorkshire police unable to act against British National Party leaflet *The Truth about Islam*, as Muslims not covered by Race Relations Act. Performance of *Behzti* suspended in Birmingham following Sikh protests.
2005	BBC screening of *Jerry Springer the Opera* leads to protests by Christian groups.
2006	Racial and Religious Hatred Act creates offence of 'inciting religious hatred'. Equality Act 2006 (Part 2) extends protection against religious discrimination to education, provision of goods and services, management of premises and exercising of public functions.
2007	October: Equality and Human Rights Commission opens, established by the 2006 Equality Act.
2008	Archbishop of Canterbury delivers speech on Sharia law to the Royal Courts of Justice.

INTRODUCTION: THE BIRTH OF MULTI-FAITH BRITAIN

The integration and assimilation of religious minorities into British society has a long and complex history, dating back to the Reformation. The Act of Uniformity, Test and Corporation Acts and Conventicle Acts of the seventeenth century established the supremacy of Anglicanism in England and Wales and curtailed the religious freedoms of the Roman Catholic and growing non-conformist communities.

Piecemeal concessions were made to the Protestant denominations in the Toleration Act of 1689, but Roman Catholics had to wait until the Catholic Relief Act 1829 to gain equal rights. This delayed acceptance of Catholicism within British society can in part be explained by the external threat of the Catholic foreign powers, notably France, as well as the unifying force of Protestantism as a central facet of British identity. The passing of the Catholic Relief Act is important, for not only did it indicate a growing toleration of Catholics in British society (allowing them to enter parliament, among other things), it also signified the symbolic end of what was known as the Anglican 'confessional state'. The predominance of the Church of England as the one Establishment religion was increasingly being challenged, and the nineteenth century saw the decline of influence of Christianity within Britain's civic institutions.

For Jews, who, like Catholics, were for centuries tolerated but constrained as a religious minority in Britain (see Chapter 2), legislative emancipation came in the Jewish Relief Act 1858. This granted Jewish citizens equal rights in respect of education (including entry to Oxford and Cambridge universities), property and voting, and the right to become members of parliament. The Liberty of Religious Worship Act 1855, enabled all religious communities to build places of worship, and Jews and Catholics were also able to establish their own educational institutions alongside the state-subsidized Anglican schools.[1] The Board of Deputies of British Jews, whose origins can be traced back to 1760, formed its constitution in 1836 and remains the main representative body for a large part of the British Jewish community. This gradual acceptance of non-Anglican faith groups grew alongside greater recognition of the rights of non-religious British citizens, including the removal of obligatory religious oaths when testifying in the law courts and in parliament.

Large-scale economic migration by Catholics from Ireland in the mid-nineteenth century prompted the Roman Catholic Church to re-establish its hierarchy of bishops and diocesan organization in England and Wales in 1850, and in Scotland in 1878. The Catholic Church's presence was focused around Britain's industrial centres, such as London, Glasgow and Manchester, where the Catholic Irish had migrated in particularly large numbers in search of work. Due to their low social and economic status, and also because of the political tensions between the United Kingdom and Ireland, Irish Catholics experienced considerable socio-economic inequality and discrimination, despite the legislative emancipation.

The concessions achieved by Britain's minority religious communities in the nineteenth century can be characterised as piecemeal reforms: there was no universal declaration of the freedom of religious expression or all-inclusive protection of religious rights. Religious diversity was tolerated, alongside an understanding that Britain remained a Christian country with a dominant established church.

The history of multi-faith Britain is inextricably connected with the history of immigration (see Chapter 2). Britain's indigenous Catholic population was small in the 1830s and it was only mass migration from Ireland in the mid-nineteenth century that re-established Catholicism as a fixed presence on the British mainland. Similarly, the integration and acceptance of Anglo-Jewry is linked to the growth of Britain's Jewish population. Between the 1880s and 1914, some 100,000 Jews escaping from persecution in Eastern Europe migrated chiefly to the East End of London, as well as establishing smaller communities in Manchester, Liverpool, Leeds and Scotland.

Jews from Eastern Europe encountered greater prejudice than immigrants of Irish descent. Differences in language, culture and religious practices meant this new community experienced severe discrimination. Fears and tensions concerning the rising Jewish population led to the passing of the Aliens Act 1905 (see Chapter 2), the first measure to restrict immigration by those without British citizenship. Faced with such hostility, British Jews relied on support from within their own community and, with assistance from Jews overseas, funded schools and welfare services to avoid being accused of making demands on British taxpayers. These schools and community organizations assisted the process of assimilation by enabling Jewish migrants to adapt to British culture (for example, by speaking English rather than Yiddish), while also helping them to maintain their faith and the essentials of Jewish culture.[2] This did not prevent further anti-Semitic aggression during World War I, mainly directed towards German Jews; in turn, this led to further immigration restrictions in the British Nationality and Status of Aliens Act 1914.

MID-TWENTIETH CENTURY: CONSOLIDATED COMMUNITIES

Suspicion and fear of religious and racial minorities was pervasive in inter-war Britain. In particular, the activities of the Black-shirts of the British Union of Fascists, led by its founder Oswald Mosley[3], an admirer of Hitler demonstrated anti-Jewish feeling. The Battle of Cable Street in 1936, in which Mosley's fascists attempted to march through London's Jewish area in East London, resulted in a confrontation between the Black-shirts and an alliance of Jews, Irish dockers and communist protesters. The late 1930s also witnessed a relatively small influx of Jewish refugees from Nazism, but, as the truth emerged about German persecution of Jews, these émigrés aroused sympathy rather than resentment.

However, an outburst of anti-Semitic riots in Britain just after World War II highlights the extent to which external events, particularly foreign affairs, influenced the treatment of religious minorities in Britain. In 1947, during the campaign against British control of Palestine, Jewish rebels bombed a British prison in Acre, capturing two British army sergeants and eventually hanging them. This incident received widespread press coverage and prompted violence against Jews in the city centres of Leeds, Liverpool, East London, Manchester and Glasgow, and even in smaller enclaves such as South End, Blackpool and Hendon. The riots lasted for five days in Liverpool, with more than 300 Jewish properties damaged and 88 people arrested.[4] Commenting on the implications of the situation in the Middle East for British Jews and the fear that such behaviour undermined Britain's moral vision of itself in the aftermath of the war, the *Manchester Guardian* observed:

> The murder of the British sergeants in Palestine was a brutal crime, the act of crazed fanatics. But . . . to answer terrorism in Palestine with terrorism in England is sheer Hitlerism. We must be desperately careful to see that we do not let ourselves be infected with the same poison of the disease we thought to eradicate.[5]

It was reported that one Jewish man in Manchester hung a sign in his shop reading: 'As a British sailor, I fought for you. This is my reward.'[6] This alluded to the fact that Jews considered themselves British, with many sacrificing themselves for their adopted country during wartime, yet they were still considered aliens by many British people. However much Anglo-Jews attempted to carve out an acceptable British Jewish identity, they remained vulnerable, particularly on the issue of Zionism, which was seen as unpatriotic and un-British. As with Catholics and their association with Irish terrorism, and more recently Muslims and Islamic terrorism, when a new external enemy/'other' is defined, the related internal 'other' becomes the focus for antagonism and abuse, regardless of the extent to which the minority has been culturally assimilated.

Anti-Semitism and attacks on Jewish properties and synagogues have occurred periodically since 1947. In the 1940s and 1950s, the Jewish community attempted to protect businesses and communities from these tensions by setting up their own institutions. The Jewish Trades Advisory Council, for example, was established in 1940 to combat anti-Semitism in trade and to gain licences for Jewish shopkeepers to work on Sundays, the Christian Sabbath. Half a century later, a report by the Runneymede Trust in 1994 titled *A Very Light Sleeper* revealed that anti-Semitism persisted in modern Britain, albeit in a less aggressive form.[7]

Both the Jewish and Catholic communities experienced increasing social mobility in post-war decades, with many moving out of inner-city enclaves to the suburbs. With social *embourgeoisement* came a greater acceptance and confidence of their place within the mainstream of British society. Following the 1944 Education Act, schools of both faiths accepted government-subsidized, voluntary-aided status. As Catholics became more tolerated, they began to express their concerns in public and political forums. In the years between the world wars, Catholic groups had campaigned against the public funding of birth-control advice and, in the post-war era,

Catholic lobbyists headed the opposition to the legalisation of abortion in the Abortion Act 1967 and lobbied MPs in subsequent unsuccessful attempts to amend it. Catholics continue to make up most of the support behind anti-abortion lobby groups such as the Society for the Protection of Unborn Children (SPUC, founded in 1966) and Life.

From the 1960s onwards, as British society in general became more secularised, British Catholicism followed this secularising trend, with many Catholics, particularly women, rejecting Catholic teaching on issues such as birth control and abortion. Neither British Catholicism nor British Judaism witnessed a comparable decline in religious observance as that experienced by the Protestant denominations, although both saw a decline of marriage within their faiths (see Tables 3.1 and 3.2).[8]

Catholics and Jews can be said to have emerged from being an 'underclass' within British society. However, just as anti-Semitism continues, parts of Britain continue to be divided along Catholic/Protestant lines and deep-rooted anti-Catholicism still exists. While such antagonism has declined since the 1950s in places where it was formerly strong, in particular in Glasgow, it survives and may even be rising. In a poll for the Scottish *Daily Herald* in September 1999, 37 per cent of readers agreed that there were 'deep rooted anti-Catholic attitudes throughout Scottish society'; a further 13 per cent agreed 'strongly', while 45 per cent disagreed.[9] A report by the Scottish Executive showed that between 2004 and 2005, the number of sectarian incidents reported to the police rose by 50 per cent, to 440, mostly in the Glasgow area and contrary to an overall decline in reported crime. Sixty-four per cent of these were offences against Catholics and 31 per cent were against Protestants, with many of them occurring at football matches where historic sectarian rivalry between Glasgow's (Catholic) Celtic and (Protestant) Rangers remains strong.[10]

1950s AND 1960s: IMMIGRATION AND CHANGE

Mass immigration from the former Empire during the 1950s and 1960s transformed Britain (in demographic terms) into a multi-faith society (see Chapter 2). Numbers are imprecise, as immigration statistics were not calculated on the basis of religion, but by 1980, Britain's Hindu and Muslim populations are estimated to have more than doubled to 120,000 and 600,000 respectively (see Table 3.3). In addition, substantial numbers of Christians of all denominations migrated from the Caribbean. By the 1970s, the religious make-up of Britain had altered dramatically, with Muslims emerging as the largest minority faith in Britain.

During the early years of their settlement, Hindus, Sikhs and Muslims organised supportive institutions and networks within their communities. For example, the 1960s saw the founding of the Federation of Student Islamic Societies (FOSIS), the Doctors Islamic Society and the Islamic Mission, which distributed literature and offered guidance at local levels.

Britain's new faith communities realized, as Jews previously had done, that although they had complete freedom to worship and practise their faith, in the context of the workplace and in wider society, their needs were not necessarily recognized or accommodated. In this way, their different customs of religious worship, dress, observance of religious festivals and Sabbath met incomprehension and prejudice. For example, when a law was introduced in 1972 making the wearing of motorcycle helmets compulsory, no allowance was made for Sikh men, who wore turbans. After a vigorous public campaign by Sikh groups, the law was amended in their favour in 1976. The following describes a Sikh woman's experience of discrimination in her workplace, a bakery:

> For 8 years, it was never a problem. Then one woman began to be picked on for wearing a bangle. Finally she was moved to a different part of the organization, and ordered to take it off, the woman refused. Representatives from the Sikh temple had a meeting with Personnel to explain, but the employer refused to yield as they classified the bracelet as jewellery. Tests were done to see if there were any bacteria on the bangle, they came out negative. This controversy had knock-on effects for other Sikh women who supported the woman's cause. The case was eventually lost at a tribunal, but after years of fighting, a special sleeve was developed, and the management and staff who had pressured the woman to stop wearing what in their view was jewellery, were required to attend diversity training.[11]

Members of religious minorities from Commonwealth backgrounds were disproportionately in low-paid work. A survey from the early 1980s, for example, revealed that unemployment among Muslim men was higher than for any other religious or ethnic group, double the rate for Hindus and Sikhs, and higher than for Afro-Caribbean men. By the end of the 1980s, the situation had not improved, with 70 per cent of Asian Muslims working in manual occupations compared with the national average of 51 per cent. Half of those aged 16–24 had no qualifications, compared with the national average of 20 per cent.

THE 1970s: 'FITTING RELIGIOUS IDENTITY INTO THE RACIAL STRAITJACKET'

Government policy during this period was largely conceptualised around race rather than religion as the chief category of difference. The passing of the Race Relations Act (RRA) in 1976, which criminalized indirect and direct discrimination and sought to build on the 1965 and 1968 Acts (see Chapter 2), did not address religious discrimination. Subsequent case law revealed that only religio-ethnic groups such as Jews and Sikhs were classified as 'races', and therefore covered by the Act and protected by the newly established Commission for Racial Equality (CRE).

This legislation emerged out of lobbying by organizations such as the Campaign against Racial Discrimination (CARD) (see Chapter 2), which were chiefly Black organizations campaigning on behalf of Black Britons. It demonstrated the extent to which concepts of race and ethnicity dominated thinking behind equality legislation. Another possible reason why religious discrimination was not considered in relation to this Act was a perceived decline in religious observance in Britain. With many Britons identifying themselves as 'non-believers', religion was not viewed as a key category of identity. As a result, equality legislation did not protect the largest religious minority in Britain, Muslims, or the smaller number of Buddhists, which were both trans-ethnic groups that identified with their religion rather than their racial origins.

One Muslim group described the 1976 Act, which was to define the principles of multiculturalism for the next 20 years, as an attempt to fit 'Muslims into the racial straitjacket.'[12] An example of its effect was the legal case *Nyazi versus Rymans Limited*[13] in 1988, involving a woman who was refused a day's leave to celebrate the end of Ramadan. She lost her claim of racial discrimination under the RRA, on the grounds that Muslims were not an ethnic group as understood by the Act. Only Muslims from racial groups in which Islam was the dominant faith could claim indirect discrimination, which excluded Muslims of European or Caribbean descent. Calling for Muslims to be recognized for their religion, not their race, the An-Nisa Society, a campaigning group established in the 1980s by Muslim women to improve the provision of Muslim-sensitive services, argued in 1992 that the RRA 'has been the one major cause for the deprivation, alienation and marginalisation of Britain's Muslim community'.[14] This classification of British Muslims in terms of their racial rather than religious origin extended to the provision of state services. For example, the application of a White English Muslim woman to adopt a Muslim Somali baby could be rejected in preference to a non-Muslim African family.

THE 1980s: BRITAIN'S ISLAMIC COMMUNITY RAISES ITS VOICE

The Satanic Verses controversy in 1988 projected Britain's Muslim population into popular consciousness. Salman Rushdie's book precipitated widespread rioting in Pakistan and India and was quickly banned in all Muslim countries, as well as in South Africa, Sri Lanka, China and India. Tensions were heightened when the Iranian leader, Ayatollah Khomeini, issued a fatwa sentencing Rushdie to death. In Britain, the controversy sparked widespread demonstrations and even book burnings, particularly in Bradford and Bolton. To alleviate the situation, Muslim groups, supported by some Christian leaders, advocated the banning of the publication and distribution of the book under the Blasphemy Act 1838. This had no effect. The demand for the extension of the Blasphemy Act to protect Islamic sensibilities was rejected by the then-Conservative government. However, the campaign did provoke widespread debate about religious concerns over freedom of speech and about the role of the Blasphemy Act in a supposedly secular nation.

The existing Blasphemy Act only protected the Anglican faith and had last been used in a court of law in 1977. That case involved Mary Whitehouse, leader of the National Viewers' and Listeners' Association (which had fundamentalist Christian origins), who brought a private prosecution against the editor of *Gay News* for printing 'A Love That Dare Not Speak its Name', a poem about homosexual desire for Jesus Christ (see Chapter 6). The editor was convicted under the Act and given a suspended jail sentence. In 1985, however, the government Law Commission suggested that a change in the blasphemy laws should be considered.

When the attempt to use blasphemy law against the publication of *The Satanic Verses* reached the courts in 1989, the Court of Appeal held that the common law offence of blasphemous libel did not extend to religions other than Anglicanism. In an open letter to influential British Muslims, John Patten MP, then Minister of State for the Home Office, set out the government's position. He argued that due to a lack of consensus on amending the blasphemy law, the government did not wish to revise it or to risk curbing freedom of speech.[15] Crucially, Muslim leaders had not called for its abolition, but for extension of the blasphemy law to other faiths. In the words of the UK Action Committee on Islamic Affairs (UKACIA): 'Abolition [of the blasphemy law] would mean negative equalisation.'[16] This statement reveals Muslim understanding of the concept of multi-faith Britain in the 1980s. Muslims did not seek the potential undermining of all religions by abolition of the Blasphemy Act, but the recognition of all faiths on equal terms through extending the Act.

If *The Satanic Verses* controversy raised the issue of religious freedom in Britain, it mobilised and united Britain's Islamic community. In 1988, when the UKACIA was established, its leader, Iqbal Sacranie, publicly urged the government to recognize the rights of Britain's Islamic community. When the government undertook a review of the RRA in 1992, UKACIA took a leading role on behalf of the Muslim community, calling for legislation banning incitement to religious hatred similar to Northern Ireland's Prevention of Incitement to Hatred Act 1970. (This legislation, confined to Northern Ireland, emerged following protests by the Catholic minority in that region that they suffered from discrimination in employment, housing and other areas of life (see below). The Act made it illegal to arouse hatred against any individual or group because of their ethnicity, race, religion or belief. The Fair Employment (Northern Ireland) Act 1976, took this further, dealing with religious discrimination in the workplace and establishing the Fair Employment Agency. In 1989, the Fair Employment Northern Ireland Act targeted indirect discrimination and removed defects in the previous law, replacing the Fair Employment Agency with the Fair Employment Tribunal and Fair Employment Commission.) Muslim representatives proposed that this legislation should act as a model for mainland Britain. In the review of the RRA in 1992, the Commission for Racial Equality acknowledged its failures in assisting religious groups. It argued that the flaws in the existing legislation prevented those subjected to religious discrimination from pursuing their claims in the law courts, and proposed a Human Rights Commission to deal with discrimination in all its forms.

Meanwhile, the call for an organization to speak on behalf of the Muslim community gathered momentum, and in 1997, the Muslim Council of Britain (MCB), an umbrella body for Islam in Britain, was inaugurated. The council opposed such labels as 'ethnic minority', describing itself as representing 'British citizens with an Islamic heritage'.[17] The establishment of a coordinating body for the British Muslim community coincided with the election of Mohammad Sarwar as the first Muslim MP (for the Labour Party in Glasgow Govan) in 1997.

Another consequence of *The Satanic Verses* controversy was an increase in what became known as Islamophobia, with the scenes of book burnings in Bradford prompting heightened hostility towards Islam and the British Muslim community. Although it was no longer deemed acceptable to criticize or make derogatory statements about Irish, Afro-Caribbean or Jewish culture, attacks on Islam and Muslim assimilation in Britain increased. The following comment from columnist Peregrine Worsthorne, published in the *Sunday Telegraph* in 1991, suggests:

> Islam, once a great civilization worthy of being argued with . . . has degenerated into a primitive enemy fit only to be sensitively subjugated . . . If they want jihad, let them have it . . . [Islam,] once a moral force, has long been corrupted by variations of the European heresies, fascism and communism – a poisonous concoction threatening seepage back into Europe through mass migration.[18]

The first Gulf War (1990–1) caused further problems for British Muslims, now defined by some as 'the enemy within'. During the war, West Yorkshire police noted a 100 per cent rise in racist attacks in Bradford. The classifying of such attacks as 'racist' rather than 'anti-religious' further demonstrated an unwillingness by public institutions to recognize British Muslim identity.[19] The introduction of a question concerning ethnic origin in the 1991 Census was further testimony to a lack of understanding within Whitehall of the predominance of religious identity over ethnic identity within the Muslim community. This was especially important for second- and third-generation immigrants (which the majority of Britain's ethnic minorities now were), whose ethnicity or place of origin was becoming increasingly distant and whose religion, whether Hindu, Buddhist, Sikh or Muslim, was their primary means of identification.

1990s–2001: RECOGNITION OF RELIGIOUS DIVERSITY

By the end of the 1980s, there were signs that Whitehall and Westminster were beginning to listen to calls from Muslim organizations for their rights as a religious community to be recognized. For example, the Children Act 1989 stipulated that any decision in respect of a child should give consideration to his or her religion as well as to racial origin and cultural and linguistic background. The Education Act 1988, also required that schools keep statistics on pupils' religion. It was increasingly the case that all faiths were represented in public institutions such as prisons, higher education, the health service and the armed services.

At the same time, there was a growing, but limited, acceptance of what were termed 'New Religious Movements', such as the Unification Church, Scientology and Paganism. Within government, there was willingness to understand these faith groups and their special requirements, such as Jehovah's Witnesses' rejection of blood transfusions. In 1988, with financial backing from the Home Office, the Information Network Focus on Religious Movements (INFORM) was established at the London School of Economics, to collect, assess and disseminate impartial information on New Religious Movements. Despite this greater official acceptance, New Religious Movements continue to be treated with a mixture of scepticism and mockery in the media and by the general population.

The increased recognition of other faith groups prompted calls from within and outside Westminster for Britain to uphold its Christian heritage. After a vigorous campaign in the House of Lords, the 1988 Education Act not only preserved the long-standing obligation for all state schools to provide daily acts of collective worship, but specified that these should be Christian in nature, which the previous, 1944 Education Act had not done. While the 1988 Act allowed parents to withdraw their children from this act of worship, the purpose behind this clause was clear: an assertion that Britain remained a Christian country. The Act also elevated religious education to a compulsory subject within the newly established National Curriculum, with a stipulation that its syllabus should reflect the 'fact that religious traditions in Great Britain are in the main, Christian, while taking account of the teaching and the practices of other principal religions represented in Great Britain'. At the same time, the Conservative government refused to grant Muslim educational establishments voluntary-aided status, and therefore parity with Jewish, Methodist, Catholic and Anglican schools. Local councils consistently rejected proposals for Muslim schools on the grounds that separate Islamic education would encourage social fragmentation.

Increasingly, faith groups formed national organizations to lobby government and business. The Hindu Council was formed in 1994, the MCB in 1997 (see above) and Sikhs in England in 2000. These organizations worked to provide services and support for their communities, to speak on their behalf and to develop a better understanding of their faith in the media and among other faiths. While the hierarchical organizational structure of Christian churches (particularly Anglicanism and Catholicism) lends itself readily to public engagement, with its leaders assuming the role of public representatives of their constituencies, other faith groups such as Islam have taken longer to create national bodies and to make their voices heard within the political sphere and in the media.

The incorporation of the European Declaration on Human Rights into English and Scottish law in the Human Rights Act 1998, provided legal recognition, rights and freedom for all faith groups in Britain for the first time. Article 9 of the Human Rights Act explicitly endorsed the rights of the individual to exercise and practise his or her religious beliefs, and in this way resolved the deficiencies of the Race Relations Act. In 2004, Muslim schoolgirl Shabina Begum won, on appeal, the right to wear the ankle-length jilbab at school, with the defence arguing that her school's policy on uniforms, which prohibited wearing the jilbab, contravened her human right to practise her religion.

The Human Rights Act was followed by a Home Office report in early 2001 that sought to explore the issue of religious discrimination separately from the issue of race. The report, *Religious Discrimination in England and Wales*, concluded that one-third of Muslims and one-quarter of Jews and Hindus had reportedly suffered unjust treatment in the workplace, compared with 16 per cent of Christians. One Muslim woman commented on her experience at a job interview: 'She knew at the end of an interview that she would not get the job because, unlike the other candidates, she did not shake the interviewer's hand. When she declined, he jolted back. He wants to hire someone he can relate to. It's very subtle.'[20] A comment from one evangelical Christian summed up the concerns of all religious groups about the nature of religious discrimination: 'The more active you are the more vulnerable you become.'[21] Referring to the situation in Wales, the report concluded that, 'because of the historical struggle to maintain and assert Welsh identity and language over and against English assimilationism, there is an additional layer of complexity in these issues'. A number of interviewees also believed that Welsh urban areas were still 20 to 30 years behind those in England in dealing with diversity issues, while in rural areas, the situation was thought to be a further ten years behind.

The Labour government announced its intention to include a question on religious affiliation in the 2001 Census. This was a major breakthrough in recognising the importance of religious identity to individuals and, more specifically, to religious communities who stood to benefit from numerical evidence of their size within British society (see Table 3.5).

JULY 2005 LONDON BOMBINGS TO THE PRESENT

The terrorist attacks of 9/11 in the United States and the London bombings in July 2005 created serious new challenges for the Muslim community, leading to a questioning of Muslim integration within British society, and of British understanding of multiculturalism and its relation to religious difference. The last decade has seen legislation offering protection to Muslims (and all religious communities) in all areas of life, such as the 2003 Employment (Religion and Belief) Regulations Act, which forbids discrimination on grounds of religion and belief in the workplace; the Race and Religious Hatred Act, and Part 2 of the Equality Act 2006, which make it illegal to discriminate on grounds of religion in education and the provision of goods and facilities.

Yet, despite these legislative changes, Muslims have increasingly been portrayed as unwilling to integrate into British society and preferring, in the words of the then-Conservative Shadow Home Secretary, David Davies, to live in 'voluntary apartheid'.[22] The issue of Muslim women covering their faces in public was raised in 2006 by the then-Labour Leader of the House of Commons, Jack Straw, as demonstrating the refusal by Britain's Islamic community to assimilate culturally. The case, also in 2006, of a British Airways employee, Nadia Eweida, who argued that, as a Christian, she had suffered discrimination for not being allowed to wear a cross at work, prompted a much wider and more sympathetic discussion of the place of religious symbols in British society.

Many have argued the need for an open debate on the integration of Britain's Islamic population, but the fact that this 'debate' often connects Islamic cultural practice (whether it be arranged marriages, wearing the veil or Islamic preaching) with a need to provide an explanation for the London bombings of July 2005 has led British Muslims to question whether it is an open debate. Indeed, many feel that any discussions of Islamic terrorism and fundamentalism should include both an examination of British foreign policy towards Muslim countries and Britain's domestic policy on multiculturalism and the separateness of the Islamic community. In 2008, the Labour government announced funding for a board of Islamic theologians to be based at Oxford and Cambridge universities, to focus on Islam's place in Britain and British Muslim citizenship identity. Although supported by some Islamic academics, this was opposed by the MCB, which raised a concern that the government was setting a dangerous precedent by involving itself in the interpretation of the Koran.

With debates about integration, security and community cohesion dominating the discussions, the level of social deprivation of many British Muslims remains sidelined. There is great socio-economic diversity among British Muslims (see Chapter 2). In particular, those from Bangladesh and Somalia continue to be among the most disadvantaged groups in Britain, experiencing the highest rates of unemployment, the poorest health and highest disability rates, the lowest educational qualifications, and more children per capita taken into care of any religious group.[23]

Increased concern for the rights of religious minorities has aroused a mixture of support and suspicion from Christian churches and communities in Britain. The Archbishop of Canterbury's speech on Sharia law in February

2008 illustrated the willingness of the established Church to support all religious traditions in Britain. The Primate recognized that the adoption of certain aspects of Sharia law in the United Kingdom was 'unavoidable' and should not be feared, since it would help to maintain social cohesion and prevent Muslims from having to choose between 'the stark alternatives of cultural loyalty or state loyalty'.[24] The subsequent controversy suggests this was not a position with which all Anglicans felt comfortable.

Certain Christian groups have become increasingly vocal in asserting their rights and concerns, arguing that Christianity has not being given the same consideration or attention as other faiths. This is suggested by the controversy surrounding the BBC's screening of *Jerry Springer the Opera* in 2005, which received the then-largest-ever number of complaints for a television show (55,000) for its use of obscene language and extremely irreverent representation of Jesus. During the regional tour of the theatre production, the organization Christian Voice organised protests and attempted, unsuccessfully, to charge its producers under the Blasphemy Act.

Such activism has not been confined to Christians. In December 2004, the play *Behzti* ('Dishonour') by the British-born Sikh playwright Gurpreet Kaur Bhatti had its run at the Birmingham Repertory Theatre terminated, following protests by Sikhs against its portrayal of sexual abuse and murder in a Sikh temple. The furore in 2005 over the publication in a Danish newspaper of cartoons depicting Muhammad, and the vigorous defence of artistic licence following the passing of the Racial and Religious Hatred Act in Britain in 2006, demonstrates, as the *Gay News* incident and *The Satanic Verses* controversy did previously, the complex tensions between maintaining artistic freedom and protecting religious sensibilities.

These episodes highlight a related theme: the extent to which religious groups can themselves promote prejudiced views and unequal treatment of minorities. The issue of homosexuality is one example, with some groups within Islam and Christianity openly refusing to accept that homosexuals should have equal legal rights with heterosexuals. Another is the perception of women's rights within some faith groups. The Human Rights Act attempts to resolve this conflict by stipulating that faith groups should be allowed to exercise their beliefs and practise their religion, but not to a point that infringes on the rights of other groups (see Chapter 6).

An established Church in Britain is perceived as an anomaly in a largely secular and multi-faith nation. Yet the Church of England, far from being an obstacle to recognizing Britain's status as a multi-faith nation, has been instrumental in making it a reality. Ecumenical initiatives from the mid-twentieth century onwards, linking Anglicans, Non-conformists, Roman Catholics and other faith groups, generated unity of purpose and understanding across the long-established faiths. During the 1980s, for example, Derek Worlock and David Sheppard, Roman Catholic and Anglican bishops of Liverpool respectively, symbolised unity in a city once known for sectarian tension. Today, the Church of England, as the main spiritual voice of the nation, considers itself duty-bound to speak for all faiths in Britain, particularly through its representation in the House of Lords. Moreover, Anglicans have led the way in liaising with non-Christian faiths. It was on the Church of England's initiative that other faith groups were invited to serve on the government-sponsored faith communities' consultative body, the Inner Cities Religious Council (ICRC), when it was founded in 1992. In 2006, it was succeeded by the Faith Communities Consultative Council, with a much broader remit. This transition is testimony to the Labour government's encouragement, since 1997, of closer collaboration between all faith communities and the state.[25] Faith communities have become recognized for their important role as service providers in sustaining communities and nurturing social cohesion. However, enthusiasm for cooperation is not universal. Some feel that the work of faith groups in the community will be compromised the more they liaise with government and become reliant on public funding, while secularists are concerned by what they see as the increasing influence of religious groups within government circles.

Despite tensions, the unity of purpose across faith groups has been crucial in fostering an understanding of Britain as a multi-faith nation. At a West Yorkshire multi-faith conference on inner cities convened by the ICRC in 1992, a resolution was passed to 'support the call for all major religions in this country to be recognized under national law and ask that legislation should be enacted to make discrimination on the grounds of religion unlawful'.[26] The increased unity among faiths in Britain is visually apparent in religious ceremonies where the major faiths are represented and each performs a ceremonial function, such as the laying of wreaths at the Cenotaph in London on Remembrance Day.

CONCLUSION

Religious discrimination has been inextricably linked to immigration. The emergence of significant Catholic, Jewish, Sikh, Hindu and Muslim communities in Britain has been a product of ongoing immigration throughout the nineteenth and twentieth centuries. Immigration of religious minorities has not ended, since the religious and cultural make-up of Britain continually changes. The 2011 Census will probably reveal a significant rise in the number of Catholics in Britain, due to immigration from Poland following its accession to the European Union in 2004. Catholic churches in many parts of the country are already experiencing higher church attendance and changes in parish life as a result, although economic recession since 2008 has shown signs of reducing the flow of migration and the inclination of Poles and other East Europeans to stay in Britain. The United Kingdom is again seeing tensions arise from European Union immigration – perhaps exacerbated by recession – similar to those that followed earlier waves of immigration from other parts of the world.

The history of new religious communities in Britain has been, first, one of survival and the establishment of identity, followed by a struggle for equality. The dominance of race as the main category of difference in equality legislation and practice of the 1970s and 1980s meant the inequalities experienced by religious minorities, particularly Muslims, were neglected. Since the 1990s, these concerns have been increasingly acknowledged and legislation passed to address them.

Religious tensions often take a localised form, irrespective of wider national developments. In this way, the 'other' religion in Glasgow is Catholicism, whereas in Bradford it is Islam and, in other parts of Britain, Hinduism is juxtaposed with Islam. External events have also impacted in major, although diverse, ways on the internal experience of religious minorities in Britain, whether it be the situation in Ireland having consequences for British Catholics; Middle East politics impacting on British Muslims and Jews; or the 9/11 terrorist attacks and international Islamic fundamentalism affecting British Muslims. External events can determine how these religious minorities are portrayed in the media, and their everyday experience.

Integration by religious minorities is only half the story; acceptance and tolerance by the majority society is also essential. The Irish and Jewish communities, despite gaining legislative recognition and freedoms, often continued to be characterized as the 'other' in British society. The inequalities they suffered a century ago have diminished, but not disappeared. Legislative changes, mainly resulting from pressure from religious groups, can be drivers for increased tolerance, but their impact can be limited by the effects of prejudices embedded within the indigenous culture.

For the last 40 years, multiculturalism in Britain has functioned on the basis that the values of the society and the cultural customs of the individual do not conflict, but are accepted and integrated within the wider social and cultural consensus. Recent observations by commentators on the perceived failure of the Muslim community to integrate into British society, and the ramifications for social unity, indicate a loss of faith in this concept. Yet the fact that multiculturalism did not originally incorporate an understanding of religious difference perhaps explains the challenge to the concept posed by the increased assertiveness of Muslims. Some propose that the adoption of a framework closer to the French model of the assimilation of minorities, which operates around a clear, secular, unifying concept of national identity, could help alleviate current tensions. However, the social fragmentation evident between ethnic and religious groups in French society is not encouraging. The formation by the government in 2007 of the Equality and Human Rights Commission, which has responsibility for protecting individuals against disadvantage on grounds of their religion or belief as well as on the already protected grounds of race, gender and disability (and age and sexual orientation) may be a hopeful sign for the future.

The main drivers and inhibitors of change for religious groups are almost identical to those relating to race (see Chapter 2). In both cases, local and regional differences in the experiences of equalities continue to be salient and should be taken into account in implementing measures to reduce inequalities.

STATISTICS

Table 3.1 Church membership of Christian denominations: 1945–85

Year	Church of England	Church in Wales	Church of Scotland	Great Britain Methodists	Roman Catholic
1945	2,989,704	155,911 (1947)	1,259,927	752,659	3,036,826
1955	2,894,710	176,000 (1956)[a]	1,307,573	744,321	3,926,830
1965	2,682,181	165,273 (1966)	1,247,972	690,347	4,875,825
1975	1,912,000[a]	133,107 (1976)	1,041,772	541,518	4,996,310
1985	1,672,000[a]	116,911	870,527	436,049	5,023,736 (1974)

Note: (a) Estimated.

Table 3.2 Non-Christian religions in Britain: 1970–85 (estimated)

Religion	1970	1975	1980	1985
Buddhist	6,000	13,000	17,000	23,000
Hindu	50,000	100,000	120,000	130,000
Muslim	250,000	400,000	600,000	852,900
Sikh	75,000	115,000	150,000	180,000
Judaism	113,000	111,000	110,915	109,150
International Society for Krishna Consciousness	500	10,000	120,000	130,000
Ahmadiyya Movement	5,000	8,000	10,000	12,000

Sources (Tables 3.1 and 3.2): Electoral Roll (Church of England); Robert Currie, *Churches and Churchgoers*, (Clarendon Press, 1977), 1975–85 Church in Wales, 1975–85 Church of Scotland; Brierley (ed.), UK Christian Handbook 1987–8 (Bible Society), as collected in A. H. Halsey (ed.), *British Social Trends Since 1900: A Guide to the Changing Social Structure of Britain* (Macmillan, 1988), pp. 524–33.

Table 3.3 2001 Census
In the 2001 Census, a question on religion was introduced for the first time. The 'voluntary' question was framed: 'What is your religion?' In the Scottish Census, the question was framed differently as (1): 'What is your current religion?' and (2): 'What was the religion of your upbringing?'

(a) Percentage of responses to 'What is your religion?' for the United Kingdom

Christian	71.8%
Muslim	2.8%
Hindu	1%
Sikh	0.6%
Jewish	0.5%
Buddhist	0.3%
Other	0.3%
All religions (total)	77.3%
No religion	15%
Not stated	7.7%

Source: Census, April 2001, Office for National Statistics, www.statistics.gov.uk.

(b) Figures for Scotland only (current religion)

Christian	3,294,545
Muslim	42,557
Buddhist	6,830
Sikh	6,572
Jewish	6,448
Hindu	5,439
Other	26,974
None	1,394,460
Not stated	278,061

Source: *Scotland's Census 2001: The Registrar General's 2001 Census Report to the Scottish Parliament* (General Register Office for Scotland, 2003), p. 31.

Chapter 4

Gypsies and Travellers

Mel Porter and Becky Taylor

TIMELINE

1888	Gypsy Lore Society founded by benevolent non-Travellers; main organization campaigning for interests of Gypsies and Travellers until dissolution in 1974.
1908	Children Act requires nomadic children to register 200 school attendances between October and March each year.
1918	*Tinkers in Scotland* examines welfare provision for Gypsies and Travellers.
1936	Public Health Act introduces regulation and licences for moveable dwellings for the first time. *Report on Vagrancy* examines welfare provision for Gypsies and Travellers in Scotland.
1947	Town & Country Planning Act aims to regularise all development, under the control of local authorities.
1950	Government survey of Chief Constables enquires into evictions of Gypsies and Travellers.
1951	Gypsy Charter published.
1960	Caravan Sites and Control of Development Act requires all caravan sites to have a licence and planning permission.
1962	Planning Circular 6/62 encourages, but does not compel, local authorities to provide sites.
1965	Gypsy census in England and Wales. Race Relations Act (& 1976 Amendment Act) does not extend protection to Gypsies and Travellers, who are not yet recognized as ethnic minorities.
1966	Gypsy Council holds its first meeting and begins campaigning for Gypsy and Traveller rights.
1968	Caravan Sites Act imposes duty (from April 1970) on county councils and London boroughs to provide sites for Gypsies and Travellers, in return for eviction powers.
1969	Gypsy census in Scotland.
1971	Oxford Conference on Gypsy and Traveller education. First International Romani Conference, hosted by Gypsy Society.

1973	Advisory Council for the Education of Romanies and other Travellers founded
1977	Sir John Cripps' report into effectiveness of 1968 Act published.
	Planning Circular 28/77 published in response to Cripps report.
1979	Biannual caravan count begins in England.
1980	Government grants available for local authority Gypsy and Traveller sites.
1983	Mobile Homes Act improves security of tenure for caravan dwellers, but not Gypsies and Travellers.
1985	Battle of the Beanfield raises profile of New Age Travellers.
1986	Public Order Act strengthens police powers to evict trespassers.
1988	Lord Swann's report on education of Gypsies and Travellers and other ethnic minorities published.
	CRE versus Dutton: Romany Gypsies recognized in case law as an ethnic minority and protected by Race Relations Act.
1990	Town and Country Planning Act strengthens local authorities' powers to tackle unauthorized developments.
1994	Criminal Justice & Public Order Act abolishes local authorities' legal duty to provide Gypsy and Traveller sites and provides tougher police powers to tackle unauthorized encampments.
	Planning Circular (01/94) sets out criteria for Gypsies and Travellers seeking planning permission for their own sites.
	Friends, Families & Travellers founded in response to Criminal Justice Act.
1995	Traveller Law Research Unit set up at Cardiff Law School (disbanded 2002).
1998	Human Rights Act incorporates European Convention on Human Rights (to which the UK had been a signatory since 1951) into UK law from 2000; used by some Gypsies and Travellers facing eviction from unauthorized sites.
	Biannual caravan count introduced in Scotland.
2000	*O'Leary versus Allied Domecq*: Irish Travellers recognized in case law as an ethnic minority and protected by Race Relations Act.
	Gypsy Site Refurbishment Grant introduced to help local authorities refurbish and build Gypsy and Traveller sites, £33 million made available by end 2006.
	Race Relations Amendment Act strengthens duty on all public bodies to actively promote good race relations.
2002	Traveller Law Research Unit publishes Traveller Law Reform Bill.
	Gypsy and Traveller Law Reform Coalition founded.

2004   Housing Act and Planning and Compulsory Purchase Act
          introduce new legal framework for provision of Gypsy and
          Traveller accommodation.
2005   Gypsy and Traveller sites become a general election issue;
          mass media coverage of 'problem' sites.
          Scottish branch of Gypsy and Traveller Law Reform
          Coalition founded.
2006   Planning Circular 01/06: Planning for Gypsy and Traveller
          Caravan Sites published, replacing circular 01/94.
          Independent Task Group on Site Provision and Enforcement
          for Gypsies and Travellers set up. Commission for Racial
          Equality and Local Government Association reports on
          Gypsy and Traveller sites.
          Gypsy and Traveller Law Reform Coalition disbanded;
          Traveller Law Reform Project founded. Caravan Sites
          Security of Tenure Bill adopted by Labour MP Meg Hillier.
          Biannual caravan count introduced in Wales. Schools
          White Paper, *Better Schools for All*, commits to removing
          inequalities in educational provision and outcomes.
2007   Establishment of Equality and Human Rights Commission;
          Gypsies and Travellers included in its remit.

INTRODUCTION

When I was growing up, we used to have what they called a horse fair in the village. Travellers and Gypsies from all over the country came, and they were fine.
They used to bring a fair with them and we had a great time, but, I think I'm a
little bit intolerant of travellers now because they've changed over the years.

(Woman aged in her mid-50s, West Midlands[1])

Over the past 60 years, the social position of Britain's travelling communities has improved far less than for many other minority groups. By almost
every measure, they remain one of the most disadvantaged groups in Britain
and the subject of intense prejudice and discrimination. This chapter refers
throughout to 'Gypsies and Travellers', except where it is relevant to identify
specific communities falling within this definition. We recognize that this
term does not fully reflect the diversity of Britain's travelling communities,
but it has been used by government, the former Commission for Racial
Equality (CRE) and the current Equality and Human Rights Commission
(EHRC) to encompass Romany, Scottish and Welsh Gypsies and Irish
Travellers. While recognizing that other travelling communities, such as
Show-people and New Age Travellers, also have a long history of inequalities, this chapter is unable to do justice to their experiences, which differ
in important ways from those of Gypsies and Travellers.[2]

Gypsies and Travellers have the poorest life chances of any ethnic minority group:

- Life expectancy for men and women is ten years less than the national average.[3]
- Mothers are 20 times more likely than the rest of the population to experience the death of a child.[4]
- More than 40 per cent of Gypsies and Travellers report a life-limiting long-term illness.[5]
- In 2006, only one in five Irish Traveller children and one in ten Gypsy children achieved five GCSEs at A*–C grades and it is estimated that more than 10,000 Gypsy and Traveller children are not registered with any school.[6]

A major reason for these inequalities is a persistent shortage of authorized transit and permanent caravan sites. Currently, between 20 and 25 per cent of Gypsy/Traveller caravans (3,000–4,000) have no authorized place to stop.[7] Other reasons include:

- the long-term failure of public services, including the education system, to reach people who move regularly
- Gypsies' and Travellers' own tendency to distrust or avoid contact with bureaucracy, reinforced by a lack of flexibility in service provision
- a long history of prejudice and discrimination from the settled community, media and – in the past – public servants who designed and delivered services.

THE POST-WAR YEARS

Central to Gypsies' and Travellers' experiences since 1945 has been the disconnection between the reality of their lives – in particular, how they have adapted to changes in modern society – and the attitudes and stereotypes of mainstream British society, which have remained largely unchanged. From the nineteenth century, an image of 'pure-blooded Gypsies' developed that located them in rural areas, typically living in bow-topped caravans, engaged in agricultural or other countryside activities, cut off from modern life, 'here today and gone tomorrow'. Those who did not conform to this image were depicted as 'half-breeds', 'pikies', or 'didikais' and seen to have no right to maintain a nomadic lifestyle. These stereotypes crystallised with the formation of the Gypsy Lore Society (GLS) in 1888 by non-Gypsy philanthropists who were concerned that 'real' Gypsy language and culture were dying out, and reinforced by a lack of empirically grounded knowledge of Britain's travelling communities – a position that continues today. They disguise a much more complex picture, including Gypsies and Travellers being located in or on the periphery of urban areas, and staying on longer-term sites or in housing over the winter, or for more extended periods.[8]

Following World War II, economic changes caused Gypsies' and Travellers' lifestyles and work patterns to change and some of the symbols that had marked them out in the eyes of settled society as 'real Gypsies' to disappear. Commentators believed that 'real Gypsies' were dying out, when Gypsies and Travellers were instead adapting to rapidly changing times. Most were abandoning horse-drawn transport and becoming motorized, and techno-logical changes reduced the demand for their seasonal labour, horse dealing and traditional crafts, while opportunities for scrap-dealing, building and garden work expanded.[9]

The idea that 'Gypsies' were dying out also stemmed from the way popular myths combined with the expansion of the state, and particularly the welfare state. Throughout the late nineteenth century and up to the end of World War II, a link had been established in both the popular imagination and official minds that while 'true' Gypsies lived in remote rural locations and sustained themselves separately from mainstream society, 'half-bred' or degenerate nomadic types were travelling in order to escape from the burdens of modern life, consequently placing an increased burden on society. Such attitudes were revealed in two early reports in Scotland – *Tinkers in Scotland* (1918) and the *Report on Vagrancy* (1936) – which examined welfare provision for Gypsies and Travellers, exposing its inadequacy, and the popular antipathy towards them. Scotland's so-called 'Tinkers' were seen as needing the atten-tion of the state in order to absorb them into mainstream society: welfare was a tool for education and assimilation. For example, the 1936 report advised local authorities to 'gradually absorb Tinkers into ordinary society by housing them and securing for their children a full time education'.[10]

Post-war efforts by the state to extend welfare provision to Gypsies and Travellers failed to break this mould of thinking. The attitudes of officials towards the calculation of National Assistance payments illustrate the puni-tive approaches to extending new welfare rights to them. In common with other groups – such as married women and long-term disabled people – under the post-war welfare state, they were disadvantaged in the National Insurance system by their patterns of irregular employment, which pre-vented their making regular contributions and reduced their entitlement to benefits such as pensions[11] (see Chapter 1). They also faced discrimination on the grounds of their lifestyle. Local officials of the National Assistance Board questioned their right to receive public money and made deductions from payments, either assuming they were not declaring their full income or that they did not need to maintain the same standard of living as settled people.[12] One Scottish National Assistance officer commented:

> ... There can be no doubt that there are undisclosed resources in most cases. A number of them have ancient cars in which they move around while our allow-ances are largely disposed of in the nearest bar that sells 'wine' ... no injustice would be done if allowances were withheld from all but the oldest and exception-ally, those with large families of young children.[13]

Local officers had discretion to make deductions, particularly in relation to rent allowances. This was also common in relation to other outsider groups that were seen as 'undeserving', notably immigrants and unmarried mothers.[14]

Similarly, Gypsies and Travellers experienced problems when they sought settled accommodation. Their access was limited both by post-war housing shortages and local authorities' reluctance to put Gypsies and Travellers on their council housing lists because they were not considered 'local'. Where councils did develop housing schemes directed at Gypsies and Travellers, such as in the New Forest, they generally provided inferior accommodation, on the grounds that Gypsies and Travellers were not ready to meet the standards of settled society, and it was their first step on the road to assimilation.[15] In some cases, this was combined with efforts to bring the children into schools and force their families to settle. Children living in the New Forest Gypsy compounds in the 1940s were enrolled in local schools, and the council rejected calls for them to be segregated because, 'to segregate the children is to make them more likely to stay Gypsies'.[16]

A general housing shortage following the war meant Gypsies and Travellers were not the only inhabitants of caravans and other temporary dwellings. Shanty towns were developed on the edges of towns and on other pieces of marginal land by people who had been left homeless by war damage. However, these people aroused public sympathy, while Gypsies and Travellers – who 'chose' this way of life – did not. In August 1946, the *Ipswich Evening Star* lamented:

> One can appreciate the stern necessity which drives normally law-abiding people to take possession of Service huts and thus become 'squatters'. When Gypsies do the same thing, the reason is not so obvious. Yes, I have seen that some of these wanderers have invaded a camp and brought their horses, dogs, chickens and a goat with them. Apart from the inconvenience caused to genuine squatters, this seems a sad reflection on the Romanies. Surely they are not losing their old love for a roving life and instead wish to settle comfortably?[17]

The government's solution to the problems of unregulated development and the housing shortage was a house-building programme combined with tighter planning laws. The 1947 Town and Country Planning Act aimed to end uncontrolled development and designate land for specific uses. Caravan sites tended to be absent from local plans, and the Act made clear that where they existed, they must be private, not state-sponsored, initiatives.[18] Tighter planning regulations plus a surge in local authority house-building increased pressure on the marginal land where Travellers had traditionally stopped. Initially, the increased motorization of Gypsies and Travellers masked the growing shortage of stopping places, but by the early 1950s it was clear that a crisis was developing.

Except for a campaign by members of the Gypsy Lore Society and others in 1936 against by-laws banning Gypsies and Travellers from Epsom Downs during race weeks, before the 1950s there was no national-level political action aiming to highlight and support the needs of Gypsies and Travellers. The first stirrings of formal political action were initiated from outside the travelling communities, in response to the closure of long-term sites. A particularly high-profile campaign in Gloucestershire in the winter of 1950–1 was led by Miss Wilmot-Ware, a tenant farmer who allowed Gypsies and Travellers to camp on her land. She vigorously resisted attempts by the local council to evict those living on her land, and drew local and national church figures into her efforts.[19] A petition generated from this campaign, signed by about a hundred Gypsies and Travellers and sent to the Convocation of Canterbury, began:

> In the coming winter many of us will be faced with certain prosecution, followed by fines or imprisonment, because we can find nowhere to stay. So many of our traditional camping sites have been declared unsuitable and closed . . . No alternative accommodation has been offered to us . . . We have seasonal occupation with which we earn an honest living through the spring, summer and autumn months as long as we are mobile. Then comes the winter and we hope to settle in one place. What shall we do this winter?[20]

At the same time, the Labour MP Norman Dodds, whose constituency included Belvedere Marshes (Kent), one of the largest long-term sites in Britain, became actively interested in the conditions of Gypsies and Travellers living in his area. Working with influential Kent-based Gypsies and Travellers, and missionaries such as William Lamour of the London City Mission, he began visiting sites in his constituency and asking questions in parliament. A high point came in May 1951, when a Gypsy Charter was issued and delivered to the House of Commons by a well-publicized deputation of Gypsies and Travellers. It called for:

1. A government survey of Gypsies and Travellers, their location, the availability of winter sites and their accommodation preferences
2. Provision of a network of camps, with water, sanitation and communal facilities
3. The compilation and dissemination of information about suitable routes and stopping places for caravans
4. 'Fair consideration' for those with 'long-established businesses' where sites were being considered for closure
5. 'A suitable scheme for the educating of Gypsy children'
6. Better liaison with the Ministry of Labour about work available in the vicinity of camps
7. Reintroduction of Gypsy Welfare Officers[21]
8. 'The recognition that there are fewer indictable offences committed by Romanies than by any other section of the community, and that their loyalty to this country is in no way inferior'
9. 'The realization that with few exceptions Romanies recognize that some re-orientation of their way of life may be justified but that this should be carried

> out in a humane way which can only be achieved by a greater understanding
> of the problem than is at present possible because of the almost total absence
> of reliable information available to the gorgios [house-dwellers]'.[22]

The efforts of Wilmot-Ware, Dodds and the charter pushed the government to commission a survey of Chief Constables in 1951 to enquire into the number of evictions of Gypsies and Travellers from winter quarters. This revealed that there were 2,084 'Gypsy camping grounds' in England and Wales – 480 of them permanent, the rest temporary – and about 7,000 Gypsies and Travellers living in the permanent camps and more than 20,000 on temporary sites. Broadly, the survey claimed that in about 90 per cent of local authority areas, there was 'no indication' of Gypsies and Travellers being moved from their winter quarters. However, the detail of the report and other evidence reveals the closure of many long-established sites, enforcement action against temporary camps, and communities' unwillingness to let them settle.[23]

The government took no action, and in May 1951, the Parliamentary Secretary to the Ministry of Housing and Local Government in the Labour government concluded:

> Our information is that the local authorities and the police are not using their powers against Gypsies as such but against the nuisances themselves, whoever causes them . . . Local authority sites are out of the question; the local authorities would not provide them and there is, indeed, no reason why Gypsies should be given priority in this way over other people . . . we don't know where Gypsies want to go, and even if we did we can't make it an obligation on local authorities and land owners to accept them on these sites. Only Gypsies themselves know where they want sites and for how long, and now that they are getting organized I suggest that they should themselves select the sites they want to have . . . [then] go and get permission from the owners to go on the land, they should then, as a body, discuss with the local authority concerned, the question of planning permission and a public health licence. If this is done by Gypsies as an organized body, it should help them get over what is, admittedly, often strong local prejudice. But it must be done by the Gypsies themselves and it must be done locally . . . if they are to avoid 'persecution' in the future, they must themselves get the thing on a proper footing with the local authorities, and convince them they are clean and respectable.[24]

This ignored the real problems faced by Gypsies and Travellers, of being hampered by illiteracy, lack of a stable address and often intimidated by local authority procedure. Some local authorities had a policy of opposing planning applications from Gypsies and Travellers, regardless of central government's intentions.[25] The fact that most of the laws affecting Gypsies and Travellers were implemented by local rather than central government meant that the 'strong local prejudice' referred to by the Minister often governed their lives. An eviction from waste ground at Leckwith Common in Cardiff in the winter of 1955–6 illustrates the powerlessness of central government when faced with local recalcitrance. Eviction proceedings began after neighbours complained about straying horses, unsanitary behaviour and harassment. One of the site residents, 68-year-old Lydia Lee, wrote to ask the Queen to intervene, generating some sympathy. However, Cardiff Council was not willing to provide another site, rebuffing the arguments of the Welsh Office that they should do so, and insisting that the site residents should be moved on and ultimately forced to settle in housing. The Welsh Office had no power to overrule the local authority.[26]

INTO THE 1960s: CRISIS

Consequently, the late 1950s and early 1960s saw an approaching crisis for Gypsies and Travellers: the availability of land for stopping places was reduced due to large-scale house-building and tighter planning controls, while social attitudes hardened towards a community that was seen as anachronistic and unruly. Two well-publicized evictions demonstrate that, while the government took a sympathetic approach to homeless members of the settled community, this did not extend to Gypsies and Travellers. In the winter of 1961–2, a Travellers' site in Darenth Woods in Kent was sold to Dartford Council, which wanted them removed, both to appease local opinion and to comply with Green Belt planning controls. A high-profile campaign was mounted with the support of the Labour MP Norman Dodds, and appeals made to the Conservative Prime Minister, Harold Macmillan. But the Travellers were evicted in mid-January and, with nowhere else to go, camped at the side of the A2 motorway for seven months.[27] In contrast, a group of non-Traveller caravan-dwellers who had rented a pitch in Egham, Surrey, only to discover that it did not have planning permission, marshalled extensive support for their cause in the winter of 1958–9. Macmillan intervened to ensure they were given alternative accommodation. The Lord Chancellor's office delayed the eviction until the end of winter, while the Ministry of Housing and Local Government pressurised Surrey County Council to provide them with accommodation. Within weeks, the caravan-dwellers had moved to a new site.

Both the Darenth Travellers and the Egham caravan-dwellers employed similar lobbying tactics, but the Travellers' pleas were ignored by central government and they were left camping on the roadside, while the Egham residents received a sympathetic hearing and were quickly rehoused.[28] A further result of the Egham case was the commissioning in November 1958 of a government survey, Caravans as Homes, which confirmed the government's more positive approach to caravan-dwellers. Gypsies and Travellers were specifically excluded from the terms of reference, on the grounds that:

> ... The Gypsies or vagrant caravanners usually move frequently about the countryside; they often park their caravans without any permission from the

landowner concerned; they are said by many local authorities to leave filth and litter where they have been, and to contain more than an ordinary share of law-breakers.[29]

The survey led to the passage of the 1960 Caravan Sites and Control of Development Act, requiring all sites to have both a licence and planning permission. It was designed to ensure that 'genuine' caravan-dwellers lived on suitable sites, but made it almost impossible to gain permission for one. Gypsies who bought pieces of land to live on or to rent to others were arrested, while councils prevented the expansion of authorized sites, moving on 'surplus' residents, who ended up camping at roadsides or trespassing. Where planning permission was given, it was often temporary and not renewed, leaving residents with no alternative but to camp illegally.[30]

By the 1960s, certain areas, such as the West Midlands, had become centres of conflict, as some local authorities adopted 'zero-tolerance' policies towards Travellers. This was particularly the case when councils perceived themselves as being at the receiving end of large numbers of recent Irish Traveller immigrants. The shift in policy towards settled sites did not change the pattern of harassment and evictions in most areas. Jimmy Connors, an Irish Traveller, recalled his experiences in Walsall, which had a reputation as one of the least tolerant councils:

> Twenty-eight times that day I produced my driving licence and insurance. The first day's summonses totalled sixty-two and the full total was three hundred. Every two minutes of the day we were summonsed for an offence. The persecution went on and on, night, noon and day. The police thought we would move away from the Midlands . . . But the question was where could we move to? All camping sites were banked up with piles of earth, and trenches dug across all open land to prevent us from camping on them. I am sure if one of those so-called policemen, councillors, or the judge was in a higher authority's chair, they would have had us put into gas chambers, every single one of us.
>
> . . . A harmless child is blown to bits at the hands of the local authorities; Ann Hanrahan, two and a half years old, crushed to death during an eviction near Dudley, two miles from Walsall.
>
> My own little son very badly injured and my caravan smashed to pieces . . . Walsall – during an eviction, three little girls burned to death.
>
> Walsall – my wife kicked black and blue by the police in her own caravan three days before her baby was born.
>
> Walsall – I was kicked unconscious.
>
> Walsall – a sister at Walsall Hospital refused to treat us.[31]

The hostility of the local authority and wider community was amplified by negative and stereotypical local media coverage. A study by UNESCO of the *Walsall Observer*'s coverage of Gypsies and Travellers from 1968–70 concluded that, although the newspaper might claim to be supporting the provision of sites for 'real Gypsies', in fact 'it differentiates between different groups of travellers when it wishes to enlist the support of one group against the other; when it is endorsing prejudicial attitudes and policies, it lumps them together'.[32]

Encouraged in part by the non-Gypsy campaigner Gratton Puxon, who had experience of working with Travellers in Ireland to prevent evictions (including using non-violent direct resistance), Travellers began actively resisting evictions in greater numbers. In December 1966, the Gypsy Council held its first meeting, in a Kentish pub displaying a 'No Gypsies' sign. The council's manifesto called for:

1. Camping sites in every county open to all Travellers
2. Equal rights to education, work and houses
3. Equal standing through respect between ourselves and our settled neighbours.[33]

The Gypsy Council had strong international links from the start, presenting Gypsies and Travellers not as 'a small minority, as many think, but a proud people 12 MILLION strong, scattered in every country' and tapping into international movements for Gypsies' and Travellers' rights.[34] It aimed to transcend the differences of opinion and experience among the travelling communities in Britain, campaigning for equal rights and collaborating with other organizations, including the National Council for Civil Liberties (NCCL) and students who supported Gypsies and Travellers camping on university land. Non-violent direct action was used repeatedly throughout England at this time to prevent evictions, in Kent, Essex, London, Leeds, Oxford, Birmingham and Bridgewater. By 1968, more than 300 complaints had been made against pubs barring Gypsies and Travellers under the new Race Relations Acts, but none was tested in court and so they remained outside the protection of the Acts, only achieving legal recognition as ethnic minorities in 1989 and 2000 respectively (see below). The council also pioneered the early caravan-school projects to improve the education of Traveller children (see below) and hosted the first World Romani Congress, in 1971.

From the beginning, the council's effectiveness was compromised by splits among the different communities. One Romany, Cliff Lee, left early on, writing to Puxon, 'I'm afraid their problems aren't mine, and, while I know most of the Irish Travellers and like them, they know and I know that we are of different blood. I think all we have in common is that we are nomadic.'[35] The international movement, led by the Comité International Tsigane, in which the Gypsy Evangelical Church was prominent, had to mediate between Gypsies and Travellers of many faiths, including Catholic, Orthodox and Muslim.[36]

Linked to political activism were moves among some Gypsy and Traveller parents, as well as supportive activists, to improve the educational experiences of their children. While the 1908 Children's Act and 1944 Education Act theoretically confirmed every child's right to education and the Local Education Authority's duty to provide it, by the late 1960s most Gypsy and

Traveller children's experiences of education was 'little different to that of their parents – short-lived, patchy, and dominated by bullying from other pupils and disdain from the teachers'.[37] Jimmy Stockins left school after two years, aged seven, in the mid-1960s:

> What did I want to go to school for? School was for gorgers [settled community]. Why should I learn to read and write? No other person I mixed with could . . . Don't ask me the name of the school . . . I hated it. Sit still. Sit up straight. Single file. Fold your arms. It was like being in a fucking cage. All silly rules and saying prayers . . . I couldn't understand why them calling 'Gypsy' or 'Gypo' across the playground was meant to annoy me. After all, that's what I was . . . Gorger [settled] kids seemed to think we didn't like being Travellers for some reason.[38]

Education authorities typically blamed their nomadic lifestyle and parents' attitudes for Gypsy and Traveller children's poor attendance, and recommended they be dispersed among several schools to lessen the 'burden' on individual schools.[39] They were treated in a similar fashion to the children of early Asian and Afro-Caribbean immigrants, who were also seen as problem under-achievers who failed to assimilate, and potentially damaging to the performance of other children.[40]

By the 1960s, some parents were demanding their children's right to education under the 1944 Act, and a public campaign in Leeds embarrassed the council into finding school places for ten Traveller children within 24 hours.[41] In other areas, by the end of the decade, a number of small, localised voluntary schemes had been launched to bring education to the children, such as the West Midlands Travellers School, operated from a bus that visited five unauthorized sites during evenings and weekends. These initiatives remained in the minority and varied in their ability to attract parental and children's interest. A conference on Traveller education in Oxford in March 1971 estimated that of 6,000 to 8,000 school-aged children, only about 2,500 attended schools. This was the highest level recorded, although some children were probably registered at several schools. Attendance levels tended to be in the range of 40–60 per cent and attainment was low.[42]

Although Gypsies and Travellers were excluded from the remit of the 1958–9 Caravans as Homes survey, a steady stream of evictions from long-term sites and pressure by Dodds led the government to issue Planning Circular 6/62 in 1962, encouraging councils to carry out surveys of Gypsy and Traveller populations (which several did) and to establish sites, using a successful public site set up in 1960 in West Ashford, Kent, as a model. The circular made clear, however, that public sites were intended as the first step towards assimilation for Gypsies and Travellers, rather than to provide a secure base from which they could continue their nomadic existence. In contrast, Travellers saw official sites as a means to continue their traditional lifestyle in an increasingly hostile climate: a refuge from constant harassment, not as a step towards absorption into settled society.[43] Jimmy Stockins recalled his family's experience:

Kennas [houses] were not for us, but there was a lot of pressure at the time to stop gypsies travelling and promises of a better life. Maybe Dad thought it best for us kids . . . [But being in a] house wasn't doing us any good at all. Dad's health was suffering from being all cooped up, and none of us could get used to having this strange thing called an 'upstairs' or going into a little cupboard to have a shit . . . neighbours didn't take too kindly to us cooking our food over an open fire in the back garden each night either, and the horses upset the local dog and cat population. Finally, Dad said 'That's enough'. He bought a new trailer and we were off travelling again.[44]

In 1965, the request for a national survey included in the Gypsy Charter (see above) was implemented by the Labour Housing and Local Government Minister Richard Crossman. The survey recorded 15,500 Gypsies and Travellers and, despite regional variations and likely under-estimation of numbers, 'it was the most uniform and general picture of the national situation that had yet been gained'.[45] The results were disseminated in a circular in June 1966, giving local authorities 'strong and detailed advice' on site provision and requesting a report on action taken.[46] However, the report on the 1965 census, *Gypsies and Other Travellers*, published in 1967, commented that the current legislative framework amounted to the 'virtual outlawing' of Gypsies' and Travellers' way of life. It has been estimated that only 75 per cent of 'Gypsies and other Travellers' were actually included in the survey, but enough detail was provided that the government could no longer ignore what was becoming a national scandal. Sixty per cent of Traveller families were found to have travelled in the preceding year and, for the majority, this was due to forced movement caused by a lack of sites or harassment from officials. Only one-third of families had access to on-site water, and the report also found systematic evidence of the impact of constant movement on Gypsy and Traveller children's education. Although there was provision within the 1960 Caravan Sites and Control of Development Act for local authorities to set up sites for 'Gypsies', only 12 local authorities had done so.[47]

The report also revealed the economic situation of Gypsies and Travellers, who continued, where possible, to choose self-employment and nomadism.

Table 4.1 Occupations of Gypsies and Travellers in England and Wales: 1965; and in Scotland: 1969

	Occupation	England and Wales	Scotland
Men	General and scrap-dealing	52%	36%
	Agriculture and horticulture	15%	19%
Women	Housewives	36%	36%

Source: MHLG *Gypsies and other Travellers* (1967), p. 34; H.Gentleman and S. Swift (eds), *Scotland's Travelling People* (1971).

Patterns of work were changing in ways that increased the potential for friction with the settled community. They reduced economic interaction and therefore familiarity, as well as increasing the length of stay in one place and therefore Gypsies' and Travellers' visibility and potential for conflict. They necessitated the storage of scrap and other materials for trade, which were seen by settled communities as unsightly 'rubbish'. The economic roles of women diminished just at the time when they were expanding in other communities, making Gypsies' and Travellers' gender patterns appear increasingly out of step with the rest of society. Increasing numbers of Irish Travellers, often living in larger, more visible communities, arrived to seek better work opportunities and living standards in Britain, particularly after 1963 when the activities of the Irish Itinerant Settlement Committee persuaded the Irish government to adopt a policy of housing all Travellers.[48]

There is debate over the influence of the Gypsy Council in the lead-up to the 1968 Caravan Sites Act, but its militancy certainly contributed to the climate in which the government accepted the need for new legislation.[49] Like many of the other liberal reforms of the late 1960s (see Chapters 2, 5 and 6), this Act was introduced as a Private Member's Bill, initiated by Liberal MP Eric Lubbock (now Lord Avebury, see below), and came into law thanks to government support for the Bill as a whole. Lubbock's Bill originally aimed to regulate bad practice among the owners of mobile home sites, but he agreed to include Part II relating to Gypsy and Traveller sites in return for the government's support.[50] The legislation affecting Gypsies and Travellers was implemented in April 1970, placing a new duty on local authorities to provide sites for Gypsies and Travellers 'residing in or resorting to' their area. Once sites were provided, councils were granted stronger powers to evict Gypsies and Travellers from any unauthorized site in their district. The Act provided a legal definition of Gypsies for the first time, as 'persons of nomadic habit of life, whatever their race or origin', but this presented fresh problems. People not of Gypsy or Traveller heritage who chose to adopt a nomadic way of life, such as New Age Travellers, were covered by the Act, while stationary Gypsies and Travellers were not. Court judgments later included in the definition Gypsies and Travellers remaining in one place over the winter, provided they travelled for work in the summer.[51]

1970s–80s: THE YEARS OF CONSENSUS?

By the early 1970s, there was a general, if grudging, consensus that local authorities should provide official sites for Gypsies and Travellers, even if there were sharp divisions over the rationale behind such provision. At the same time, there was increased activism and coordination within and among travelling communities, and a willingness to engage in public debate and use the law to force change.

Crucially, the 1968 Act gave no deadline by which local authorities were required to provide sites, and district councils retained the right to object to individual sites, but once sites were provided, the council was 'designated' and it became a criminal offence to camp elsewhere in the district. This 'carrot and stick' approach created an incentive for councils to make at least some site provision, but effectively criminalised the way of life of all Gypsies and Travellers in designated areas (which included most of London), who did not have a legal stopping place.[52] By 1973, between one-fifth and one-quarter of the sites needed were built. However, the Gypsy Council claimed that before the Act came into force, councils tried to evict Gypsies and Travellers in their area to avoid providing for them.

Despite ongoing confrontations with local authorities, police and bailiffs at evictions, the Gypsy Council became accepted as a representative organization.[53] Nevertheless, there was continued fracturing of Gypsy and Traveller groups, with some grouping round a specifically Romany or Irish Traveller banner and others concentrating on particular issues, such as education. There was also a split between groups formed and led by Gypsies and Travellers and those formed from outside the travelling communities. In addition, local leaders or spokespeople, such as Tommy Doherty in Leeds, emerged in response to specific circumstances, typically over a campaign to prevent an eviction, but also to fight more generally for Traveller rights. While there is rarely any question that the individuals involved in these activities aimed to improve the status of their community, none of them can necessarily be taken as 'representative' of Gypsies and Travellers in any wider sense.

There was and remains a wider democratic deficit: Travellers have not, generally, participated in mainstream politics; indeed, many are not registered to vote,[54] and they have not developed strong representative organizations of their own. During this period, there were attempts to campaign on their behalf. One of these was the Labour Campaign for Travellers' Rights, set up in 1980 by trade unionists to fight anti-Traveller prejudice in the unions as part of a wider involvement of trade unions in minority issues at this time, but it had limited success.

By 1976, the Labour Local Government and Planning Minister, John Silkin, was aware that the 1968 Act was not delivering enough sites, to the detriment of both settled and travelling communities:

> It has become apparent that the rate of site provision is seriously inadequate. In consequence, unauthorized encampments continue to proliferate in most areas, with all that they mean in terms of nuisance, public health hazards, community tension and law enforcement problems, as well as misery for the Gypsies themselves who live under constant threat of eviction.[55]

Sir John Stafford Cripps (son of the former Labour Chancellor Sir (Richard) Stafford Cripps), who campaigned for improved quality of life in rural areas, was appointed by the Labour government in 1976 to investigate why provision of sites was tailing off. His report, *Accommodation for Gypsies*, found that 133 local authority sites had been created in England and Wales since

1970, containing 2,131 pitches, but leaving approximately 6,000 caravans with no legal stopping place. Cripps also found a lack of provision for Gypsies and Travellers 'resorting to' an area while on the move.[56] Although there was nothing in the 1968 Act to indicate that the creation of sites 'was to be a stage in enforced settlement or assimilation', he found many local authorities implemented it with this goal in mind.[57] Furthermore, Cripps revealed that sites were often:

> ... Excessively close to sewage plants, refuse destructors, traffic laden motor-ways, intersections of these and other busy highways, main railway tracks and other features contaminating the environment by odour, noise and so on. No non-Gypsy family would be expected to live in such places.[58]

Residents of such sites could hardly avoid feeling that they were 'unwelcome, marginal and deserving of the bare minimum'. They were also isolated from basic services such as shops, schools and surgeries.[59] Cripps highlighted the weight of public opposition – 'bordering on the frenetic' – against new and existing sites, which sometimes erupted into violence and vandalism and was often rooted in stereotypical assumptions about Gypsies' habits and beliefs.[60] He was clear that the current 'duty' of local authorities to provide sites was ineffective and said central government must take a greater role in providing funding, land and, if necessary, the coercion that had so far been lacking.[61]

Judith Okely's fieldwork in the 1970s revealed the mismatch between Gypsies' and Travellers' needs and local authorities' motives for site provision. While residents wanted more temporary sites, with basic facilities, low rents and flexibility, some official sites charged up to 70 per cent of council house rents and provided 'a brick chalet for each pitch, with living room, bathroom, w.c. and store room. Electricity, immersion heater and coal-fired courtier stove were provided.'[62]

Planning Circular 28/77 was issued in 1977 in response to Cripps' findings. This aimed to discourage local authorities from referring decisions on Gypsy and Traveller sites to the Secretary of State to avoid taking responsibility in the face of local opposition. It warned that local people's objections often related to their experience of unauthorized sites, not council-run sites, and recommended 'close cooperation between county and district councils', reminding district councils of their powers to provide sites independently of the counties. It ignored Cripps' recommendation that the government should create a national plan specifying the number and location of new sites.[63]

The Labour government introduced 100 per cent grants for local authorities to build sites (available from 1980), which led to an increase of about 200 to 300 pitches per year. By the beginning of 1985, of the estimated 9,900 Gypsy and Traveller caravans in England, 4,600 were on local authority sites, 1,900 on private sites and 3,400 on unauthorized sites. But as they created sites, local authorities were rewarded by becoming 'designated' as effectively 'out of bounds' for Gypsies and Travellers on the road and in need of a stopping place. Groups representing Gypsies and Travellers described this as a form of 'apartheid'.[64]

By the mid-1980s, a more stationary lifestyle on council-run sites was part of Gypsy and Traveller culture for many. This was partly through necessity, as the shortage of pitches made families reluctant to travel once they had secured one, but stable residence also afforded better access to education, health and welfare facilities. However, the large number of pitches on many council sites made conflict with the wide community more likely. Sites were generally designated for residential use only, so that work, such as car-breaking and scrap storage, had to be conducted elsewhere. Kinship networks were weakened because pitches were allocated by wardens on the basis of need – for example, having school-aged children, or being known as 'good tenants'. There was no security of tenure, as Gypsies and Travellers were exempted from the 1983 Mobile Homes Act, which protected other caravan-dwellers from summary eviction. Also, inhabitants experienced a lack of interaction with and visibility to settled communities because council-run sites were often positioned outside towns and villages.[65]

For those who did not want, or were unable, to live on council sites, unauthorized sites remained a major feature of the Gypsy/Traveller experience, with a third of Gypsy/Traveller caravans still on unauthorized sites by the mid-1980s. These families often found themselves trapped in a cycle of conflict and eviction:

It's a terrible business just finding a space to stay. We just go round and round like a game of dominoes and things are getting worse. Even getting a bit of land is difficult. We go round in a convoy and sometimes we get ten to fifteen of us on the bit of land and the police come and stop the rest of us getting on. There's a lot of argument then and sometimes we all get on but it's bad if we don't, as the others have to go on the roadside. Then when we get onto the land the police will be onto us. Sometimes they dig a trench all round with JCB diggers and say we can't get off unless we take our caravans with us. Well we're trapped then. Can't take out cars to get food even and we can't get out to get to work. Then they will come into our trailers and ask for receipts for all the stuff there. Might have to go a hundred miles back to the shop to get a receipt for the television, for example, and what do you do about the Crown Derby you've been given for the wedding? And there was one morning at six o'clock when they had warrants to search for firearms and we were all out of the trailers standing in a row while they searched. Tore the carpet up as well. It's all a kind of bluff to get us off as quickly as possible . . . Sometimes people are ill: one time they hitched up a trailer and the midwife looked out and said that a baby was going to be born . . . The local people we don't see directly but a few have waved sticks at us when we try to get onto a piece of land but that's not important. The worst is what the papers say about us. People panic automatically when we first arrive and too much is written in the papers to frighten people against us.[66]

This account highlights how, by the 1980s, fear of and resistance to the appearance of unauthorized sites was becoming embedded in the public imagination. However, the picture was complicated by the growing numbers of New Travellers[67] whose roots lay in the 1960s free-festival movement. An increase in their numbers in the 1980s, due to high unemployment and homelessness, hardened official and popular attitudes to travelling communities generally. In June 1985, police intercepted several hundred New Travellers en route to an unlicensed festival at Stonehenge. In an attempt to avoid attacks by the police, the travellers trampled on a nearby field in an incident that was much publicized as the 'Battle of the Beanfield'. Gypsies and Travellers were often inaccurately included in public and media discussions about the 'problem' of New Travellers. In fact, Gypsies and Travellers generally distanced themselves from New Travellers; ironically, these newer communities were more likely to fall within the 1968 Act's definition of 'nomads' than Gypsies and Travellers who had settled in housing or on council sites and were perceived to have 'forfeited' their ethnic status. The Gypsy Council laid the blame for the continuing inequality experienced by so many of them at the door of local authorities that had failed in their duty to provide sites.

As well as being increasingly organized and using sophisticated lobbying techniques, since the mid-1970s Gypsies and Travellers have turned increasingly to the courts to challenge inequalities and site evictions. In particular, they have used the judicial review process to challenge both local authorities' practice of evicting them from unauthorized sites while providing no legal place for them to go to, and the failure of central government to direct councils to provide sites.[68] Early court decisions did not always go in the Travellers' favour, but in a seminal case in 1986, West Glamorgan County Council's decision to evict a group of illegally camped Gypsies was quashed by the court on the grounds that the council had failed in its duty to provide sites.[69]

1990s: THE END OF 'CONSENSUS'

By 1990, there was a sense of optimism that the Conservative government might introduce stronger legislation to increase pressure on local authorities to provide sites for Gypsies and Travellers. The 1989 Local Government and Housing Act ring-fenced the capital grants for local authorities, so that Gypsy and Traveller sites no longer competed for resources with other housing priorities.[70] In 1990–1, the Department of the Environment commissioned a flurry of research and evaluation of site provision. During a parliamentary debate in July 1990, the Housing Minister, Christopher Chope, indicated that he would consider withholding site funding from councils that did not produce site plans, forcing them to provide sites at their own expense. He agreed that the current legislative framework was not working, raising expectations of a new Bill.[71] But within months of winning the 1992 general election, John Major's government introduced the most aggressive and restrictive legislation aimed at travelling communities for many decades. What had changed?

The 1992 election, in combination with a tidal wave of anti-Traveller feeling, quashed any hope of a drive to increase public site provision. By the early 1990s, New Traveller culture crossed over with the growing 'rave' sub-culture, drawing large crowds to giant parties at rural sites (most infamously at Castlemorton in the summer of 1992), adding to public panic about anarchic hordes of 'nomads'. The official and popular perception, fuelled by tabloid headlines, was that nomadism was running out of control. The government was under pressure to act, and saw a crackdown on travelling communities as an issue that would shore up its image as the party of law and order, while few people sprang to the defence of Gypsies, Travellers and New Travellers. A Conservative party pre-election press release promised swifter, tougher action against unauthorized campers, claiming the number of Gypsy caravans had grown by 30 per cent since 1981 and there were between 2,000 and 5,000 New Travellers camping illegally in England and Wales.[72] This conflation of separate issues and communities reinforced the perception of all travelling communities – old or new and regardless of where they stopped – as a problem.

Soon after the Conservatives' re-election, a Consultation on Changes to the 1968 Caravan Act was launched. It proposed:

- repealing the duty on local authorities to provide sites, replacing it with a discretionary power
- encouraging Gypsies and Travellers to move into private and public sector housing
- reforming the provision for 100 per cent grants to local authorities for new sites, enabling ministers to target grant-aid as they saw fit
- tougher measures to remove people camping on unauthorized sites, including the seizure and removal of vehicles
- withdrawing the 'privilege' that allowed Gypsy and Traveller sites to be located on Green Belt land.[73]

While the timing suggested this was a response to raves and New Travellers, there were clearly financial and philosophical considerations at play. Sir George Young, the Housing Minister, described the 1968 Act as 'an open-ended commitment to provide sites', 'a drain on the taxpayer's money' and a disincentive for Gypsies 'to provide for themselves'.[74]

In the parliamentary debates that followed, there was widespread concern about the logic of removing the duty to provide sites when it was acknowledged that more sites were needed. It emerged that virtually all the 1,000 known responses to the consultation (which the government never published) were critical – including those that might have been expected to support the proposals, such as the Country Landowners Association, the Council for the Preservation of Rural England and the National Farmers Union. The Department of the Environment's own unpublished analysis of the responses 'referred to the common perception that "the proposals present an attack on basic human rights and are designed to stop [Travellers] travelling for good . . . the phrase 'ethnic cleansing' was used by several respondents".[75]

An analysis of local government responses to the consultation by the Advisory Council for the Education of Romanies and other Travellers (ACERT)[76] revealed a high level of opposition to the new proposals. The vast majority of county and district councils and London boroughs did not believe the government's proposals provided workable solutions; more than half wanted to retain the statutory duty to provide sites and the majority also wanted to retain 100 per cent government funding for new sites.[77]

Although the combination of the duty under the 1968 Act and capital grants was not providing enough sites and – without modification – never would, the consensus among those consulted was that the government was going too far. Abolishing the duty and leaving the local planning system to determine individual site applications would worsen the vicious cycle of unauthorized stopping and increasingly violent evictions. And, as both history and the ACERT evidence showed, local authorities had little appetite for an increased role as referees between their travelling and settled residents.

However, the government insisted that the planning system was 'perfectly capable' of making adequate site provision,[78] arguing – as the government had in the 1950s – that Gypsies and Travellers should take responsibility for finding and developing their own land. The inclusion of the government's proposals in the Criminal Justice Bill, alongside measures directed at rapists, murderers and terrorists, signalled to Gypsies and Travellers that they were perceived as a trouble-prone minority that needed to be coerced into conformity. Apart from the withdrawal of the proposal to confiscate caravans and to offer financial assistance for Gypsies and Travellers to move into housing, the Bill hardly differed from the consultation proposals.[79]

As well as the remonstrations of interest groups – including Save the Children Fund, which was concerned at the impact of evictions on travelling children's health and welfare, and the National Housing and Town Planning Council, which criticized the conflation of unlawful occupation of land with site provision for Gypsies and Travellers – there were passionate parliamentary debates in the spring and summer of 1994.[80] Lobbying by ACERT resulted in an eleventh-hour Lords' amendment to postpone repealing the duty on local authorities to provide sites and the 100 per cent grant for five years. However, this was defeated in the Commons and arguments that the Bill would breach the European Convention on Human Rights fell on deaf ears. In November 1994, the Criminal Justice and Public Order Act (CJPOA) received royal assent. It introduced powers that made life more difficult for all travelling communities: travelling or stopping in groups of more than six vehicles (with towing vehicles and trailers counted separately) became a criminal offence, and evictions from unauthorized sites were made easier, while local authorities no longer had any obligation or ring-fenced funding to provide public sites.

At the same time, changes to planning policy caused further difficulties for

Gypsies and Travellers. The 1990 Town and Country Planning Act strengthened councils' enforcement powers against unauthorized development (on land owned by Gypsies and Travellers without planning permission). From 1994, Planning Circular 1/94 (which applied in England and Wales) set out the criteria for Gypsies and Travellers to develop sites on their own land, as the government argued they should. A second circular (18/94) called on local authorities to consider tolerating unauthorized Gypsy and Traveller encampments (on other people's land) where they 'cause no nuisance', but this 'was frequently ignored or wilfully misinterpreted'.[81]

The planning system can be a minefield for the average citizen – who does not usually have to build his or her home from scratch and does not risk seeing the entire dwelling torn down for any planning infringements – let alone Gypsies and Travellers who have high levels of illiteracy. Without the benefit of planning advice, many purchased land that was unsuitable and did not secure planning permission before moving onto sites, or failed to meet the strict and sometimes discriminatory criteria set down by local authorities. Green Belt land was excluded from consideration, creating a major hurdle because Gypsy and Traveller sites were traditionally on marginal land on the edge of towns and villages. In some areas, local criteria made it virtually impossible for planning applications to succeed – including bans on sites combining residential and employment uses, arbitrary maximum limits for the number of caravans, banning applications from people without proven 'local connections'[82]. Or planning conditions were applied that conflicted with traditional practices, such as banning additional trailers moving onto a site for large family gatherings such as weddings and funerals.[83]

The post-1994 regime was a disaster for Gypsies and Travellers. Local authorities, many of whom had already proved reluctant to give permission for council-run sites under the 1968 Act, were now expected to decide planning applications by individuals, often in the face of community hostility. Up to 90 per cent were rejected, and a rapidly growing number of Gypsies and Travellers faced eviction from their own land for breaching planning regulations.[84] By 2006, about 1,200 such sites were subject to council enforcement action.[85] Most local authorities stopped building new sites and many allowed existing ones to fall into disrepair, with a net loss of 596 pitches between 1995 and 2002.[86] Figure 4.1 (below) illustrates how the policy changes of 1994 began to bite in the late 1990s. There has since been a drop in the number of caravans on unauthorized encampments, replaced by a rise in the number on unauthorized developments, as many Gypsies and Travellers find themselves trapped on land they own, without planning permission and living under the shadow of potential eviction.

It should not be underestimated how threatening and destabilising the post-1994 climate has been for Gypsies and Travellers. For many law-abiding members of the settled community, the CJPOA and planning changes represented a much-needed crackdown on a deviant community. For the increasing number of homeless but otherwise law-abiding travelling families, it represented a sustained assault on their identity, ethnicity, culture and capacity to provide for their families. In parts of the country where the law has been rigorously applied, it has meant a daily cycle of harassment and eviction, with barely time to maintain vehicles or prepare food for children before being moved on.[87]

LATE 1990s ONWARDS: FORCES FOR CHANGE

These policy changes caused a crisis in site provision, but also stimulated a new spirit of organization, cooperation and determination among Gypsies and Travellers and their advocates. Friends, Families & Travellers (FFT) was established in response to the CJPOA and developed from an informal support group and network primarily helping New Travellers into a formal advice, information and training organization providing a wide range of services to all Gypsies and Travellers. FFT now aims 'to work towards a more equitable society where everyone has the right to travel and to stop without constant fear of persecution because of their lifestyle'.[88]

The Traveller Law Research Unit (TLRU) at Cardiff University, led by Phil Thomas, Luke Clements and Rachel Morris, became a hub for research, lobbying and advice for Gypsies and Travellers and those working with them.[89] From 1995 to 1998, the Telephone Legal Advice Service for Travellers (TLAST) was based at the unit, providing advice for individual Gypsies and Travellers and related service providers such as health visitors, educators, planners, landowners and the police. In 2000, TLRU and the Rural Media Company received Comic Relief funding to support production of *Travellers' Times*, now well-established as the national magazine for Britain's travelling communities and an important lobbying tool.[90]

The TLRU also organised conferences in 1997, 1999, 2000 and 2002, bringing together hundreds of Gypsies and Travellers and service providers to 'create a common platform to take forward the reform debate'.[91] Lobbying by the TLRU achieved important policy changes in relation to planning advice, toleration of unauthorized encampments, health care and voting rights. The unit's activities culminated with the launch in January 2002 of the Traveller Law Reform Bill, bringing reform proposals together into a single, draft Parliamentary Bill.[92] Its major innovation was the proposal for a new Gypsy and Traveller Accommodation Commission to assess the need for sites in England and Wales, which would remove decisions from local politicians about the need for and provision of sites. The Bill turned on its head the 'carrot and stick' approach to site provision, proposing that a local authority's failure to provide sites should affect its powers to evict Travellers from unauthorized sites and be taken into account when deciding planning applications from Gypsies and Travellers.[93] The Bill also aimed to remove 'discriminatory statutory provisions', for instance by extending the powers of the Housing Corporation to support the development of caravan sites as well as bricks-and-mortar housing.[94]

In December 2002, the TLRU closed, passing the baton of law reform to the Gypsy and Traveller Law Reform Coalition (G&TLRC), founded in September 2002. The coalition marked a watershed in the history of political representation, acting as an umbrella body for various groups representing Gypsy and Traveller communities and bringing together those from different ethnicities and backgrounds to lobby against their common disadvantages. It campaigned for legal reform to tackle accommodation problems and established a parliamentary wing, the All Party Parliamentary Group for Traveller Law Reform, chaired in 2009 by Labour MP Julie Morgan, with Lord Avebury (former MP Eric Lubbock) as its secretary. The Traveller Law Reform Bill was introduced several times in the House of Commons as a Private Member's Bill, but never attracted the government support it needed to progress through parliament. In 2004, a Scottish wing of the G&TLRC was established, aiming to introduce a similar Bill into the Scottish parliament.

This combination of an effective umbrella body and active parliamentary lobbying succeeded in raising awareness among policymakers, politicians, other lobby groups and the media of the inequalities facing Gypsies and Travellers. In recognition of its achievements, the G&TLRC received Liberty's Human Rights Award in 2004.[95] In April 2006, the G&TLRC was disbanded and reincarnated as the Traveller Law Reform Project (TLRP), which carries on its aim of legal change through parliamentary lobbying.[96]

Since the late 1990s, growing numbers of Gypsies and Travellers have battled for planning permission to stay on sites they have bought. Cases in which some Gypsies and Travellers have moved onto land – occasionally at night or over the weekend, when council offices are closed – quickly establishing a site with hard standings and then seeking retrospective planning permission, have been points of conflict and contention, particularly in the east, south-east and south-west of England, where Gypsy and Traveller communities are concentrated.

... travellers in their thousands are deliberately breaking the law by illegally setting up home overnight – and blighting rural communities across Middle England ... [there is an] increasingly common trend for gypsies to flout planning rules by developing unauthorized camps near some of the country's most picturesque villages.[97]

Some cases, such as the large unauthorized sites at Dale Farm near Basildon in Essex and Cottenham in Cambridgeshire, escalated into battles of wills lasting many years, with local authorities determined to evict and the well-informed residents using every legal tool possible to stay in their homes. There have been brutal showdowns between Travellers barricaded on their land and bailiffs and police aiming to evict them. In one tragic case in May 1998, six-year-old Patrick Dooley died during an eviction in Edmonton, North London, after being run over by a vehicle while attempting to hide.[98]

Pressure was growing on the new Labour government to address both the repression and inequalities faced by Gypsies and Travellers and the rapidly rising number of unauthorized sites. From 2000, Gypsies and Travellers had recourse to both the Race Relations Acts (RRAs) and the new Human Rights Act. The courts had been used successfully, although belatedly, to secure protection for English Gypsies and Irish Travellers under race relations legislation. A 1988 test case brought by the CRE identified (English) Romany Gypsies as an ethnic minority (*Commission for Racial Equality versus Dutton*) and an independent case in 2000 achieved the same for Irish Travellers (*O'Leary versus Allied Domecq*). No test case has yet clarified the position of Scottish and Welsh Gypsies under the RRAs, although the Scottish Executive recognizes Scottish Gypsies as an ethnic minority.[99] The RRA 2000 (see Chapter 2) introduced a new requirement on public bodies not just to prevent racial discrimination, but to positively promote good race relations. This means that, at least in theory, local authorities, primary care trusts and other public bodies can no longer simply designate Gypsies and Travellers as being 'hard to reach'; they must actively ensure they have equal access to public services.

However, the practical application of race relations law to protect Gypsies and Travellers has been chequered. In a 'classic' discrimination case brought by the CRE in 1998, Cheltenham Borough Council was found to be in breach of the RRA for refusing to allow two Gypsy women to hire a hall for a wedding reception without stringent conditions.[100] In two far more shocking cases in 2003, no prosecutions were brought, despite the efforts of the police. Firle Bonfire Society in East Sussex burned an effigy of a caravan with a Gypsy family painted on the side and the registration plate 'P1 KEY',[101] but denied racism and avoided prosecution after claiming the village had experienced problems with Travellers camping on local farmland.[102] When 15-year-old Irish Traveller Johnny Delaney was kicked and stamped to death in Ellesmere Port, Liverpool, several witnesses testified that his killers had shouted racist abuse. However, Justice Richards dismissed the case made by Cheshire police that the murder was racially motivated; Johnny's killers were found guilty of manslaughter and sentenced to just four-and-a-half years in prison. Although comparisons were made with the racist murder of Black teenager Stephen Lawrence in London in 1993, the case did not spark a similar bout of societal and institutional soul searching.[103]

Recourse to European law has had similarly patchy results for Gypsies and Travellers. The European Convention on Human Rights (ECHR) was incorporated into British law in the 1998 Human Rights Act (HRA), which came into effect in 2000. Prior to that, anyone wishing to challenge a decision under British law had to take their case to the European Court of Human Rights (ECtHR) in Strasbourg; since 2000, the process has become easier and cheaper. Some Gypsies and Travellers have attempted to use human rights law to overturn planning decisions against them, usually under Article 8, the right to respect for private and family life, or article 14, prohibition of discrimination.[104] One of the first cases of this kind was *Buckley versus UK* (1996),[105] in which Mrs June Buckley claimed that South Cambridgeshire

District Council's refusal of retrospective planning permission for a site on land she owned prevented her from pursuing her way of life as a Romani Gypsy.[106] The European Court of Human Rights found against her, primarily because the council had not used 'disproportionate means' to enforce its decision.[107] In the later case of five Gypsy families who owned their land, *Chapman versus UK (2001)*, the court found there had been no violation of their human rights under any of the five articles they claimed.[108]

However, other cases have produced results that were favourable to Gypsies. A 2001 High Court judgment[109] found against a planning inspector who, when rejecting a Gypsy family's planning appeal, had taken into account Tunbridge Wells Borough Council's offer of conventional housing:

> If [an immutable antipathy to conventional housing] be established then, in my judgement, bricks and mortar, if offered, are unsuitable, just as would be the offer of a rat infested barn. It would be contrary to Articles 8 and 14 to expect such a person to accept conventional housing and to hold it against him or her that he has not accepted it, or is not prepared to accept it, even as a last resort factor.[110]

In the case of *Connors versus UK* (2004), the ECtHR criticized the British government for failing to address the lack of security of tenure experienced by Gypsies and Travellers on public sites compared with residents of council housing and mobile home parks. The government, also under pressure from the TLRP, has belatedly taken action under the Housing and Regeneration Act 2008, which includes measures to improve security of tenure for Gypsies and Travellers on local authority sites. In late 2008, the government was consulting on how to bring this into effect.[111]

However, the perception that European law is 'over-riding' British law and setting the rights of minorities above those of 'the silent majority' is widespread, damaging and regularly reinforced by the popular media:

> This 'chancer's charter' as Mr [Michael] Howard has correctly dubbed it, is being used by gypsies to openly defy our planning laws. It is being called upon by failed asylum seekers to stay in this country and leech off our benefits system. Because of it, criminals are now rewarded instead of punished for their crimes. Indeed, anyone who wants to sidestep British justice just needs to bleat 'human rights' and they are given a passport to do as they please . . . We must listen before everything that we in Britain hold dear crumbles completely.[112]

RECENT TENSIONS AND CONCLUSIONS

Under the 2004 Housing and Planning Acts, the Labour government took action to solve the shortage of Gypsy and Traveller sites, requiring local authorities to identify the accommodation needs of Gypsies and Travellers in their communities and take steps through regional and local plans to provide for them, as for the rest of the community. There was now an opportunity to effect real change, with an effective and respected lobbying organization active (the TLRP), increasing levels of legal awareness among travelling communities, and strengthened human rights and race relations legislation in place. What followed, however, was a full-blown moral panic over 'problem' Gypsy and Traveller sites.[113]

In November 2004, the Select Committee on the Office of the Deputy Prime Minister (ODPM) called for the reintroduction of the statutory duty on local authorities to provide sites, and expressed concern that the new regional planning system would take too long to deliver results:

> There must be a national response with a duty imposed on all local authorities based on assessment of need at regional level. The Government should establish a Gypsy and Traveller Taskforce to ensure site vacancies are co-ordinated across the region and throughout the country. The Minister has outlined his hopes that regional spatial strategies and regional plans will be used to assess and provide for that need. We recommend he goes one step further and places a requirement on local authorities to meet that need. The Government must provide a statutory framework, political leadership and capital funding.[114]

The following month, after a long policy review, the ODPM published a new planning circular for consultation.[115] This aimed, without bringing back the duty, to address some of the obstacles to the provision of new sites and to remove the inherent inequalities in the current circular 1/94.

National and local media were already sensitised to 'problem' Gypsy and Traveller sites, whose residents were blamed for antisocial behaviour such as fly-tipping, noise and environmental damage. The new, draft planning circular was perceived as evidence that the government was 'going soft' on Gypsies and Travellers and giving them 'special treatment' to create 'eyesores' in the countryside. This, combined with growing public and political hostility to unauthorized sites, provoked an explosion in media (especially tabloid newspaper) coverage of Britain's Gypsy and Traveller communities, which became increasingly politicized during the general election campaign of spring 2005.

In January 2005, an ICM poll for the *Sunday Express* found that:
- almost three-quarters of 'householders' believed they should pay lower council tax if Gypsies 'set up camp' nearby
- 74 per cent of 'taxpayers' thought they should get a reduction to compensate for any slump in their house prices caused by 'Gypsy blight'
- three in five said the government should 'toughen its approach in dealing with Gypsies', while 28 per cent said it should be more lenient
- 18 per cent thought current policies were successful and more than half thought them unsuccessful
- 63 per cent said 'Labour's stance on Gypsies' was 'lacking in common sense' and 'ruled by political correctness and fear of accusations of racism'

- 63 per cent said 'the law of the land' was not being applied to the 'growing nuisance of unofficial Gypsy camps which sprout up overnight'
- more than a third were 'incensed' at current government policy and law enforcement, believing 'Gypsies have more rights than others to set up home wherever they choose'
- nearly three in five said the police were 'not tough enough'.[116]

A 2005 MORI poll conducted for Stonewall (before the 2005 media coverage) found that Gypsies and Travellers were the group that respondents were most likely to feel 'less positive towards', while pointing out that 'these are just the people admitting their prejudices and wearing them on their sleeves'. This suggests that the proportion of people prejudiced against Gypsies and Travellers is likely to be even higher.[117] The poll revealed that the percentage of respondents feeling 'less positive' towards a selection of social groups was:

Travellers/Gypsies	35 per cent
Refugees/asylum seekers	34 per cent
Ethnic 'minorities' (including White, Asian, Black/Afro-Caribbean)	18 per cent
Gay or lesbian people	17 per cent[118]

'The two groups identified as the most threatening – asylum seekers and Travellers – were the only two groups with whom most interviewees had had no contact.'[119] For many respondents, the media was the source of their knowledge and opinions. Forty-three per cent said television influenced their views of refugees and asylum seekers, and 40 per cent cited newspapers.[120] There are no equivalent figures for Gypsies and Travellers, but in the absence of personal contact, it is reasonable to assume that the media is similarly powerful in shaping public opinions about them.[121]

With public opinion apparently on his side, the Conservative leader Michael Howard made the 'Gypsy problem' an electoral issue, pledging to prevent Gypsies and Travellers using the Human Rights Act to stall eviction proceedings and to toughen the enforcement powers against unauthorized sites that he had introduced as Home Secretary in 1994. The cocktail of tabloid frenzy and electoral politics created the impression that rural communities all over Britain were 'at war' with marauding Travellers.[122]

On 9 March 2005, the *Sun* launched its 'War on Gipsy free-for-all'. The 'full story' was carried on a double-page spread under the headline 'Stamp on the camps', with a photo of the Travellers' site at Crays Hill in Essex. Part of it has planning permission, and the rest is one of the largest unauthorized sites in the country. An editorial labelled the Human Rights Act 'the villain of the piece', portraying the government as blinkered by political correctness, while the *Sun* stated the 'obvious truth'.[123]

Andrew Ryder of the G&TLRC brought a complaint against the *Sun* to the Press Complaints Commission (PCC), on the grounds that it breached the commission's rules on accuracy and discrimination. The PCC ruled there had been no breach. Despite Ryder's evidence that the CRE 'recorded an increase in incidents of discrimination against Gypsies and Travellers after publication of the articles', the discrimination complaint was dismissed.[124] The PCC stated that the discrimination clause is 'designed to protect the rights of the individual and is not applicable to groups of people'; as 'no individual has been referred to in the article in a prejudicial or pejorative manner', there was no breach.[125]

This was the most dramatic and contentious example of the extensive media coverage of Britain's Gypsies and Travellers in 2005. At least 400 national newspaper articles were published that year, as well as bouts of national broadcasts and regional media coverage, about a community representing just one in 1,200 people in the United Kingdom.[126] The reports included such comments as:

> Yet again the rights of hard-working taxpayers have come second to those whose only contribution to society is to put a drain on it. Gypsies are treated as victims, but it is the rest of the community who are the real victims. Until gypsies respect our way of life as they expect us to respect theirs, they will be unwelcome everywhere. (*Daily Express*, 24 May 2005)[127]

> For people who describe themselves as travellers they are strangely averse to travelling. If gipsies love the open road so much why don't they stay on it and save us all a lot of trouble . . . and money. (*Sun*, 13 August 2005)[128]

> Newspapers such as *The Sun* and *The Daily Mail* have presented an entirely bogus image of Middle England being overrun with illegal encampments, and repeated vile slurs about the Gypsy way of life. (*Independent*, 12 March 2005)[129]

Both the scale and vehemence of the tabloid coverage were questioned at the time by some broadsheet newspapers, broadcast media and observers, including the CRE, campaign groups and individual MPs but, as the PCC decision demonstrates, no action was taken. A study of the national press coverage found:

- a widespread failure to capitalise 'Gypsies' and 'Travellers' as proper nouns, in defiance of guidelines published by the National Union of Journalists and the CRE
- a tendency by the right-wing tabloids to question Gypsies' and Travellers' ethnic status, implying that they were not 'real' ethnic minorities and that to consider them as such was 'political correctness gone mad'
- the use of terms that were, at best, mildly offensive and, at worst, racist, ranging from 'itinerants' and 'tinkers' through to 'gyppos' and 'pikies'
- routine stereotyping of all Gypsies and Travellers as threatening,

dirty and lazy, with the over-riding message that they were invading and destroying the countryside through the stealthy and deliberate development of 'illegal' and unwanted sites

• some use of the binary stereotype of the good/bad and real/fake Gypsies to excuse racist reporting

• routine stereotyping of the settled community as law-abiding, decent and hardworking, drawn together by the *Express* newspapers under the 'Middle England' label, to sharpen the contrast with Gypsies and Travellers

• many of the hallmarks of a moral panic, including the portrayal of the Gypsy 'problem' as national rather than local, 'calls for action' in some newspapers, predictions the problem would snowball, and linking with other social problems as evidence that Britain was 'going to the dogs'

• very few voices, including that of the CRE, challenging the stereotypes or criticising the abuse of Gypsies and Travellers.[130]

Ironically, all political parties claimed to agree that the solution to the tensions was to increase the number of authorized public and private Gypsy and Traveller sites and to clamp down on unauthorized ones. The 2004 Housing and Planning Acts and Planning Circular 01/06, *Planning for Gypsy and Traveller Caravan Sites*, are intended to achieve this in the long term, obliging local authorities to assess the accommodation needs of Gypsies and Travellers in their area and bring forward sites through the planning system, as they would do for bricks-and-mortar housing. By late 2008, two local authorities, Epping Forest and South Gloucestershire, had been directed by the Communities and Local Government Secretary to produce plans for Gypsy and Traveller sites in their area.

Concerns were expressed by both the Select Committee (see above), and the Independent Task Group (set up by the government in 2006 to investigate the problems of Gypsy and Traveller accommodation) that the new framework was too slow and cumbersome. In its final report, the Task Group warned that:

> [The framework] is not delivering at a pace that will meet the needs of either Gypsies and Travellers or the settled community. Unless the pace of delivery increases, it will fail the children who today have nowhere to call home, no base from which to access education or healthcare, and whose families have no stake in the economic success of their communities. If we are to improve the life chances available to those children's children, and to address the community tensions fuelled by unauthorized sites, there must not be further delays to the implementation of the policy framework now in place.[131]

The chair of the Task Group, Sir Brian Briscoe, noted that 'the problem' is small, with only about 4,000 caravan pitches and less than one square mile of land required in total to solve the current shortage.[132]

Both recent and long-term history suggests that implementing this ideal will be problematic. How will settled communities – whose response to house-building is often 'not in my back yard'– be persuaded to accept new Gypsy and Traveller sites? As the local surveys of the 1950s demonstrated, when it comes to taking responsibility for site provision, councils will look first to the interests and prejudices of their electorates, among whom Gypsies and Travellers are under-represented. Furthermore, there is a question mark over whether policies designed to treat – and which expect local authorities to treat – Gypsies and Travellers 'the same' as the rest of the community can promote equality. It has long been recognized in relation to women and other minority ethnic groups that different treatment is sometimes needed to create equal opportunities and outcomes for disadvantaged groups. The ongoing 'carrot and stick' approach to site provision continues to offer stronger eviction powers to cajole local authorities into providing sites, and does little to persuade local politicians or the wider public that Gypsies and Travellers are valued members of the community with a right to stable, secure homes.

The continued presence of 'No Travellers' signs in some areas and the persistence of headlined stereotypes in the media suggests that anti-Gypsy prejudice is the last bastion of respectable racism at many levels of society. Gypsies and Travellers have a long way to go before their theoretical legal protection becomes embedded in popular culture. Restricted contact with other social groups helps these barriers and prejudices to survive. The persistence of outdated images of 'true Romanies' living in bow-topped caravans, which are used to undermine the rights of 'travellers' to a nomadic lifestyle, local authority attitudes that continue to portray them as outsiders rather than as constituents, and the under-representation of Gypsies and Travellers in political and social life are still barriers to equality. It is to be hoped that the formation of the Equality and Human Rights Commission in 2007, with a broad remit to address all forms of inequality and discrimination, including the needs of Gypsies and Travellers, will be a step towards dismantling these barriers.

Gypsies and Travellers suffer the greatest inequalities, on all measures, of any social group in Britain. Improvement in their situation over the past 60 years has been slight compared with other groups. The main inhibitors of change have been:

• their relatively small number compared with other groups suffering inequalities, the diversity of travelling communities, their shifting location, relative poverty, poor educational attainment and reduced cultural contact with 'settled society'. All of these features have limited the capacity of Gypsies and Travellers to campaign effectively on their own behalf. In all of these respects, inequalities have reinforced inequality

• strong and enduring hostility from other sections of the community, reinforced by the popular media.

But there have been improvements, mainly driven by:

- campaigning and use of the law by Gypsies and Travellers since the 1970s
- targeted government support designed to reduce inequality, and recent legislative changes designed to drive up site provision at the local level and improve educational attainment
- Labour governments' greater willingness than their opponents to act to diminish inequality
- recourse to European Union law and Europe-wide movements for reform.

STATISTICS

Statistics on the number and location of Gypsies and Travellers have always been seriously inadequate, due to these people's high mobility and a historic lack of interest in measuring their populations or needs. The only official measure is the government's biannual caravan count, which has taken place in England since 1979. All local authorities are required to count the number of Gypsy/Traveller caravans on two days each year (in January and July), classified according to their location in one of these categories:

- private authorized site
- public authorized site

and, since 1996:

- unauthorized encampment (on someone else's land)
- unauthorized development (on their own land, but without planning permission).

The statistics are collated and published by central government (see Figure 4.1). Almost 18,000 Gypsy/Traveller caravans were recorded in January 2008, compared with just over 8,000 in 1979.[133] Of the caravans recorded in 2008, 25 per cent were in the east of England, 19 per cent in the south-east and 14 per cent in the south-west.[134] However, there are some caveats to note about the count:

1. **Caravans are counted, not people.** If an average of three people per caravan is taken as reasonable, this would give a figure of between 51,000 and 54,000 Gypsies and Travellers living in caravans in 2008, compared with 25,000 in 1979.[135] However, many Gypsies and Travellers now live in settled housing for at least part of the year and are statistically invisible. They could account for half of the total population, which would bring the totals to almost 100,000, compared with about 50,000 in 1979. The caravan count almost certainly under-estimates numbers, and it is believed that the Gypsy/Traveller population has increased more quickly than the population as a whole due to lower marriage age and higher fertility, although improved recording practices may account for some of the apparent increase.[136]

2. **Definitions vary locally and over time.** The count depends on accurate

recording by local authorities and on which caravan-dwellers they count as Gypsies/Travellers – some include New Travellers, others do not. Although now recognized in case law as minority ethnic groups (see above), neither English Gypsies nor Irish Travellers have ever been included as ethnic categories in the national census held every ten years. Activist groups have long campaigned for their inclusion, and the Office of National Statistics proposes to introduce a category of 'Gypsy or Irish Traveller' in Census 2011, pending parliamentary approval of the census in 2010.[137]

3. **Seasonal fluctuations.** The January caravan count is always slightly lower than that for July. Some Gypsies and Travellers live in settled housing during the winter, but go on the road in the summer.

4. **Regional variations.** The caravan count has taken place since 1979 in England only. Scotland undertook one-off counts in 1969 and 1992, and has conducted a biannual count only since 1998. The Scottish count returns more detailed information than the English version, providing some insight into the number of people in each household, their ages and their length of stay on public sites. The estimated population of Gypsies and Travellers living in caravans in Scotland in July 2007 was 2,800, the highest recorded since 1998, and 1,547 in January 2008.[138] Counting in Wales has also been ad hoc. It was suspended in 1997 and a biannual count like that in England was reinstated in July 2006. The 1997 count recorded 732 Gypsy and Traveller caravans: 217 on unauthorized sites, 502 on local authority sites and 13 on private sites. The most recent count, in July 2008, recorded 798 Gypsy and Traveller caravans, of which three-quarters were on authorized sites. Of the remainder, 9 per cent were on unauthorized sites owned by Gypsies and 16 per cent on unauthorized sites not owned by Gypsies.[139]

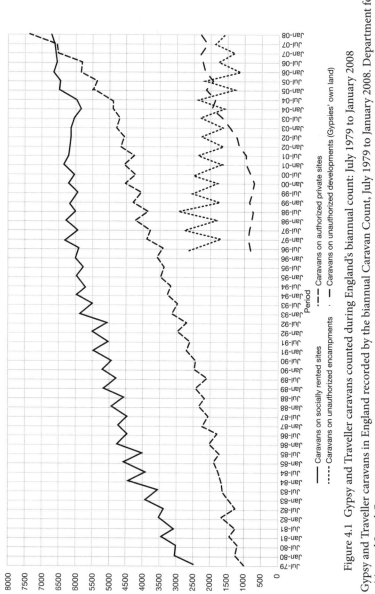

Figure 4.1 Gypsy and Traveller caravans counted during England's biannual count: July 1979 to January 2008

Source: Gypsy and Traveller caravans in England recorded by the biannual Caravan Count, July 1979 to January 2008. Department for Communities and Local Government.

Chapter 5

Gender equality

Helen McCarthy[1]

TIMELINE

1792	Mary Wollstonecraft's *A Vindication of the Rights of Women* published, launching modern demands for gender equality.
1869	Female householders gain vote in local elections.
1870	Married Women's Property Act, a milestone in women's campaign for equality.
1918	Most women aged over 30 gain vote in national elections, following lengthy campaign. Women allowed to stand for election to parliament from age 21.
1928	Women gain right to vote on same terms as men at age 21.
1945	Family Allowances Act.
1955	Women in public service win equal pay.
1967	Abortion Act legalizes abortion up to 28 weeks in certain circumstances.
1968	Female sewing machinists strike for equal pay at Ford Motors, Dagenham.
1969	London Women's Liberation Workshop formed. Divorce Reform Act establishes principle of no-blame divorce. Women's National Commission established.
1970	Equal Pay Act passed (in force 1975). First Women's Liberation Movement conference at Ruskin College, Oxford. Feminists disrupt Miss World competition at Albert Hall.
1971	Erin Pizzey opens first women's refuge, in Chiswick.
1974	Families Need Fathers formed to campaign for equal parental rights.
1975	Sex Discrimination Act and creation of Equal Opportunities Commission. National Abortion Campaign launched to defend 1967 Act.
1976	Domestic Violence and Matrimonial Proceedings Act. First Rape Crisis centre opens in North London.
1977	First Reclaim the Night march.

1979	Margaret Thatcher becomes first female prime minister. Trades Union Congress demonstration against Corrie Bill (to reverse 1967 Abortion Act) attracts 100,000 marchers. Dame Josephine Barnes first female president of British Medical Association, and Agnes Curran first female governor of a male prison.
1981	First women's peace demonstration, at Greenham Common.
1984	Brenda Dean first woman leader of a major trades union (Society of Graphical and Allied Trades).
1988	Legislation to allow spouses to be assessed separately for tax purposes.
1989	Valerie (later Baroness) Amos, first Black chief executive of Equal Opportunities Commission (until 1994).
1993	Labour Party adopts All Women Shortlists for next election.
1997	Record 120 women MPs elected. Women's Unit formed in Cabinet Office. Marjory Scardino first woman to head a FTSE 100 company.
1999	Scottish Parliament establishes standing Equal Opportunities Committee. Fathers Direct formed.
2002	Scottish Executive's Equality Strategy commits to mainstream all forms of equality. Fathers4Justice formed. Employment Act empowers parents with the right to request flexible work arrangements and requires employers to consider requests.
2003	All government departments required to carry out equal pay reviews.
2006	Public Sector Duty for Gender Equality introduced. Margaret Beckett becomes Britain's first female foreign secretary.
2007	Equality and Human Rights Commission takes over Equal Opportunities Commission responsibilities.
2008	Parliament votes to retain 24 weeks as upper limit for abortions, following calls for a reduction from right-to-life campaigners.

INTRODUCTION

Gender differs from the other aspects of equality and inequality discussed in this volume in that women, who are more likely than men to experience disadvantage attributable to gender, are not a minority but a majority of the population. In 1951, there were 24 million males and 26 million females in Britain. In mid-2006, there were an estimated 29.6 million males and 30.8 million females.[2]

Individual women have protested against various forms of inequality throughout history, especially since the late eighteenth century. A sustained movement for equal rights for women began throughout Britain in the 1850s. By the end of the nineteenth century, there had been gains in legal rights and access to education, and some women could vote and stand for election at local level.[3] These changes came about chiefly because women campaigned for them, often against fierce opposition. Further, more militant campaigning gained them the national vote in 1918, but only at age 30, whereas men could vote at the age of 21. Women were a majority of the population and, explicitly, the government was wary of allowing them to become a majority of the electorate. Further campaigning achieved equalization of the voting age in 1928, although few women were elected to parliament between the world wars and for long afterwards. They complained persistently, then and since, of discrimination by selection committees, including by female selectors.[4] The very active women's movement of the 1920s and 1930s achieved greater, but still far from complete, equality before the law and in access to the professions, although women continued to experience difficulty in making headway in the legal, medical and other established professions.[5]

1945 TO THE 1960s

It is often believed that, after they gained the vote, women's activism largely declined until the emergence of Women's Liberation in the late 1960s. But there was more continuity in women's campaigning than this suggests. Between the wars, equal pay was an important issue for many women. Although their efforts to achieve this failed, the issue continued to be salient throughout World War II. There were some successful strikes for equal pay in factories, as women took advantage of their importance to the wartime economy. Women teachers, who demonstrably did the same work as male teachers, succeeded with the help of female and male MPs of all parties in inserting a clause granting equal pay into the Education Bill 1944. However, despite the pressures of war, the Prime Minister, Winston Churchill, chose to veto the clause and it was removed. Women's continuing demands led to the establishment of a Royal Commission on Equal Pay, which reported in 1946. The report carefully documented the differences in male and female pay where these could be established. The differences were clear in large areas of the public sector, where men and women did the same or similar work, but in much of the private sector and a substantial part of the public sector, work was strictly gender divided – for instance, there were no male typists. The majority report acknowledged inequalities, but concluded that measurement of inequality was difficult due to the problems of establishing equivalence of work between men and women. The commission's four female members issued a minority report asking the government to take steps to establish equal pay, initially in the public sector. Throughout its time in office, from 1945–51, Labour refused to move to equalize pay, on the grounds that it would increase labour costs and undermine the government's chief priority: rebuilding the economy after the war and the inter-war Depression.

Women of all classes were substantially represented in the labour market during the war, and a few had been able to take advantage of the absence of men to advance to senior positions. The post-war government was concerned about an unprecedented peacetime labour shortage. Before the end of the war, the Ministry of Labour was urging older women whose children were no longer dependent to remain in or re-enter the labour force. The pre-war 'marriage bar', which had banned married women from working in such occupations as teaching, the civil service, banking and many factories, was lifted. For the first time, it became socially acceptable for middle class married women to take paid work, and more of them sought to do so. However, the opportunities open to women in general and for older 'married women returners' in particular, did not noticeably expand and there were few opportunities for women to retrain after a career break for parenting. Nevertheless, the number of women recorded as economically active rose. Especially noticeable was a rise in part-time work, mainly among older women. However, official statistics may be misleading: much of women's part-time work was not officially recorded before the war. After the war, records are more reliable. Part-time work accounted for 11 per cent of women's employment in 1951 and 25 per cent in 1961.[6] But although older married women were more active in the labour force than before, this did not lead to a noticeable shift of household responsibilities to their male partners, or in the gender division of labour in the workplace.

After the war, the government encouraged younger women to leave the labour force, to marry and have children. It was concerned that a pre-war decline in the birth rate would continue. In fact, marriage and birth rates rose after the war. During the 1930s, about 15 per cent of all women and 8 per cent of men never married. After World War II, marriage was almost universal. The average age at marriage and first childbirth fell, the former to a historically low level of about 22 for women (compared with 25 previously) by the early 1970s.[7] Levels of illegitimacy were low and unmarried motherhood was a highly stigmatized source of inequality.

Early marriage and childbirth restricted the opportunities of women to be active in public campaigning or to become established in a career before taking a break to care for children. There was strong social disapproval of mothers of young children who took paid work, reinforced by popular psychological theories of the time, which stressed the damage caused to young children by the absence of their mother.[8] A 1965 opinion poll found that 80 per cent of those surveyed thought women with children under school age should always stay at home.[9] Limited child-care provision, other than support from grandmothers and other family members, left most mothers with little other option. This may help to explain women's slow progress in occupational terms and the relative inactivity of younger women in public campaigning compared with earlier decades: they were more likely to be involved with child-rearing. Even those who were better off could no longer easily recruit servants to free them for activities outside the home, as they previously had. Working class women who had previously worked as domestic servants after the war had access to a wider range of employment offering them more independence.

Women's career prospects were also held back by the fact that their opportunities for training did not noticeably improve. In 1945, only 1.8 per cent of British 18-year-olds attended university, and only 25 per cent of these were women. Higher education expanded a little after the war, but mainly in the sciences, which disproportionately recruited males. By the early 1960s, only 4 per cent of the age group (and very few older students) attended university, and the proportion of women had fallen slightly. The occupations open to women graduates expanded only a little: the majority became schoolteachers, as they had done before the war. Females were more likely than males to leave school at the minimum age (raised to 15 in 1947 until 1973, when it rose to 16), and less likely to take national examinations – not surprisingly, given the absence of obvious occupational gain from doing so and a general lack of encouragement for girls to aim to be other than wives and mothers. The 11+ examination (which was introduced by the 1944 Education Act as the mechanism for selection for entry to 'academic' grammar schools – the route to higher status occupations – or, for the majority, secondary modern schools) was weighted against girls. For historical reasons (fewer grammar schools had been provided for girls in the past), there were fewer grammar school places for girls than for boys, and as a result, girls in many areas had to gain a higher exam score than boys to enter a grammar school. This inequality persisted, largely unnoticed, until comprehensive schools were introduced in the mid-1960s.

The women's movement was more quiescent in the 1940s and 1950s than before and less attractive to younger women, but it did not disappear. Older women who had been active in organizations before the war, such as the Fawcett Society, the Women's Co-operative Guild and the British Federation of Business and Professional Women (BFBPW), continued to campaign on such issues as improved health and welfare, improvement of science education for girls (to improve their career chances) and equal pay. Between 1946 and the mid-1950s, these organizations, together with women in the larger public sector unions and staff associations, the Joint Committee on Women in the Civil Service and the Equal Pay Campaign Committee (formed 1943), lobbied Ministers and MPs and used the press and film to publicize their cause.[10]

In 1955, the Conservative government granted equal pay to about 155,000 women employed in the non-industrial civil service, to be implemented through six annual increments, with parity to be achieved in 1961. Equal pay for teachers and for National Health Service employees followed shortly after. This was undoubtedly a step forward, but because it applied only to grades that recruited both men and women, large numbers of women in gender-specific posts were unaffected, such as typists, cleaners and female manual workers in the nationalized industries. The private sector, in general, did not, as was hoped, follow the government's lead.

The government's change came about, probably, because the Conservatives were anxious to hold the votes of middle class women, whom they had attracted in large numbers in the 1951 election.[11] Also, there was a shortage of recruits to a number of traditionally female public sector jobs, such as teaching, due both to the expansion of education services and of the public sector generally after the war, and to the early retirement from full-time work of younger women due to marriage and childbirth. There were also international influences. The United Nations Commission on the Status of Women adopted a resolution in 1948 calling upon the International Labour Organisation (ILO) to take action on the issue of equal pay for equal work. Three years later, this principle was enshrined in Convention 100 of the ILO.

Throughout the late 1950s and 1960s, an array of groups, most with roots in the pre-war period, cooperated to keep the gender equality agenda alive. Two victories were won in the sphere of politics. The first came in 1958, when the Life Peers Act allowed the creation of both male and female life peers, admitting women to the House of Lords for the first time, for which there had been a campaign since women were admitted to the House of Commons in 1918. This campaign was fully successful in 1963, when hereditary peeresses were admitted to the House of Lords on the same terms as men.[12]

In 1966, an alliance was formed of the Six Point Group, the Status of Women Committee, the Suffrage Fellowship, the Association of Headmistresses, the BFBPW and the National Council of Married Women to produce a set of election demands concerning equality at work, in pensions and other benefits and taxation.[13] In 1967, the Abortion Act legalized abortion. This owed much to lobbying by the Abortion Law Reform Association, founded in 1935 by women, with support from male and female doctors who had witnessed the death and damage caused by illegal abortions.[14] The change in the law was achieved through an alliance between campaigners and backbench MPs, notably David Steel, and with the tacit support of the Labour Home Secretary, Roy Jenkins, and was one of a remarkable series of pieces of liberalizing legislation (see Chapters 2, 4 and 6) that characterized this period. In 1966, Labour won a majority of female votes, as it had in 1945, which may have influenced this move and the introduction of the Equal Pay Act (see below). A succession of unsuccessful attempts through the 1980s and 1990s to repeal or restrict abortion (see Chapter 3) met strong opposition.

These activities pre-dated the birth of the Women's Liberation Movement from 1968. The movement was active throughout Britain and included women from most minority ethnic groups, although not evidently Gypsies and Travellers. It had different concerns from the older women's movement, being less focused on influencing government and changing legislation, and more on achieving cultural change – in particular, protesting against the sexual exploitation of women and violence against them, issues that had not previously been prominent. For the first time, women placed rape and sexual and domestic violence firmly on the political agenda, where they have remained as prominent public issues. Generally, the movement operated in localized, non-hierarchical groups, rather than as a mass movement holding big demonstrations on the model of the early twentieth-century movement, although some spectacular demonstrations occurred, particularly when a group of feminists disrupted the televised Miss World contest at the Royal Albert Hall.

1968 TO EARLY 1980s

The trend towards married women's greater participation in the workforce continued, as did the growth in part-time employment: part-time work accounted for 39 per cent of women's employment in 1975 and 42.8 per cent in 1985.[15] More women were entering universities, although by the 1970s, when about 7 per cent of all 18-year-olds went to university, the proportion of women was still about 25 per cent and subjects studied were still gender-divided, most science students being male and arts students female. Generally, segregation and low pay remained a common feature of women's employment, over-represented as they were among lower professionals (such as teachers and nurses), technicians, clerical workers, sales staff and shop assistants.

However, women workers were becoming more assertive, primarily through the trade union movement. Between 1964 and 1970, 70 per cent of new union members were women, reflected in the increasing number of trade union campaigns with a gender focus.[16] In the 1970s, these included efforts to unionise night-time office cleaners, who were low-paid as well as working unsociable hours. In 1974, the London Trades Council issued a ten-point Charter for Working Women, adopted by the Trades Union Congress (TUC) in 1975, which formed the basis for a widespread campaign by women's groups. It included equal pay and equal opportunity, 18 weeks' paid maternity leave, a minimum wage, increased family allowances and an end to social security and tax discrimination against women.[17] At this time, trade unions were giving increasing support to equality campaigns (see Chapters 1, 2 and 4). In 1976, the TUC gave some support to an unsuccessful strike at the Grunwick photo-processing plant in North London, in which most of the strikers were Asian women (see Chapter 2). This was by no means the last industrial action by Asian women.

Growing discontent among unionized women about pay differentials was almost certainly one reason for the Labour Party's 1964 manifesto pledge to legislate on equal pay. Once in government again in 1964, Labour Ministers set up a working group of government, trade union and employers' representatives, which reached agreement on the principle of equal pay by 1967. Labour was reluctant, however, to legislate, for fear of undermining its own policies to hold back prices and incomes.[18] In 1968, female sewing machinists at Ford's in Dagenham went on strike, demanding their jobs be upgraded from unskilled to a skilled classification, to achieve parity of status and pay with their male co-workers.[19] The media furore that followed convinced Barbara Castle, the Employment Secretary, that legislation was needed.[20] The strike also led to the formation of the National Joint Action Committee for Women's Equal Rights (NJACWER), which brought trade unionists and women's groups into alliance. The committee adopted a charter calling on the TUC to lead a campaign for equal pay and equal opportunities, and a rally in Trafalgar Square in May 1969 attracted much media interest.[21]

As in 1955, wider international forces helped to force the equal pay issue up the agenda. This time, the influence came from the European Community (EC), whose member states were bound by Article 119 of the Treaty of Rome to promote equal pay, partly to ensure that member countries in which female labour was especially cheap did not have an unfair competitive advantage. Women's groups across Europe later used Article 119 to support their campaigns for equal pay.[22] Although Britain did not join the EC until 1973, it aspired to do so, and Ministers were aware both that future membership would require action on equal pay and of attempts by feminists from other European nations to have Article 119 applied.[23]

In 1970, the Equal Pay Act (EPA) gave individuals the right to the same contractual pay and benefits as persons of the opposite sex where both performed 'like work', work 'rated as equivalent under an analytical job evaluation survey', or 'work that is proved to be of equal value'. Claims were to be brought through an employment tribunal, and awards for claims that were upheld could result in back pay of up to two years (amended to six years in 2003). The EPA also introduced the concept of indirect discrimination, covering cases where pay differences were due to a condition or practice applicable to both sexes, but adversely affected a larger proportion of one or other. The Act would not come into force until 1975, a delay much lamented by equality campaigners but an improvement on the 7- or 8-year grace period requested by employers' organizations. Castle hoped that employers would use this time to take voluntary measures to bring men's and women's wages into line, and that improvement would begin to be seen almost immediately.

There was some evidence that this occurred. An Office of Manpower study commissioned by the Conservative Party in 1971 revealed that in about 20 per cent of national agreements and Wages Council orders covering manual workers, discrimination had been removed or was on track for removal by 1973. In most cases, this was achieved by levelling women's wages up, rather than levelling male wages down. The study also identified substantial progress in insurance and banking.[24] Ten years later, a team from the London School of Economics found that women's relative pay had increased by about 15 per cent, and argued that this could not be attributed to women's migration from lower- to higher-paying sectors; rather, it had occurred across all sectors and industries.[25]

However, the EPA was passed in a hurry before the 1970 election and had serious weaknesses, of which opponents took advantage. Some employers used the delay between passage of the Act and its enforcement to restructure and regrade jobs to avoid its provisions.[26] One chain of shoe stores regraded all male but not female shop assistants as 'managers', retaining the pay differential without changing the undifferentiated work. Another tactic was to sack ancillary workers (such as cleaners) and replace them with workers employed by contractors, to avoid 'like work' issues among their own employees.[27]

Shortcomings in the legislation were corrected to some degree by an Amendment to the EPA in 1983, forced upon Britain by judicial action at EC level.[28] The new Act replaced 'like work' with work 'of comparable value', which enabled women to make the case that their jobs were as valuable to their employers as those performed by men, even where the jobs were very different in nature. One of the earliest cases brought under the Act, and resolved only at EC level in favour of the woman on whose behalf it was brought, involved a female cook arguing that her work was comparable to that of a painter, a joiner and a thermal insulation engineer employed by the same company.

Although this was an important step forward, the amended EPA did not and could not address many of the deeper underlying factors behind pay differentials, such as the impact on women's work experience and career prospects of breaks from employment due to caring responsibilities, men's tendency to work longer hours, and women's over-representation in lower-paying, lower-status occupations (often due to constraints on mobility and time because of their domestic responsibilities) and in part-time employment, which tended to be paid at a lower rate and to include fewer benefits (such as pensions) than full-time work. The New Earnings Survey (NES), which began in 1968, revealed women to be heavily over-represented among the lowest-paid groups.[29] The great majority were concentrated in a small number of occupations in which the labour force was predominantly female. Women's jobs were generally repetitive and uncreative, their need for skills or responsibility was low, and situations in which women might be required to supervise male workers were avoided by employers wherever possible. Surveys suggested considerable employer resistance to women holding authority over men in the workplace.[30]

Recognition of the need to attack broader processes of discrimination other than pay drove the Sex Discrimination Act (SDA). Passed by Labour in 1975 on its return to government, this was the outcome of a similar combination of feminist pressure, political expediency and impetus from Europe. It outlawed discrimination on the basis of sex in employment, education and advertising, or in the provision of housing, goods, services or facilities. It created the Equal Opportunities Commission (EOC) to oversee the implementation of the legislation and gave it powers of investigation.[31]

These changes would almost certainly have occurred if the British Women's Liberation Movement (WLM) had not existed, given the strength of other drivers of change. However, the WLM was a significant assertion of the independent voices of women and part of an international movement that helped to drive these changes, and it brought new issues to the public agenda and new groups of women into activism. Black feminists, organized through the Organisation of Women of Asian and African Descent (OWADO) and Southall Black Sisters, campaigned in particular against immigration laws, virginity tests imposed on women arriving in Britain to join men, and against police brutality (see Chapter 2).[32]

Domestic violence became a prominent and enduring public issue for the first time. Its existence had been regularly exposed since at least the mid-nineteenth century, but the justice system, including the police, was reluctant to take it seriously. The first refuge for wives who were victims of violence in the home was established in Chiswick in 1972 by Erin Pizzey, who obtained grants from government, charitable and private sources and focused media attention on the issue. Her model was adopted by women's groups throughout Britain. In 1975, 111 such groups were represented at a national conference, and by 1980 about 200 refuges were in operation.[33] The Women's Aid Federation (NWAF), with branches throughout Britain, provided a national infrastructure for the movement, based on the principles of local autonomy, open-door policies at all refuges and the right of women residents to self-determination.[34] This grassroots activity drove the passage of the Domestic Violence and Matrimonial Proceedings Act 1976, which for the first time enabled a wife to obtain a court injunction to restrain a violent husband. The NWAF provided expert evidence to the 1975 Commons Select Committee on Violence in Marriage, which laid the groundwork for the Act.[35]

Around the same time, feminists were also working effectively to support the victims of rape and to raise public awareness of this issue, about which there had previously been near public silence, despite women's efforts, especially since the inter-war years, to convey the seriousness of the issue.[36] The first Rape Crisis centre opened in North London in 1976, funded by a mix of state and charitable grants to provide counselling for victims. As with the refuge movement, the model was quickly replicated, with 16 centres, alongside rape crisis telephone lines, operating by 1981. Like the refuge movement, a woman-centred approach was crucial. A similar model underpinned the Reclaim the Night movement, founded in 1977, which organized women to march through cities late at night to assert their right to walk the streets unmolested.[37] These activities helped to ease the passage of the Sexual Offences (Amendment) Act in 1976, which improved the safeguards for women giving testimony at rape trials.

Feminists achieved considerable success in the 1970s in widening the terms of the gender-equality debate and putting new issues relating to sexuality, violence, abortion and race onto the national political agenda. Less prominently, many of them continued to be active in the 1980s, in, for example, the anti-nuclear camp and demonstrations at Greenham Common, and in the campaign against pornography and use in the media of images seen as degrading to women, such as 'page 3' girls. Many 1970s activists also became active in conventional politics and were among the drivers of moves in the 1980s and 1990s for more equal representation by women among Labour Party parliamentary candidates and in the devolved Welsh Assembly and Scottish Parliament established in 1999.[38]

1980s TO THE PRESENT

The government led by Britain's first female Prime Minister, Margaret Thatcher, was not evidently sympathetic to gender equality. There were, however, important changes in the 1980s. The EC Directives of the 1970s created a momentum for further extending administration and law relating to gender equality. The EOC took the lead in the United Kingdom. It faced criticism in the late 1970s from feminists, who feared it was under-resourced and over-eager to please government. In the 1980s, strong leadership, better relations with the trade unions and a succession of legislative amendments and court decisions increased the effectiveness of the EPA and SDA.[39] An investigation by the EOC into alleged discrimination at Barclays Bank in 1983 focused the banking industry's attention on inequalities women faced in promotion, training and fair treatment in other respects, and prompted the emergence of 'equal opportunities' policies in large companies.[40] Again, judicial decisions at the European level, on cases often brought with the support of the EOC, were an important driver. A ruling in 1983 judged unlawful the exemption from the Equal Treatment Directive of employees in private households, businesses with fewer than five employees and partnerships with fewer than five partners. This resulted in a new Sex Discrimination Act in 1986, which outlawed discrimination in collective bargaining agreements and extended anti-discrimination law to small businesses.[41] The appointment in 1989 of Valerie Amos, a Black woman, as chief executive (until 1994) helped to boost the EOC's credibility on race issues and also to cement stronger links with the Commission for Racial Equality (CRE).

There was a relatively weak relationship between the equality experts, lawyers and policy advisers, and the WLM. The movement's activists tended to focus on local rather than central government or big business. They experienced particular success in London, where the Greater London Council (GLC) provided funding to a number of women's groups and projects and set up the first Local Government Women's Committee to give women a formal voice in decision-making.[42] In 1984, the GLC spent nearly £8 million on gender equality activities, as well as holding open meetings and setting up working parties to deal with issues relevant to women, including employment, sexuality, disability, race and ethnicity and child care.[43] There were similar successes in Edinburgh, and hubs of feminist activity developed elsewhere, usually in urban centres with Labour-controlled councils, where structures were created that brought women more fully into decision-making processes.[44] Such successes could be fragile, as the abolition of the GLC in 1986 demonstrated. In Scotland, where Conservatism was weaker, local women's committees appear to have survived the 1980s more successfully. Most notably, in 1992, the Edinburgh District Zero Tolerance Campaign initiated active campaigning against domestic violence, which was progressively taken up by Scottish local authorities, the police, the Scottish Office and, since devolution in 1999, a major national strategy on domestic abuse for Scotland.

Other new challenges for women appeared in the 1980s. Public spending on child care and child benefits was reduced; and privatisation, 'flexible' employment policies and growing unemployment made it more difficult for single mothers, and many married couples, to earn enough to support their families. The real value of pensions fell, particularly disadvantaging women since most pensioners were, and are, female because women outlive men on average, and women are more likely than men to be dependent upon state, as distinct from private or occupational, pensions (see Chapter 1). Growing social inequality during the 1980s also impacted disproportionately on women. Privatisation of certain state services, such as hospital cleaning, resulted in poorer working conditions for low-paid and/or part-time workers who were previously employed by the state, most of whom were female. The Wages Councils, which safeguarded the lowest-paid workers against exploitation, were weakened in 1986 by legislation that exempted people aged under 21 from Wage Council rates and lifted protection on holiday pay, weekend pay, shift premiums and skill differentials for workers of all ages.[45]

Major changes in marriage and birth rates became evident in the early 1970s and continued at a faster pace in the 1980s and 1990s. The birth rate began a steady decline, falling below the replacement rate (the number of births required to replace the number of deaths) from 1972, although it has been rising since 2001 and by 2007 was approaching replacement. The mean age at first birth rose from 23.9 in 1972 to 26.5 in 1996 and 27.3 in 2005.[46] Childlessness also rose. Unmarried cohabitation, often including parenting, increased markedly and, for the first time in the twentieth century, became publicly acceptable in the White population, as it had long been in the Black Caribbean population, although it was by no means acceptable among Muslims. In the late 1980s, one-third of babies were born to unmarried parents, who were often living together. The divorce rate rose significantly following the Divorce Act 1969, which made divorce easier to obtain. Most divorces were initiated by women, despite the fact that this was likely to leave them financially worse off than their former partners, especially if they had young children.

These demographic patterns have continued to the present. The sharp cultural shift that they imply is hard to explain. It was not a direct outcome of government action, which in the 1980s focused on promoting 'Victorian values' and involved the most insistent governmental support for 'traditional family values' of the entire period since 1945. The shift was probably the outcome of a number of parallel changes. The introduction of the birth control pill, which became widely available from the mid-1960s and was provided free by local authority clinics from 1974, enabled people to engage in sexual relationships without fear of pregnancy – a fear (and a reality) that had brought about many of the early marriages of the previous generation.[47] The rise in divorce – mainly among the early-married generation – from the early 1970s on perhaps created caution among younger people (who were often the children of divorced parents) about entering into permanent relationships. High unemployment during the 1980s revived the poverty and insecurity that had been a reason for late or non-marriage before World War II. Longer hours, pressure and insecurity at work,[48] which became evident in the 1980s and continued since, put strains on partnerships. Unmarried motherhood and unmarried cohabiting parenthood were more common among women from low- than high-income families.[49] Other, more privileged women were gaining more education and aiming for ambitious careers, and they preferred to delay childbirth until they were established in a career. The length of time taken in career breaks for reasons of motherhood fell until, by about 2000, the majority of mothers of children aged under five were in paid work, despite the continuing inadequate availability of child care.

There are also signs that, by the 1980s, parents had higher expectations than before of their daughters' educational performance and career prospects. This may have been due in part to the increasing instability of marriage; a woman could no longer expect to be supported by a husband throughout her adult life. At least as important, although very hard to measure, was real cultural change towards a greater acceptance of gender equality. Increasing numbers of girls took national school examinations, and by the 1990s, they were outperforming boys. This was widely discussed as a 'problem' of boys' underperformance, although the 'underperformance' of girls had not previously been perceived as a problem. There is good evidence that the tendency of boys to be inattentive and less diligent at school than girls had been recognized since at least the mid-nineteenth century.[50] An influential 1967 study of primary education pointed out that teachers 'assessed the girls as having a more serious attitude to their work and as being more satisfactory pupils than the boys, who were more often reported as restless and inattentive in class. The teachers also thought that a larger proportion of the girls than of the boys would benefit from a grammar school education; indeed they would have sent nearly a third more girls than boys to grammar schools. The actual distribution of places, of course, did not follow this pattern.'[51] Boys were doing badly at a time when family life was more stable and boys were more likely to have a male role model at home than at any time in history, to cite reasons often given for the relatively poor performance of many boys in the recent past.

Poor performance did not hamper the relative success of males at all educational levels or in the employment market while girls had limited opportunities and prospects. By the 1980s, females were taking educational qualifications far more seriously than before, regarding them as the avenue to real advantages. This suggests that the very real problem of the underperformance in education of many males, especially those of low income and from all ethnic backgrounds (including White), compared with females from similar backgrounds (see Chapters 2 and 4), may be deeper-rooted than contemporary discussion assumes.

Admission to higher education expanded rapidly from the 1980s, reaching about 40 per cent of 18- to 21-year-olds by 2006. The proportion of female students rose from 28 per cent in 1970 to 38 per cent in 1980, and to more than 50 per cent by the mid-1990s, where it remains. However, university courses remain gender segregated: the number of women studying the sciences or engineering remains low, despite recent efforts by the government and independent bodies to achieve an increase. People from higher socio-economic groups remain more likely to attend university than those from lower groups, and there are large differences among ethnic groups (see Chapter 2). Broadly, in 2002, the participation rate at universities of White 18- to 19-year-old females was 31 per cent and of White males of the same age 27 per cent; of all ethnic minority groups, it was 59 per cent and 48 per cent respectively, but with wide variations between groups (see Chapter 2). From the 1980s, more older students attended universities. This especially benefited women who often had not had the opportunity for higher education when younger and found it easier to enter university after a career break than did men in mid-career. In general, opportunities for retraining in middle life became somewhat greater for women, although they remained limited.

Nevertheless, women remain remarkably underrepresented in the 'top jobs', given that they outnumber men in the population. In 2007/8, they made up 11 per cent of directors of FTSE 100 companies (executive and non-executive), up from 8.3 per cent in 2003; and 13.6 per cent of editors of national newspapers, an increase from 9.1 per cent in 2003. The comparable figures for other occupations are: local authority chief executives, 13.1/19.5; senior ranks in the armed services, 0.6/0/9; senior police officers, 7.5/11/9; senior judges, 6.8/9.6; civil service top management, 22.9/26.6; head teachers in secondary schools, 30.1 in 2003 and 34.1 in 2006 (2007/8 figures are not available for this group).[52] There has been progress, but it is very slow.

There is also a continuing gender pay gap at all levels of employment, currently 17 per cent, on average, in the United Kingdom. This is comparable with Denmark (also 17 per cent), Norway (16 per cent) and Sweden (16 per cent), and better than the United States (22.4 per cent), but worse than Australia (14.1 per cent).[53] The gaps at specific levels of employment in 2003 are shown in the table below:

Table 5.1 Average hourly earnings of full-time employees: 2003

Occupation	Women (£)	Men (£)
Managers and senior officials	15.60	21.00
Professionals	17.47	19.12
Administrative and secretarial	8.91	9.99
Skilled trades	7.71	9.80
Personal service	7.19	7.90
Sales and customer service	6.99	8.03

Source: *Interim Update of Key Indicators of Women's Position in Britain*, Women and Equality Unit (London, Department of Trade and Industry, 2004).

There have not been noticeable improvements in these rates since 2003.

Another outcome of the cultural and economic changes since the 1970s was a growth in lone parenthood, and especially lone motherhood.[54] In 1971, 7.5 per cent of all families were lone-parent families. Unmarried motherhood was still heavily stigmatized. The stigma has since diminished, but the economic penalties remain. Forty-two per cent of all poor children live in one-parent families, and lone parents continue to be among the poorest people in Britain. In 2006, there were 1.8 million one-parent families, caring for almost 3 million children, although lone parenthood is often a transient stage in the life cycle and lasts for about five years on average. Nine out of ten lone parents are women. Three out of five lone parents were previously married. Only 3 per cent of lone parents are teenagers. One-third of lone mothers has a child under five. Lone parents from Black or minority ethnic groups make up 12 per cent of the total, although there are considerable differences across these social groups. From 1991, with the creation of the Child Support Agency, the government made greater efforts to make absent fathers support their children. But fathers were often themselves poor or unemployed, or had second families to support; and mothers might be reluctant to comply with the requirement that they name the father, especially if they were victims of domestic violence. Some fathers felt unfairly discriminated against, especially by the courts in custody cases, and in the early years of the twenty-first century, there was a short-lived flurry of very public activism by groups such as Fathers4Justice.

Among women, as with the general population, the 1980s saw a widening gap between the more and the less privileged, with a minority entering a wider range of careers and a substantial number living in poverty, with wide regional, ethnic, age and socio-economic differences among them. Women have been especially vulnerable to poverty in old age (see Chapter 1). At a time when it appeared that wider opportunities were opening up to women, rising divorce, unemployment and long hours for those who were in work made combining motherhood and a career increasingly difficult. This may in part explain the falling birth rate, combined with the evidence that fathers in two-parent households took only marginally more responsibility for child rearing than in the 1970s. Mass male unemployment exposed the fragility of the male-breadwinner ideal, the emotional and psychological impact of which was conveyed in the television series *Boys from the Black Stuff*. Although many women were also unemployed, rates were lower than among men, and women's participation in the workforce continued to increase, mostly in low-paid, often part-time, employment.

Opinion surveys testified to changing public attitudes to women's careers. In 1984, 43 per cent of people interviewed for the British Social Attitudes survey agreed or strongly agreed with the statement: 'A husband's job is to earn the money; a wife's job is to look after the home and family.' By 1990, the figure had fallen to 25 per cent.[55] The notion that men might play a more active role in the home gained in popularity. In 1984, 50 per cent of interviewees believed that looking after a sick child should mainly be the mother's role. This figure fell to 37 per cent by 1991, and the percentage that believed the task should be shared equally rose from 47 to 60. Actions did not necessarily change equally with expressed beliefs, but there is every sign that the changes were real, if slow.

The institutionalization of gender equality regained momentum in the 1990s in response to a combination of new pressures from Europe and initiatives on the part of the modernising Labour Party. The European Commission developed bureaucratic structures for devising and promoting gender-equality initiatives, and other European states, notably France and Germany, established dedicated ministries for women.[56] Britain was a laggard in this respect, delegating responsibility for sex equality to junior Ministers in the employment and health departments before setting up a Sex Equality Branch in the Department of Employment in 1992.[57]

In opposition, the Labour Party developed policy ideas that were more in line with the European trend. In 1987, Labour established a Shadow Minister for Women (unusual in that there was no government counterpart) and promised in its election manifesto to create a Ministry for Women, along with a Cabinet Minister for Women to monitor a gender audit of all government legislation.[58] This last objective reflected a wider interest in the new concept of 'gender mainstreaming', which appeared in the late 1980s and early 1990s. It found much support within the European Commission, which applied the concept to the structural funds programme.[59] Mainstreaming involved integrating the promotion of gender equality within all policies and programmes, ensuring that women's needs and interests were represented at all levels of government, and measuring the differential impact of legislation and policy initiatives on men and women.

The Women's Unit, established in 1997 after Labour returned to government, was committed to mainstreaming, as were the Equality Units formed in 1999 by the Scottish and Welsh Executives following devolution. While the Women's Unit signified a new commitment to gender equality on the part of government, significant differences distinguished it from the vision of a Ministry for Women included in the 1987 manifesto, under John Smith's leadership of the Labour Party, before his death in 1994. Under Tony Blair's leadership, these ambitions were reined in. The 1995 party policy document *Governing for Equality* downgraded the Ministry to a unit located in the Cabinet Office. One independent assessment of the unit's impact between 1997 and 2001 concluded that, while useful research had been commissioned and a number of successful initiatives launched, compared with the other policy units created by New Labour (the Social Exclusion Unit and the Prime Minister's Strategy Unit), the Women's Unit's remit was ill-defined and its influence weak.[60] The attitudes of the party leadership significantly affected the implementation of equality measures.

However, there can be little doubt that the political sphere has become increasingly feminised under the Labour governments since 1997, in particular due to the increased representation by women in the House of Commons. The number of female MPs barely moved between 1945 and the 1980s, hovering between 24 and 27 before rising to 41 in 1987 and then 60 in 1992, out of a total of between 630 and 650 MPs.[61] The leap to 120 in 1997 (102 of them representing Labour), out of 657, was dramatic. The Labour Party had committed itself to applying All-Women Shortlists (AWS) in half of all key seats (defined as winnable on a 6 per cent swing) and in half of all vacant safe seats.[62] The policy was adopted largely in response to a long internal campaign carried out by women inside the party, with support from John Smith's leadership. The Labour Women's Network was established in 1988 to promote women's progress within the party. Quotas were introduced in 1990, ruling that 40 per cent of all party offices and delegations were to be composed of women. AWS were adopted by the party conference in 1993.[63] The election defeat the previous year provided the trigger, as analysis of voting patterns revealed that the Conservatives had been more successful in securing women's votes under John Major's leadership, having lost them under Margaret Thatcher. This paved the way for key women within the Labour Party, including Margaret Prosser of the Transport and General Workers' Union (TGWU), Maureen Rooney of the Amalgamated Engineering and Electrical Union (AEEU), and Claire Short MP to make the case for AWS as part of wider efforts to make the party more appealing to women electors.[64]

Without AWS, the progress made in 1997 would not have been possible. As a report for the Hansard Society remarks:

> Where significant gains have been made [by women] in British politics, whether at the 1997 general election or the elections to the Scottish Parliament or National Assembly for Wales in 1999, the overriding explanation points to the use by (some) political parties of equality guarantees – measures that require a particular number or proportion of women to be elected.[65]

The report points out that it has required similar measures of positive discrimination to increase representation of women in the elected assemblies of other countries. The willingness of parties contesting elections in Scotland and Wales to use techniques aimed at achieving gender equality in selection of candidates, such as 'twinning' and 'zipping', helps to explain how the Scottish Parliament and Welsh Assembly produced ratios of 39.5 per cent and 50 per cent female membership respectively in 2003. By contrast, women were only 13.6 per cent of Scottish MPs. These improved gender ratios were a direct result of campaigning by women in both countries[66] and have led to further institutional developments such as the establishment of a standing Equal Opportunities Committee in the Scottish Parliament. In 2000, the Scottish Executive committed itself to an Equality Strategy that mainstreamed a commitment:

> . . . To ensure the prevention and elimination of discrimination between persons on grounds of disability, age, sexual orientation, language or social origin, or

of other personal attributes including beliefs or opinions, such as religious or political beliefs.[67]

The dropping of AWS at the 2001 general election followed a court ruling on a case brought by men aspiring to be Labour candidates, which found the policy unlawful under the SDA. This caused the number of female MPs to drop slightly in the elections of 2001 and 2005. The government swiftly legislated to exempt AWS from the provisions of the SDA, but so far Labour has still been the only party prepared to introduce AWS, and it has not been employed since 2001. The policy remains highly controversial in all parties.[68]

Many gender-equality campaigners continue to support AWS, partly for reasons of justice, since they believe that prejudice and discrimination prevent women having a fair chance of selection as party candidates, and partly because they believe the presence of more women in politics will result in policies promoting gender equality. A larger pool of Labour women MPs has resulted in more women Ministers, including some in Cabinet posts, and a more equal gender balance among members of select committees and in the parliamentary Labour Party. Issues of particular interest to women, such as work–life balance, equal pay, maternity and paternity leave, child care, and domestic violence have become more central to political debate, championed by senior Labour women such as Tessa Jowell, Margaret Hodge, Harriet Harman and Patricia Hewitt.

CONCLUSION[69]

The changed position of men in the workplace and the home since the 1940s has influenced gender roles and relationships. Broadly, from the late 1940s to the 1970s, male full employment, high marriage rates and the tendency of married women to take time out of the workplace to care for children, followed by part-time employment, reinforced the already strict gender division of labour in and outside the home. The restructuring of the labour market in the 1980s polarized male (and full-time female) workplace experiences between unemployment and 'over-employment', with increasing hours and workplace stress, while in some areas more women than men could find paid employment. This appears to have had little effect on the division of labour in the home, except among a minority of mainly highly educated men, whose domestic role has increased, although not dramatically. Time-use surveys showed that in the 1980s, men married to women in full-time employment increased their contribution to domestic work to a greater extent than those married to women in part-time work, but that the gender division was by no means equal. Overall, since 1945, the relationship of women to the paid labour market has changed far more radically than that of men to unpaid work in the home, and many women's attitudes to and expectations of their social roles have changed more profoundly than those of most men. Housework and child care are not generally allocated efficiently to the person with the most time available to do it; unemployed men have been shown to do little housework.

Since 1945, the media has played an ambiguous role. More women have been employed in print and broadcast media in both senior (although as a minority) and junior roles, and in 'serious' (such as financial) and, like many men, less serious specialties. Women have been portrayed in publicly active, powerful roles while objectification of women's bodies (presenting them as essentially sexual objects) has become much more explicit (especially since the 1960s), has no male equivalent and shows little sign of declining, despite persistent protest by a minority of feminists. As the rest of this volume shows, gender inequalities are experienced in all ethnic and religious groups and by older, disabled (both of which generally have lower incomes than men in similar situations), lesbian and trans women.

The main drivers towards increased gender equality over the past 60 years have been:

- women's activism, sometimes explicitly feminist and sometimes eschewing the label while promoting gender equality. It was weak but still had some influence – for example, in achieving equal pay in parts of the public sector – in the 1950s, and has been continuously strong since the 1960s, although with shifting goals and methods of campaigning. Both insider lobbying and public campaigning have been effective on different issues
- government institutions, notably the EOC, using their powers to promote further legislation and to achieve implementation
- Labour governments generally doing more than Conservatives to promote equality
- international or supranational norm-setting. Pressures from the UN and ILO in the 1950s encouraged moves towards equal pay. Direct pressure from the EU, and the use of European courts by EOC and British campaigners, led to action in Britain on equal pay and equal treatment
- the less tangible, but broad and real long-term shift in Britain and elsewhere towards expectations of gender equality in the workplace, education and at home, propelled by the drivers listed above and reinforced by women's own experiences of increasing equality.

Inhibitors of change have included:

- demographic factors – early marriage and childbirth from around 1945 to the early 1970s; divorce and lone parenthood since the 1970s; gender inequality in responsibility for child care throughout the period – holding back women in the labour market, despite the expansion of opportunities overall. The growth of a 'long hours' culture since the 1980s has created further difficulties
- media reinforcement of gender stereotypes.

Chapter 6

Gender identity and sexual orientation
Mel Porter[1]

TIMELINE

1533	Buggery Act makes sodomy punishable by hanging.
1861	Offences Against the Person Act formally abolishes death penalty for buggery in England and Wales.
1885	Labouchère amendment to Criminal Law Amendment Act creates offence of 'gross indecency'.
1895	Oscar Wilde sentenced to two years' prison with hard labour under 1885 Act.
1898	Vagrancy Act makes importuning 'for immoral purposes' an offence, used primarily against gay men.
1914	British Society for the Study of Sex Psychology founded.
1921	Failed attempt to bring lesbianism within scope of 1885 Act.
1928	World League for Sexual Reform founded. Radclyffe Hall's *The Well of Loneliness* banned.
1948	Alfred Kinsey publishes *Sexual Behaviour in the Human Male*. Norman Haire publishes first edition of the *Journal of Sex Education*.
1949	Mass Observation's 'Little Kinsey' the first survey of British sexual attitudes.
1953	Kinsey publishes *Sexual Behaviour in the Human Female*.
1954	Wolfenden Committee appointed to review laws on homosexual offences and prostitution. Trial of Montagu, Pitt-Rivers and Wildeblood. Roberta Cowell's account of her gender transition published.
1956	Sexual Offences Act recognizes crime of sexual assault between women.
1957	Report of Wolfenden Committee published.
1958	Homosexual Law Reform Society founded.
1959	Street Offences Act enacts Wolfenden recommendations on street prostitution, but not homosexuality.

1963   Minorities Research Group founded.
1964   North West Committee of Homosexual Law Reform Society
         founded by Alan Horsfall.
1967   Sexual Offences Act (England and Wales) decriminalizes
         private, consensual homosexual acts between two men aged
         over 21 and tightens the law on street offences.
1969   Scottish Minorities Group founded.
         Stonewall riots in New York lead to formation of Gay
         Liberation Front. Committee for Homosexual Equality
         formed from North West Committee.
1970   London Gay Liberation Front founded.
         Corbett versus Corbett decision prevents post-operative
         transsexuals from changing gender stated on birth certificate.
1971   Gay Liberation Front manifesto published; first march.
         Lesbians invade Women's Liberation Conference platform.
1972   *Gay News*, Britain's first gay newspaper, founded.
         Scottish Minorities Group launches campaign to
         decriminalize homosexuality in Scotland.
         First Gay Pride march in London.
1974   Unsuccessful appeal to European Court of Human Rights to
         decriminalize homosexuality in Northern Ireland.
         First national lesbian conference, in Canterbury.
         London Gay Switchboard launched.
         First International Gay Rights Conference held, in
         Edinburgh. Action for Lesbian Parents founded.
         National Transvestite and Transsexual conference organized
         in Leeds by Beaumont Society.
1975   Committee for Homosexual Equality, Scottish Minorities
         Group and Union for Sexual Freedom in Ireland publish
         sexual reform bill aimed at equalizing the law.
1976   Sexual Offences (Scotland) Act reinforces criminalization of
         homosexuality.
1977   Bills to reduce gay age of consent to 18 and decriminalize
         homosexuality in Scotland fail.
         Mary Whitehouse instigates successful prosecution of *Gay
         News* for blasphemy.
1979   Scottish Homosexual Reform Group (formerly Scottish
         Minorities Group) brings case for decriminalization to
         European Court of Human Rights.
         Self Help Association for Transsexuals formed.
1980   Criminal Justice Bill decriminalizes male homosexuality in
         Scotland.
         Northern Ireland's laws against homosexuality ruled in
         breach of European Convention on Human Rights.
1982   Male homosexuality decriminalized in Northern Ireland.
         Terence Higgins Trust launched.

1983	Labour candidate Peter Tatchell defeated in Bermondsey by-election.
	First Department of Health report on AIDS.
1984	Chris Smith first MP to come out as gay.
	Terence Higgins Trust organizes first national conference on AIDS.
1986	Some London boroughs promote positive images of homosexuality to school pupils.
1987	Government leaflet on AIDS delivered to every household.
1988	Section 28 of Local Government Act comes into force; protests in London and Manchester. Lesbian protesters abseil into House of Lords and invade BBC Six O'clock News.
	First national conference for lesbians and gay men with disabilities.
1989	Stonewall founded, organizes first lesbian and gay receptions at party conferences.
	FTM Network for female-to-male trans people formed.
1990	Direct action group Outrage! set up after murder in London of gay actor Michael Boothe.
1991	Failed attempt to prohibit lesbians and gay men from adopting or fostering.
1993	Stonewall launches first challenge to European Court of Human Rights on age of consent with three gay teenagers aged 16–18.
	Transsexual lobby group Press for Change formed.
1994	Age of consent for gay men reduced to 18.
	Criminal Justice and Public Order Act makes male rape an offence.
	First *National Survey of Sexual Attitudes and Lifestyles* published.
1997	Chris Smith Britain's first 'out' gay Cabinet Minister.
	Labour MP Angela Eagle first British MP to come out as lesbian.
	Equality Network founded in Scotland to campaign for lesbian, gay, bisexual and transgender rights.
1998	House of Commons votes to equalize age of consent; defeated in Lords.
	Suicide of Justin Fashanu, first professional footballer to come out as gay.
1999	Bomb explodes in Admiral Duncan gay pub in Soho, killing three people.
	Government lifts ban on lesbians and gay men serving in the armed forces after European Court of Human Rights ruling.
	Sex Discrimination (Gender Reassignment) Regulations make it illegal for employers to discriminate against trans people.

2000	Scottish parliament repeals Section 28.
	European Court of Human Rights rules transsexuals' lived gender should have legal status.
2001	Age of consent for gay men reduced to 16.
	Second *National Survey of Sexual Attitudes and Lifestyles* published.
2002	Equal rights granted to same-sex couples applying for adoption.
	European Court of Human Rights finds Britain in breach of rights of trans people to marry and to respect for private life.
2003	Section 28 repealed in England and Wales; Employment Equality (Sexual Orientation) Regulations make workplace discrimination illegal;House of Lords rules male-to-female transsexuals cannot marry under British law.
2004	Sexual Offences Act abolishes crimes of buggery and gross indecency.
	Gender Recognition Act gives people legal right to live in their acquired gender.
	Civil Partnership Act gives same-sex couples same rights and responsibilities as married heterosexual couples.
2005	First civil partnerships formed.
	First gender recognition certificates awarded.
	First transsexual marriages take place.
2006	Equality Act outlaws discrimination on grounds of sexuality in provision of goods and services.
2007	Equality and Human Rights Commission, with sexual orientation included in its remit.

INTRODUCTION

In 1806, more men were executed in Britain for homosexual offences than for murder.[2] Two hundred years later, gay men and lesbians can register civil partnerships and have legal protection from discrimination, and transgender people have their identity recognized in law. The past two centuries have witnessed major strides towards equality for Britain's lesbian, gay, bisexual and trans (LGBT) communities. In addition to landmark legal reforms, people can now publicly express their gender identity and sexuality in ways that were impossible even 30 or 40 years ago.

There have never been robust statistics on gender identity or sexuality in Britain. They have never been included in questions in the census and the Office of National Statistics is unlikely to do so in 2011.[3] The statistics available are described in the following narrative, with the necessary qualifications.

The changing definition and understanding of gender identity and sexuality and the language used to describe and categorise people, further complicates the picture. It is only within the last 30 years that the terms gay, lesbian, bisexual, transsexual and transgender have entered everyday discourse. The subtle distinctions between different sexualities, or the range of identities that any one person might experience, were not understood or recognized in the early twentieth century. For instance, men who might now identify as transgender were often assumed to be homosexuals and could be successfully prosecuted for sodomy, even if their only transgression against norms of accepted behaviour was to dress in women's clothes and wear make-up. It was not until the major sex surveys of the 1940s that there was significant appreciation of the shades of grey in many people's gender and sexual identities.

To avoid imposing twenty-first century terminology that would not have been recognized in earlier periods, the historical terms appropriate to the time are used here, and explained where possible. This poses certain problems in relation to transgender and transsexual people and transvestites, for the reasons indicated above. The term 'trans people' is used by lobby groups, including Press for Change and the Gender Trust, to encompass all people experiencing gender identity issues, and will be used in this chapter where relevant.

LONG SHADOWS: THE NINETEENTH CENTURY LEGACY

Until the late nineteenth century, the legal framework controlling homosexuality (specifically, sexual acts between men) was based on King Henry VIII's law of 1533, which first brought buggery within the scope of statute law. In the early nineteenth century, men were still executed for buggery, but from 1830, the death penalty was no longer enforced, and in 1861, it was replaced with prison sentences ranging from ten years to life.

The Labouchère Amendment to the Criminal Law Amendment Act 1885, set the legislative framework for the next 80 years. Although the Act primarily targeted prostitution, it brought all forms of male homosexuality within the scope of the law for the first time. It addressed homosexuality alongside prostitution, underlining that both were perceived as deviant sexual behaviour. From 1885, men could be, and regularly were, prosecuted for homosexual sex, even if it was consensual and in private. The writer Oscar Wilde, convicted in 1895, was the most celebrated victim. Ironically, the publicity surrounding Wilde's trial raised public awareness of homosexuality and created a 'community of knowledge' among other gay men, although this was still highly secret.[4] The shadow of the 1885 Act meant that homosexual men lived furtive lives, subject to persecution, blackmail, guilt and shame, which in turn could lead to suicide.[5] From 1885, cross-dressing, which appears previously to have been relatively tolerated, was likely to be used as evidence of sodomy, and transvestite men had to be more circumspect in their behaviour.[6]

Lesbianism, meanwhile, was not criminalized and was virtually ignored in public discourse, at least until the 1920s. Because women had fewer opportunities for independent lives and close friendships between women did not attract suspicion, most lesbians probably remained inconspicuous.[7] Even the term 'lesbian' was rarely used until well into the twentieth century. It was known in some upper class and medical circles that same-sex activity could and did happen between women. It might be described as 'Sapphism' or 'inversion', or more likely evaded and not named at all.

There was a failed attempt to criminalise 'gross indecency between women' under the 1922 Criminal Law Amendment Act, but some parliamentarians expressed concern that doing so would spread knowledge of and therefore temptation into 'lesbian vice' among women.[8] The Lord Chancellor claimed 'the overwhelming majority of the women of this country have never heard of this thing at all . . . I would be bold enough to say that of every thousand women, taken as a whole, 999 have never even heard a whisper of these practices.'[9] However, the Act did make consensual sex with *anyone* under the age of 16 an offence, where previously the law had assumed a male offender and female victim. Arguably, this established an 'age of consent' for lesbian activity.[10]

During the 1910s and 1920s, there was a small but growing body of support for legal reform, not only in Britain but also in mainland Europe and the United States, which began to coalesce in new sexological associations. Those involved tended to be middle or upper class, well educated, often themselves homosexual, and aware of the growing body of international research about sex. They aimed to remain respectable and believed that a major public education exercise should precede calls for the amendment of laws relating to sexuality. The most prominent organization in the United Kingdom was the British Society for the Study of Sex Psychology (BSSSP), which was founded in 1914 and became the British Sexological Society (BSS) in the 1920s. It remained the major organization concerned with sexual law reform in Britain until the 1930s.[11]

Australian-born medical practitioner Norman Haire emerged as one of the leading figures in the early movements for sexual law reform, and was involved in many of the early sexological societies in Britain and Europe, including the BSSSP. He also practised at one of the earliest birth-control clinics in Britain, the Walworth Women's Welfare Centre. Haire was secretary of the World League for Sexual Reform and organized its third congress in London in 1929. Following the demise of the league in 1936, he accepted the presidency of its British offshoot, the Sex Education Society (see below).[12]

In the late 1920s, lesbianism emerged into public consciousness, in particular due to Radclyffe Hall's novel, *The Well of Loneliness*, being banned and successfully prosecuted for obscenity. During the first two weeks after its publication in 1928, *The Well* was well received by critics. It was a tragic story of love between two women, but the content was not overtly sexual. It was then attacked in a vitriolic editorial in the *Sunday Express*, as part of the paper's wider campaign against 'degeneracy and decadence'. 'I would rather give a healthy boy or girl a phial of prussic acid than this novel. Poison kills the body, but moral poison kills the soul,' ranted the editorial.[13] This publicity raised awareness of the book among MPs, the civil service, ministers and the judiciary. It was then prosecuted as an obscene publication because it 'had not stigmatized this relationship [between two women] as being in any way blameworthy'.[14] However, in the weeks following the editorial, there was a marked increase in sales and about 5,000 copies were in circulation by the time proceedings began.[15] Many media commentators were highly critical of the *Sunday Express'* stance, both for its vehemence and for the perverse publicity it gave *The Well* and its risqué subject matter. Despite – or perhaps because of – the ban, the episode provided a name and an identity for lesbianism.[16]

THE 1940s AND 1950s: WAR, SEX SURVEYS AND REASSERTION OF 'NORMALITY'

It has been argued that World War II facilitated the emergence of more confident homosexual subcultures[17] and some case-study evidence suggests there were new, if temporary, sexual freedoms and opportunities.[18] The evidence is contradictory, however. For example, the number of illegitimate births more than doubled between 1940 and 1945, but the number of children born within eight months of marriage fell, suggesting, as Richard Titmuss put it, that 'the proportion of premarital conceptions did not differ very much from that obtaining before the war', but that war, separation and death prevented or delayed many marriages.[19] Official estimates of venereal disease rose by 70 per cent from 1939–42. It is difficult to know how much of this was a real increase in infection or the outcome of more people coming forward for treatment, because during the war the government made a determined attempt, through publicity, to break the prevailing secrecy and shame surrounding these diseases, and made treatment more widely available and free of charge.[20]

For some people at least, being uprooted by war from their normal surroundings did provide opportunities for new freedoms. Frith Banbury described both the wartime opportunities for gay men and the disillusionment with civilian life afterwards:

> Let's face it, people were in different circumstances, away from their families so the what-will-the-neighbours-say factor didn't come into it. And there were lots of foreigners – Poles, Czechs, the French – all around the place so there was a good deal of sex to be had for people on the loose. I know of a respectable clergyman who came from Canada and had the time of his life even though he had a wife and four children at home. When he went back after the war, the marriage broke up in three months. And later, the poor chap came back to London hoping and thinking it would be like it was during the war and of course it wasn't.[21]

There were attempts to 'weed out' homosexuals from the armed services – including the writer and actor Quentin Crisp – during enlistment interviews; and from 1939–45, there were more courts martial for 'indecency between males' than for any other category of offence, rising from 48 in 1939–40 to 324 in 1944–5.[22] The military authorities commissioned reports on the behaviour of homosexual soldiers, one of which observed that homosexual recruits were 'less resistant to trauma and demonstrated excessive grief for comrades-in-arms'.[23]

In the absence of criminal sanctions against lesbianism, the authorities' only recourse was to make life difficult for them. Nurse Monica Still described how, after her relationship with another female nurse was discovered, they were separated: 'They put her on the male military ward. I suppose they thought that this would make her normal, and they saw to it that we were never on the same ward or had the same time off.'[24]

It is difficult to make comparisons with the pre-war period, for which evidence is slight. Wartime relationships had still to be highly secret and the relatively conservative cultural climate of the post-war years inhibited the further development of any gains in open sexual expression that might have been achieved during the war.[25] From 1945, the norm of the stable, nuclear family was reasserted, wartime 'indiscretions' were swept under the carpet and gay men and lesbians were expected to return to their closets. From 1946, there was a spike in marriages delayed by war, and in divorces, some prompted by wartime relationships, hetero- and homosexual, or by estrangement due to absence.[26]

In 1948, the American biologist Alfred Kinsey published *Sexual Behaviour in the Human Male*, the first output from his ground-breaking attempt to survey American sexual behaviour, involving 12,000 people over several years. This caused a public sensation in Britain and the United States. Kinsey found that at least 60 per cent of his male subjects had experienced homosexual sex play as boys, and 37 per cent had climaxed with another male. He proposed a sexual scale, from 0 for men who had never had a homosexual experience (about 50 per cent), to 6 for men who had only experienced same-sex relationships (about 4 per cent). The remaining 45 per cent had experienced both forms of sexual activity at some point in their lives. He dismissed the traditional approach of classifying people as heterosexual, homosexual or bisexual. His findings suggested that half the population would be categorised by current laws, moral codes and psychiatry as 'perverts'.[27] For the first time, sex reformers had a scientific justification for arguing for the normalization and decriminalization of homosexuality. *Sexual Behaviour in the Human Female* followed in 1953, and Kinsey's findings on lesbianism were equally shocking. Twenty-eight per cent of his female sample had had sexual contact with another female, and the incidence (or at least admission) was higher among more highly educated women.[28]

In autumn 1947, the Sex Education Society revived in the United Kingdom under Norman Haire's leadership and adopted homosexual law reform as one of its aims. In August 1948, Haire published the first edition of the *Journal of Sex Education*, which included details of Kinsey's study of male sexual behaviour. Like the earlier sexological societies, Haire aimed to change public opinion gradually, in order to pave the way for reform.[29] The society kept its members informed about developments both in Britain and abroad. Early in 1951, a regional branch was set up in Manchester. Haire viewed the lack of open media discussion about homosexuality as a problem 'here in England, where no commercial stations exist, where the BBC has a monopoly, and where broadcasting suffers under the dead hand of the Churches'.[30]

Haire's response to a reader's request for information about books on transvestism hints that by 1949 an organized transvestite subculture existed, and makes clear that the term was in current usage:

> Before the second World War there was a weekly magazine published in London, which devoted a large part of its space to stories and articles about transvestists, [sic] and to letters from them and which published advertisements from wig makers, dress-makers, shoe-makers and corset makers who catered specially for transvestites.[31]

In 1952, Haire died, and with him both the journal and, for the time being, the reform cause.

Kinsey also stimulated the British research organization Mass Observation, in 1949, to conduct a qualitative survey, which became known as 'Little Kinsey'.[32] A question about homosexuality (defined as 'sex relations between two people of the same sex') was only included in the pilot survey, so the results are limited. Nonetheless, they give a flavour of popular understanding of and attitudes to homosexuality in the late 1940s. The researchers commented that:

> There is no doubt but that homosexuality in one form or another is at least not an unusual form of sexual behaviour. Yet popular feeling against it is very strong. It was Mass Observation's original intention to include a questionnaire on homosexuality in the present survey . . . Results of the pilot surveys, however, suggested that about a third just did not understand what homosexuality was, 'it never occurred to me'. About a quarter just represented themselves as generally against it, and another third showed very violent reactions, calling homosexuality 'disgusting', 'terrible' and 'revolting' . . . Another reaction, less revolted, was the 'rather vulgar isn't it?' . . . A few people, on the other hand, look at the matter from a more or less clinical angle and suggest some form of treatment . . . But on the whole people regard homosexuality as a revolting or incomprehensible form of behaviour; many would even seem never to have heard of it. It is, of course impossible to generalize from such limited results as these; but the isolationist manner in which homosexual groups appear to function makes extensive ignorance of their existence at least a possibility.[33]

One of the researchers explained why the question was not repeated in the full study:

There was found a more genuine feeling of disgust towards homosexuality . . .
than towards any other subject included . . . partly as a result of this . . . no questions were asked to the general sample on this subject . . . [in the pilot survey]
however, 8 per cent admit to having had homosexual relations and a further
12 per cent to having had homosexual relations at some point in their life.[34]

These attitudes must be understood in the context of the widespread sexual
ignorance revealed by Little Kinsey, with many respondents stating that
they had received no sex education. Some displayed what now appears an
astounding level of ignorance about the 'facts of life', including a midwife
who apparently did not know that the production of babies had anything
to do with men.[35] These findings were followed by a case study of a 'homosexual clique' of four young men aged between 19 and 30: Arthur, John,
Michael and Peter. John and Michael lived together as a couple, but both
had relationships with other men, moving only in 'queer' circles and, where
possible, avoiding the company of non-homosexuals, 'except for neuters,
borderline cases and possible converts'. They held 'soirees' at their flat 'at
which unknown queers . . . are introduced and weighed up'.[36] It is not known
how these men were selected for the study and they cannot necessarily be
considered representative, but this snapshot of their lives shows that in 1949,
at least in London and Brighton, it was possible to lead what would later
be described as a gay lifestyle. It also illustrates the range of sexualities that
could be expressed within the 'queer' subculture and the language used to
describe them – 'queer' being a common synonym for homosexual at the
time, and 'camp' describing men who 'flaunted' their homosexuality.

Later sex surveys paid little attention to exploring experiences or attitudes concerning homosexuality. In *Exploring the English Character* (1955),
Geoffrey Gorer noted that 'of those not interested in sex, quite a number
volunteered the statement that they were homosexual'. But this was not
explored further. In Gorer's later study, *Sex and Marriage in England Today*
(1971), homosexuality is barely mentioned.[37] In his 1965 study, *The Sexual
Behaviour of Young People*, which involved interviews with almost 2,000
15–19-year-olds, Michael Schofield revealed that more than one in five boys
knew of homosexual behaviour among their school friends, and one in 20
had been involved themselves. The figures for girls were one in ten and one
in 40 respectively, but Schofield did not examine the issue further.[38] Since,
at this time, homosexuality was criminalized and considered a threat to
young people, the reluctance of researchers to question subjects further is
perhaps not surprising.

FROM THE WOLFENDEN COMMITTEE TO REFORM: 1950s AND 1960s

During the 1950s, several factors created political, social and media concern
about declining moral standards and threats to the family and public health.

In addition to the rising divorce and illegitimacy rates mentioned above, the visibility of prostitutes in Mayfair and the West End during the Festival of Britain and the Queen's coronation in 1953 was an embarrassment to Churchill's Conservative government.[39] There had been a steep increase in recorded homosexual street offences, from an annual average of about 2,000 in the 1930s to more than 10,000 by 1952 and 12,000 by 1955.[40] This did not necessarily indicate an increase in homosexual activity, as the number of indictable homosexual offences for which people could be arrested increased five-fold in the same period. However, prosecutions were concentrated in a few police districts,[41] and the increase was partly due to Home Secretary David Maxwell-Fyffe's drive for greater uniformity in prosecutions and the use by the police of entrapment techniques and conspiracy charges to ensnare homosexual men.[42]

The press sensationalized and disseminated the details of a series of successful prosecutions of prominent men, often on flimsy evidence. In 1952, the mathematician Alan Turing, who received an Order of the British Empire (OBE) for his work on cracking the Enigma code during the war, was arrested for homosexual offences. He accepted hormone treatment instead of a prison sentence, but committed suicide in 1954.[43] In 1953, the novelist and playwright Rupert Croft-Cooke was sentenced to nine months in prison on the testimony of two sailors. While in prison, he wrote *The Verdict of You All*, describing the climate of fear at the time:

> As the witch-hunt of homosexuals ordered, or at least countenanced by the Home Secretary raised its disgusting hue and cry, the prisons began to house a new kind of victim, men of the highest probity and idealism who'd been dragged from useful lives . . . found themselves stunned and baffled in prison.[44]

Shortly before his release from prison, Croft-Cooke was asked, but refused, to return his war medals.[45]

The most spectacular scandal was the trial and conviction of Lord Montagu of Beaulieu, his cousin Michael Pitt-Rivers and *Daily Mail* diplomatic correspondent Peter Wildeblood for homosexual activity in 1954. The use of letters as evidence led to a 'bonfire of memories' by gay men, terrified they might suffer the same fate.[46] Wildeblood described the atmosphere within his own profession:

> I could hardly have chosen a profession in which being a homosexual was more of a handicap than it was in Fleet Street. Its morality was that of a saloon bar: every sexual excess was talked about and tolerated, provided it was 'normal'.[47]

However, there was now a responsible body of opinion arguing for the decriminalization of private homosexual acts, disgusted by the trail of blackmail and suicides that accompanied the wave of prosecutions. Perhaps surprisingly, pressure came from the Church of England Moral Welfare Council (CEMWC), which, in 1952, published a report by clergy and doctors recommending an inquiry and calling for the separation of the homosexual 'sin' from the criminal law. The council highlighted the legal anomaly that male homosexual practices were the only 'private actions of consenting adults' to be criminalized, and expressed concern at the 'human tragedy' of suicides caused by the current law.[48] However, the traditional concerns about predatory homosexuals and contagion among young people remained. The council believed that 'one effect of the present law is that the fear of blackmail by adults may drive homosexuals to seduce boys', and recommended that the age of consent be set at 21 to protect young men during their National Service.[49] In 1948, the Labour Party Research Department had also advocated decriminalization in a paper on law reform.[50]

Maxwell-Fyffe recognized that, in view of the crime statistics, the public mood would not accept action on prostitution if homosexual offences were ignored. It took him several attempts, in early 1954, to persuade Prime Minister Winston Churchill to agree to an inquiry. Churchill and other Ministers feared any suggestion that the law might be liberalized would cost Conservative votes, but Maxwell-Fyffe won the argument, although the inquiry was downgraded from a Royal Commission to a Departmental Committee.[51] The result was the Wolfenden Committee on Prostitution and Homosexual Offences, which started work in 1954 and, after 62 meetings and evidence from more than 200 organizations and individuals (of whom only three were professed homosexuals), published its report in 1957.

Sir John Wolfenden (whose own son, Jeremy, was openly homosexual[52]) and his colleagues started from the premise that the function of the law was to maintain public order and decency, not to enforce any moral code. They were not interested in liberalizing the law, but in making it work more effectively.[53] From this standpoint, the criminalization of private consensual homosexual acts seemed anomalous. This did not mean that homosexuality was considered acceptable, but it was now being explained by doctors and psychiatrists as an unfortunate mental disability that required treatment, rather than punishment. The committee briefly considered lesbianism, but found themselves unable to discover any example of female homosexuality 'which exhibits the libidinous features that characterize sexual acts between males'.[54]

They recommended:
- decriminalization of homosexual activity in private between consenting adults over the age of 21 (effectively repealing the Labouchère Amendment)
- a time limit on prosecution of other homosexual offences, to prevent the dredging up of old cases, which were often fodder for blackmailers
- exemption from prosecution for cases revealed in the course of blackmail investigations
- entitlement to jury trial for those accused of importuning
- oestrogen treatment being made available to those convicted of homosexual offences

- further research into homosexuality and the effects of various treatments
- increased penalties and a tightening of the law relating to street offences.

The recommendations fulfilled Wolfenden's intention to clamp down on homosexual offences *in public*, which matched his approach to prostitution, and to decriminalize *private* behaviour that could not be said to impact on public order. Not surprisingly, it was a compromise among conflicting views, but it has rightly been described as 'a crucial moment in the evolution of liberal and moral attitudes'.[55]

Wolfenden and several of his committee members were wary of public opinion, which they fully expected to be hostile to their proposals.[56] Like the early twentieth century reformers, they believed that a process of public education was needed to prepare the ground for reform. They did not expect immediate legislation, and they did not get it. The clampdown on street prostitution was more appealing to the Conservative government than decriminalization of homosexual offences. Home Secretary R. A. Butler feared that this would be misinterpreted as giving approval to homosexuality, which was neither the government's nor Wolfenden's intention. The proposals on homosexuality were not implemented, except the reintroduction of oestrogen treatment for prisoners (which had been discontinued in England and Wales, although not in Scotland, under the Attlee government, due to fears that it could cause sterility). The proposals clamping down on street prostitution became law in the Street Offences Act 1959.

However, the issue did not go away. In March 1958, a letter appeared in *The Times* calling for implementation of Wolfenden's recommendations, with the 33 signatories including Lord Attlee, Bertrand Russell and the Bishops of Birmingham and Exeter. In April, a similar letter followed from 15 'eminent married women', including novelists, academics, women active in public and political life and wives of leading politicians and other public figures.[57] Wolfenden was reported as saying '... the majority of the British people, as well as the House of Commons, agreed with the recommendations, but the Government, with 18 months of their term left, did not want to alienate some of their supporters'.[58] These fears were not surprising, given the precariousness of Macmillan's new government after the Suez Crisis and Anthony Eden's resignation. The Conservative MP H. Montgomery Hyde, who spoke in favour of the Wolfenden reforms in the House of Commons in 1959, was deselected by his local party for having 'condoned unnatural vice'.[59]

The Homosexual Law Reform Society (HLRS) was founded in 1958, led by, among others, university lecturer A. E. Dyson and the Rev Andrew Hallidie Smith, to campaign for implementation of the Wolfenden proposals. It was one of many single-issue pressure groups that were active during the 1960s (see Chapters 1, 2, 4, 5 and 7). Like its predecessors, the HLRS sought a respectable public image, aiming to promote the public and political education that the Wolfenden report advocated by focusing on legal reform and eschewing an overtly homosexual identity.[60] The society's first public meeting, in London in May 1960, attracted more than one thousand people. A charitable arm, the Albany Trust, focused on research, counselling and publications.

When the House of Commons debated the Wolfenden report in November 1958, an editorial in *The Times* summarized the public and political mood that made reform unlikely in the immediate future, but unavoidable in the longer term:

> It is a foregone conclusion that the homosexual laws will not be reformed yet. It is equally a foregone conclusion that reform must eventually come. For the majority of well-informed people are now clearly convinced that these laws are unjust and obsolete in a society which refuses to punish lesbian practices, adultery, fornication or private drunkenness.[61]

A Gallup poll conducted shortly after the debate showed 47 per cent against Wolfenden's recommendation to decriminalize private, consensual homosexual behaviour, and 38 per cent in support, with women slightly more disapproving than men.[62]

Wolfenden did, however, have an impact in the cultural sphere. In 1957, the Lord Chamberlain, who was responsible for licensing (that is, censoring) stage plays, discussed with the Home Secretary, R. A. Butler, how to treat plays dealing with homosexuality. He recognized that some had artistic merit, and they agreed that prosecutions would further stimulate already growing public criticism of censorship. In 1958, in the absence of government action, and to deal with the growing number of plays that pushed the boundaries, the Lord Chamberlain published guidelines on the dramatisation of homosexuality for the first time:

> I . . . propose to allow plays which make a serious and sincere attempt to deal with the subject . . . Licences will continue to be refused for plays which are exploitations of the subject rather than contributions to the problem . . .
> a. Every play will continue to be judged on its merits. The difference will be that plays will be passed which deal seriously with the subject.
> b. We would not pass a play that was violently pro-homosexual.
> c. We would not allow a homosexual character to be included if there were no need for such inclusion.
> d. We would not allow any 'funny' innuendos or jokes on the subject.
> e. We will allow the word 'pansy', but not the word 'bugger'.
> f. We will not allow embraces between males or practical demonstrations of love.
> g. We will allow criticism of the present Homosexual Laws, although plays obviously written for propaganda purposes will be judged on their merits.
> h. We will not allow embarrassing display by male prostitutes.[63]

This compromise silenced pressure neither for homosexual law reform nor for censorship. The 1961 film *Victim* was passed by the censor after a struggle. It centred on a married barrister (Dirk Bogarde), who was black-mailed following homosexual liaisons with young men, and it discussed and endorsed the Wolfenden proposals.

In 1960 and 1962, Labour MPs Kenneth Robinson and Leo Abse both proposed unsuccessful Bills in parliament to make minor changes to the law to legalize private homosexual behaviour. The climate of sexual scandal – notably the Profumo affair, involving a Conservative War Minister, John Profumo, who had a affair with a young woman, Christine Keeler, who appeared also to be having a relationship with an attaché at the Soviet Embassy, in the midst of the Cold War – made reform impossible during the later years of this Conservative government, although it also exposed the lack of moral consensus at the top of society.[64] However, major social and cultural changes were in progress that would break down popular conservatism about sexuality, particularly the increasing availability of the birth-control pill during the 1960s (see Chapter 5).[65]

The election of a Labour government in 1964, albeit with a tiny majority, aroused optimism among reformers,[66] although the government was divided and – officially – strictly neutral on the issue.[67] In 1965, Roy Jenkins was appointed Home Secretary and shifted the government's position to one of 'benevolent neutrality', arguing for assistance in drafting and more parliamentary time for reform Bills such as that put forward by the Conservative MP Humphrey Berkeley. Berkeley's Bill was interrupted by the 1966 general election, and it was believed he subsequently lost his seat in Lancaster because of his support for homosexual law reform.[68]

After the election, the Wilson government had a comfortable majority and Jenkins' reforming instincts were given more licence. Lord Arran put forward a Bill that successfully passed the Lords in June 1966, and Leo Abse received Commons approval for a Ten Minute Rule Bill. However, there was still strong resistance in the Labour Party to what some called the 'Buggers Bill', partly out of a fear of alienating working class voters and partly from a longstanding perception that homosexuality was associated with an artistic, upper class elite.[69] The leader of the House, R. H. S. Crossman, recalled:

> Frankly it's an extremely unpleasant Bill and I myself didn't like it. It may well be twenty years ahead of public opinion; certainly working class people in the north jeer at their Members at the weekend and ask them why they're looking after the buggers at Westminster instead of looking after the unemployed at home.[70]

Nevertheless, he agreed with Jenkins to allow time for the Bill to be fully debated, and encouraged him to raise the matter in the Cabinet. The uncertainty had made the existing law increasingly difficult to administer, and the Director of Public Prosecutions had ruled in 1964 that all cases be referred to him before prosecutions were pursued.[71] In 1967, Leo Abse made compromises to get his Bill through the Commons, assisted by Harold Wilson's agreement to extra parliamentary time both for this Bill and that sponsored by David Steel to legalize abortion (see Chapter 5). Important concessions included setting the age of consent at 21 rather than 18, and excluding the armed forces and merchant navy from its provisions. It passed the Commons on 3 July after a marathon 20-hour session, and was steered through the Lords by Lord Arran.[72]

The 1967 Sexual Offences (England and Wales) Act decriminalized private homosexual activities between consenting adult men, changing the lives of many gay men – particularly those living quietly in long-term relationships, who had lived in fear of prosecution. But it also tightened the restrictions on street offences, resulting in a doubling of reported incidents of indecency from 1967–76, a trebling of prosecutions and quadrupling of convictions.[73] Lord Arran's comments on the new law demonstrate that no more than grudging toleration was intended, even by its parliamentary supporters:

> Homosexuals must continue to remember that while there may be nothing bad in being a homosexual, there is certainly nothing good. Lest the opponents of the new Bill think that a new freedom, a new privileged class has been created, let me remind them that no amount of legislation will prevent homosexuals from being the subject of dislike and derision, or at best of pity.[74]

The HLRS did not feature prominently in the final push for reform. It subordinated itself to the parliamentary reformers, acting as their secretariat, and was largely ignored by Arran and Abse. The secretary of the HLRS, Antony Grey, believed that, 'the Society's chief contribution had been made before the debates of 1965 began, in creating the climate of opinion in which they could be held at all'.[75] Given the shift in public opinion, with polls reporting that 63 per cent of the population supported reform by 1965, this seems a fair assessment. After 1967, support for the society declined, although it was reincarnated as the Sexual Reform Society in 1970. However, the North West branch founded in 1964 by Labour Councillor Allan Horsfall continued to flourish and later developed into the Committee for Homosexual Equality (see below). And the Albany Trust continued to provide counselling, including for lesbians, receiving a £30,000 government grant in 1974.

After 1967, men who looked for partners in public places still risked not only prosecution but homophobia and violence, and continued to attract sensationalist tabloid coverage. On 25 September 1969, Michael De Gruchy was murdered by four youths in a homophobic attack on Wimbledon Common. It has been argued that recent coverage in *The People* (in particular, an article headlined 'The Sick Men of Hampstead Heath') influenced the attackers and provided advice on how to spot homosexuals signalling to each other with cigarettes, which they used to identify De Gruchy as a target.[76]

The tortuous path to homosexual law reform was of little direct relevance to lesbians, although their situation also changed during this period. The 1956 Sexual Offences Act recognized for the first time the crime of sexual assault between women. In 1963, the first British lesbian social and political organization was founded, innocuously titled the Minorities Research Group (MRG) to deflect unwelcome attention. The group produced a magazine, *Arena Three*, and provided counselling and contact for isolated lesbians. Like the early homosexual societies, it aimed to inform public opinion and promote research. Several regional outlets were created, similar to Kenric in West London, which provided a respectable alternative social focus for lesbians to the emerging bar and club scene.[77]

THE ROAD TO REFORM IN SCOTLAND

Perhaps the most significant of the concessions made to get the Sexual Offences Act through parliament was the exclusion of Scotland and Northern Ireland from its provisions. Scotland had a different legal framework for homosexual offences from the pre-1967 regime in England and Wales. Sentences were generally lighter, with fewer offences attracting prison sentences. There was an automatic time limitation on prosecution of 'stale offences' and a higher standard of proof was required, with most cases requiring at least two witnesses. In practice, this meant that it was rarely possible to prosecute private homosexual behaviour between two consenting adults.[78]

In 1955, only 80 convictions for homosexual offences were recorded in Scotland, compared with 2,293 in England and Wales. From 1953–6, 480 men in England and Wales aged over 21 were convicted of consensual, homosexual offences in private; the comparable figure for Scotland was nine. The population of Scotland was approximately one-ninth that of England and Wales at this time. Consequently, the Scottish administration did not believe that homosexuality constituted a significant issue. It was seen as a southern and, more particularly, a London problem.[79] This did not mean that homosexuality was condoned in Scotland. It was regarded as a predatory and infectious activity that corrupted the young. While Scotland's lighter legislative regime, which provided a model for the Wolfenden report, meant that homosexuals suffered less *legal* persecution, homophobia appears to have been more evident than in England and held law reform at bay for longer.

There was a scathing reaction to Wolfenden from some of Scotland's opinion-formers. In contrast to sympathetic sections of opinion in the Church of England, Scotland's churches were implacably opposed. The Free Presbyterian Church of Scotland was the most vitriolic, lamenting in 1954 that 'the voices of Sodom and Gomorrah . . . appear to be rife among us'.[80] It criticized the activities of the HLRS, the Bills introduced from 1965 and the Church of England's support for reform. James Adair, a long-serving elder of the Church of Scotland, was a member of the Wolfenden Committee and violently opposed homosexual law reform. He also ensured that a Church of Scotland sub-committee report supporting law reform was overruled. The General Assembly opposed the argument that won reform in England, that criminal law should not concern itself with moral behaviour, concluding:

In our opinion there are certain kinds of behaviour that are so contrary to Christian moral principles, and so repugnant to the general consensus of opinion throughout the nation that, even if private and personal, they should be regarded as both morally wrong and legally punishable . . . Homosexual offences seem to us to fall within this category. If so, it is surely right that they should be regarded not only as sinful but as criminal.[81]

A contrast was drawn with 'other cripples'. Homosexuals were perceived as being proud of their 'disability' and seeking to spread their 'perversion'.[82] In 1966, a further attempt by a Church working group to support limited homosexual law reform was also rejected.

Adair's stridently homophobic views were influential within the Church, the press and parliament, and often cited in policy briefings and parliamentary debates as representative of Scottish public opinion, although evidence of popular attitudes is thin.[83] However, a poll conducted by the *Scottish Daily Record* in 1957 found 85 per cent of respondents opposed to the Wolfenden Report. The Scottish media reflected and reinforced negative attitudes. In 1959, the *Scotsman* called for 'an immediate campaign of police repression' and, as late as 1967, the *Scottish Daily Express* insisted that 'the evil professionals who indulge in this filthy trade must continue to be punished and their misguided and diseased associates be forced to take treatment'.[84]

In parliament, 'an influential cluster of Scottish peers sustained an unrelenting opposition to legislation', including former Home Secretary David Maxwell-Fyffe, now Lord Kilmuir.[85] There was also a marked lack of support for reform among Scottish MPs. The Scottish Home Department and Scottish Office adopted a negative posture, arguing that, because prosecutions were rare in Scotland, reform was not required and public opinion would not tolerate it.[86]

TRANS PEOPLE'S EXPERIENCES, 1950s TO 1970s

By the late 1950s and 1960s, there was a growing public awareness of and access to treatment for transsexuals.[87] 'Sex change' operations were made possible by developments in hormone research and plastic surgery, and patients' experiences were widely, and rather pruriently, publicised, especially in the popular press from the 1950s onwards. Christine Jorgensen's story of her 'sex change' was serialised in the *Sunday Pictorial* in 1953. Roberta Cowell's account of her transition from male RAF fighter pilot to woman attracted widespread publicity in 1954. April Ashley was another prominent transsexual who became a model and celebrity. This publicity led to the development of a 'small, but influential lobbying community of transsexuals demanding surgery'.[88] However, surgery did not remove the obstacles to equality for transsexuals, who acquired none of the legal rights of their reassigned sex, were unable to marry and often experienced discrimination in society and dismissal from work.

An analysis of twentieth century newspaper coverage reveals a persistent fascination with 'sex change' stories.[89] Before 1950, stories focused on men 'masquerading' as women, with the use of the term 'drag' (to describe anything from transvestism to fancy dress), and 'sex change' being introduced from the 1960s.[90] By the 1970s, there was a shift towards more serious discussion of the legal and social issues faced by transsexuals, due partly to April Ashley's high-profile divorce case in 1970 and the debates on the Nullity of Marriage Bill in 1971, but not of the day-to-day issues faced by transvestites.[91] Throughout the twentieth century, coverage focused overwhelmingly on male-to-female transsexuals, although it is not clear whether this was due to there being more cases or to their apparently making more exciting news copy.[92]

Roberta Cowell's experience illustrates how, in the 1950s, the tabloid press accorded some sympathy to 'genuine hermaphrodites' whose sex had been 'confused' since birth and required corrective surgery, but distinguished them from people who *chose* to have surgery for psychological reasons, describing them as 'freaks' who ended in limbo, neither 'truly' male nor 'truly' female. The *Sunday Pictorial* 'revealed' that Cowell was not a 'complete woman', listing eight characteristics separating the sexes and concluding that 'Cowell is probably a "transvestist" – a man who is compelled by an overwhelming impulse to act as a woman and feels driven to stop at nothing to bring about and encourage all possible necessary changes'.[93] And *The People* revealed 'the ghastly truth at last':

> The change was purely outward and artificial. There was no physical condition that called for the operations. They were done purely to meet Cowell's abnormal craving. When all this work was complete the horror that was Robert Cowell released himself on the world as 'Roberta'.[94]

In 1959, John B. Randell published an analysis of 50 transsexuals (defined by 'the wish to change the anatomical sex') and transvestites (defined by 'the impulse to wear the clothing of the opposite sex'). Most had presented at Charing Cross Hospital in London, which was gaining a specialist reputation in this new field. Randell defined his patients as either 'homosexual' or 'obsessive compulsive', fitting them into existing medical paradigms and refusing to accept their 'claims' that their sex had been mistaken at birth.[95] His analysis demonstrates that although there was growing medical interest in and awareness of trans people and their circumstances, this did not necessarily translate into sympathetic treatment.

Comments by plastic surgeons who worked with male transsexuals during the early 1980s reveal the persistence of unsympathetic and prejudiced attitudes within the medical profession:

> I would rather not have anything to do with them. They are overdressed, too camp. They upset other patients and the nursing staff. If I hadn't inherited them,

I wouldn't do them. I've said I won't do any more, though being soft-hearted I
probably will.[96]

However, others found their prejudices challenged by the experience: 'I have
always been worried that they were going to be manipulative and difficult
and I have been very pleasantly surprised.'[97]

GAY AND LESBIAN POLITICISATION AND
SELF-REPRESENTATION IN THE 1970s

Like other groups experiencing inequalities, gay men and lesbians found a
new, more assertive, public voice in the 1970s. The catalyst for the formation
of the Gay Liberation Front (GLF) in the autumn of 1970 was the Stonewall
riots in New York, sparked in June 1969 by a police raid on a gay bar. The
GLF's first meeting, held by student activists Aubrey Walker and Bob Mellors
at the London School of Economics, involved nine people. Just a few months
later, 400–500 people were attending weekly meetings.

The GLF rejected the leadership and organizational models of the HLRS,
as well as its cautious aims. It defined itself as 'a revolutionary organization'
and aimed to confront the persecution, discrimination and oppression of
the gay community.[98] Subgroups pursued specific activities, including the
production of the magazine *Come Together*, the organization of 'Gay Days'
in London parks and a successful campaign to have homosexuality removed
from the United Kingdom's register of psychiatric illnesses.[99] The GLF spe-
cialised in direct action, 'zapping' high-profile events, such as a rally by the
Christian Festival of Light in 1971.[100] It also established new mass tactics,
such as Gay Pride marches, the first of which took place in July 1972 and
involved 1,000 people. As well, the GLF actively supported contemporary
campaigns by other groups experiencing inequalities: for women's rights,
against racism, industrial relations disputes (marching with the Trades
Union Council against Ted Heath in 1971 and supporting striking miners
in South Wales with a 'Pits and Perverts' fundraising effort) and protests
against the Vietnam War.

Individuals were encouraged to change their way of life, by publicly
acknowledging their sexuality ('coming out', as it was now known), rejecting a guilt-ridden, furtive double life and demanding not just equal legal
rights, but the right to enjoy an open and sometimes radical gay lifestyle. A
number of experimental communes were established in London.[101] The term
'gay'(Good As You) became current in the United Kingdom and internationally, describing a collective cultural identity, as distinct from 'homosexual',
which referred simply to sexual behaviour, or 'queer', which was seen an
oppressive, hostile definition.[102]

However, the unstructured and diverse nature of the GLF soon caused
divisions and fragmentation. Within months of its first organized march in
August 1971, the movement had fragmented. Small local groups continued

in south London, Lancaster, Leeds and Bradford, but by the end of 1972, the ideal of a mass movement under one banner was over. Gay people, like other groups suffering inequalities, had diverse interests and were not identified solely by their sexuality. The GLF asserted gay identity in contrast to hetero-sexuality and was accused of excluding bisexual and trans people.[103] Its 'us and them' attitude also alienated gay people who felt unable to embrace its radical and public approach for fear of family, work or community reaction, or due to other responsibilities.[104]

Tom Walker Brown, a member of the GLF Youth Group, recalled 'a certain amount of unfair resentment towards the few young lesbians in the group . . . a lot of the men's attitude was, we're more oppressed than you.'[105] For many lesbian women, sexism appeared as prevalent in the gay community as in wider society, and they found their interests taken more seriously by the Women's Liberation Movement (see Chapter 5). In early 1972, the women in London's GLF formed a separate group. Socialist and Marxist groups saw their struggle as part of the wider labour movement and channelled their efforts into the trade unions. By the early 1980s, race and ethnicity were also more prominent issues, with a particularly strong Black lesbian and gay subculture developing. People from minority ethnic groups sometimes found the radicals' anti-family rhetoric unhelpful, as family often provided their only support against racism, as an Asian gay man described in 1989:

> Our community provides a nurturing space . . . [families] are often bulwarks against the institutional and individual racism that we encounter daily . . . And then we discover our sexuality. This sets us apart from family and community, even more so than for a white person . . . More often than not, we live two lives, hiding our sexuality from family and friends in order to maintain our relationships within our community, whilst expressing our sexuality away from the community.[106]

Later movements tended to coalesce around these diverse allegiances, rather than attempting to cut across them, with new organizations emerging, including the Gay Christian Movement (1976), Gay Teenage Group (1979), Gay Black Group (1981) and the disabled lesbian and gay organization REGARD (1989).[107]

The self-help principles and 'the cultural context for a mass coming-out' established by the GLF, rather than its political radicalism, proved to be its lasting legacy. The campaign for further reform was taken up by new organi-zations, including the Committee (from 1971, Campaign) for Homosexual Equality (CHE), the Scottish Minorities Group (SMG), which organized the first International Gay Rights Congress in Edinburgh in December 1974, and the Union for Sexual Freedom in Ireland (USFI). Other gay rights groups continued to use direct action, such as the Gay Activists Alliance (GAA), which picketed the bookseller W. H. Smith for refusing to stock *Gay News*, campaigned against police harassment in Manchester and sup-ported the anti-fascist league after National Front attacks on gay venues in the mid-1970s.[108]

By 1972, CHE was the largest gay organization in Britain, lobbying rather than 'zapping' political parties, churches and other organizations, which consequently felt they could 'do business with it'.[109] In July 1975, it drafted a Bill, together with the SMG and USFI (see below), proposing measures to equalize the law between homosexuals and heterosexuals by lowering the age of consent to 16; applying the 1967 Sexual Offences Act to Scotland, Northern Ireland and the armed forces; abolishing the homosexual offence of gross indecency; creating a new importuning offence for heterosexuals, comparable with that applied to homosexuals; and establishing freedom for homosexual magazines to publish in Britain.

Despite the momentum of its early years, which drew more than 1,000 people to its national conferences, by 1976 CHE was facing criticism for its narrow focus. It did not know how to react when several openly gay men were sacked from their jobs in 1976.[110] Its focus on the law relating to gay men failed to meet the needs of lesbian women, who were heavily under-represented at its conferences.[111] New organizations and support groups for lesbians emerged during the 1970s, including *Sappho* magazine in 1972, which became the focus of regular meetings, and Action for Lesbian Parents in 1976, which campaigned for lesbian women's rights to custody of their children.[112]

Smaller, locally focused, groups proved more durable than the mass movement, with many counselling and befriending services emerging, including London Icebreakers in 1973. This phone service received between 4,000 and 5,000 phone calls a year, one-sixth of them from unmarried women, one-tenth from married people and one-twentieth from transvestites. The London Gay Switchboard, set up in 1974, received 200,000 calls in its first year and expanded to offer a 24-hour service. Even these new services exposed divisions, with the longer-established Albany Trust criticizing the lack of professional counselling offered.[113]

By 1976, all the major political parties had formed gay groups, which acted as support networks and focuses for reform pressure, as did similar groups in many of the professions and trades unions. Jewish and Christian groups also formed. In 1972, the weekly magazine *Gay News* was founded, and within four years it had a circulation of more than 20,000. While there was no shortage of activity, it was uneven geographically, with London and other large cities having the most vibrant networks, mainly serving middle class gay men.[114] These new grassroots organizations had profound social effects, but made little political progress.[115]

There was also a growing counter-movement from Mary Whitehouse and her Christian moralist supporters in the National Viewers' and Listeners' Association. In 1977, Whitehouse brought a successful private prosecution against *Gay News*, reviving the archaic Blasphemy Act in response to the publication of a poem, 'The Love That Dares to Speak its Name', in which a Roman centurion expressed his homosexual fantasies about the crucified Christ. Whitehouse and her colleagues explored the potential of both existing law and possible law reform to attack not only homosexuality, but a range of 'deviant' behaviours (see Chapter 3).[116] Public opinion remained broadly hostile towards homosexuality. An opinion poll for *Gay News* in 1975 found support for the 1967 legislation, but little support for further legal change.[117] The ugly spectre of homophobic attacks and murders was ever-present. A week after the *Gay News* blasphemy case, 32-year-old Peter Benyon was murdered when leaving the Rainbow Rooms in North London, and in 1978, Roy Phillips was killed outside a gay bar in Liverpool.[118] The problem of homophobic bullying in schools was also becoming recognized, although there was no government agenda to protect or support gay school children until the mid-1980s.[119]

Nevertheless, groups representing LGBT people began to have a voice in policy-making. In December 1975, Roy Jenkins, again Home Secretary in a new Labour government, set up the Policy Advisory Committee on Sexual Offences to revisit the laws on the age of consent. In contrast to the Wolfenden Committee, which had heard evidence from only three homosexuals, this committee received lengthy submissions from many LGBT groups.[120] Although campaigners' arguments for equalising the age of consent for gay men to 16, or even lowering it to 14, were unsuccessful, and Margaret Thatcher's government ignored the committee's recommendation that it should be lowered to 18, clearly the policy climate had changed since World War II.[121]

TRANS POLITICISATION AND SELF-REPRESENTATION IN THE 1970s

Trans people, on the whole, were still confronted by public contempt and police harassment but, from the late 1960s, groups were developing that provided counselling, support and opportunities to socialize. Like the GLF, British trans groups took their inspiration from the United States, where, in about 1960, the Foundation for Personality Expression (FPE) and its magazine, *Transvestia*, were founded. The FPE provided an anonymous means of communication for transvestites, access to sympathetic suppliers to enable cross-dressing, and an ideology that promoted 'guilt-free expression' rather than medical 'cures'.[122]

In 1963–4, three British transvestites set up a British branch of the FPE, which in 1967 became the Beaumont Society and is still active. It began to publish a newsletter in the following year, and attracted about 100–150 members. In March 1974, the society hosted a national transvestite and transsexual conference in Leeds, attended by more than 100 people (including some involved in the GLF, Icebreakers and CHE), but aroused little interest or support from the gay movement. By the end of the decade, the Beaumont Society had about 700 members, although another 2,000 had passed through. It developed a more formal organization, with a constitution, an elected executive and regional officers. The Beaumont Society was criticized by sections of the gay and women's movements and other trans groups for its low-profile approach, operating as a 'closed closet', failing to engage with contemporary sexual politics and criticism of marriage and family structures, and for the exclusion of transsexuals, homosexuals and fetishists from its membership.[123] However, one of the society's founders, Alice L100, explained that the society dissociated itself from the gay movement to overcome the assumption that cross-dressing men were necessarily gay (many of its members were married, and support for wives was a central part of the society's activities) or touting for sex.[124] The Beaumont Society now allows homosexual transvestites to join, but an offshoot, the Seahorse Society, retains the original focus on heterosexual transvestites.

Other organizations representing trans people were active during this period, including regional groups, for example in London and Leeds, and some operated under the umbrella of gay organizations.[125] The Isis Commune in London housed a transsexual Liberation Group in the early 1970s and, about 1977, a small British cell of the American Transsexual Action Organisation was founded, again active mainly in urban centres. In 1979, the Self Help Association for Transsexuals (SHAFT) was formed, primarily as an information-collecting and disseminating body, a focus it retains now as the Gender Trust. Unlike transvestite groups, transsexual organizations had 'concrete targets to aim for': to remove the legal inequalities relating to marriage and birth certificates, and to campaign for better medical treatment.[126]

Change was slow but, by the 1970s, it was becoming possible, at least in London and other urban centres, to be part of a wider transvestite or transsexual community, sharing information and experiences and enjoying social and emotional support.[127]

EQUALISING THE LAW ACROSS BRITAIN

While gay men in England and Wales enjoyed, and pushed the boundaries of, the limited new freedoms allowed by the 1967 Act, their counterparts in Scotland and Northern Ireland were still constrained by the nineteenth century legal framework. The Scottish Minorities Group (SMG) was predominantly a moderate, middle class reform organization focused, like CHE and HLRS, predominantly on legal reform rather than broader sexual liberation.[128] It distanced itself from radical groups such as the GLF, but from the early 1970s mounted a vigorous campaign for legal reform. In 1972, the SMG drafted a reform Bill, but it proved difficult to find a parliamentary sponsor. In 1974, it changed tactics, joining the wider movement for gay rights, and dropped its Scottish Bill in favour of a British-wide Bill proposed by CHE (see above), which sought equality between homosexual and heterosexual law throughout the United Kingdom. An important driver was that the continued criminalization of all homosexual activity in Scotland and Northern Ireland compromised the legality of the advisory, counselling and welfare services now provided by both the SMG and other voluntary agencies.[129] And, as Mary Whitehouse had demonstrated, the forces of conservatism were willing to deploy apparently moribund legislation to suppress what they considered to be immoral activities.

The campaign was launched at a London rally in November 1974, attracting more than 2,500 men and women.[130] CHE's Bill found sponsors in Dr J. Dickson Mabon, the Labour MP for Greenock, and the Liberal peer Lord Beaumont, but it failed in the House of Commons. The possibility of Scottish devolution also presented a strategic problem, as the Westminster government considered it inappropriate to introduce controversial legislation on a matter that might soon be devolved. However, devolution did not occur at this stage.[131]

A major setback came in 1976, when the Labour government introduced a Sexual Offences (Scotland) Bill to consolidate the law, restating the illegality of all homosexual acts. The government's defence, that there would be no prosecutions for acts that were now legal in England and Wales, united Labour supporters of reform, such as Robin Cook and the Conservative spokesman Malcolm Rifkind (both of whom were Scottish MPs), against a law that would not be enforced.[132] Despite press and parliamentary campaigning by the SMG, the Consolidation Bill was passed and the nineteenth century legacy remained. The SMG had, however, gained visibility for the Scottish cause, and the Labour government's majority was reduced to only ten on what should have been a non-controversial Bill. Robin Cook observed that the majority was due entirely to 19 Scottish MPs voting for the Bill.[133] Unsuccessful Bills to amend the law followed in the Lords and the Commons, meeting opposition in particular from Scottish peers and the Free Church of Scotland.[134]

Thereafter, the SMG's agenda became more radical, with a name change to the Scottish Homosexual Rights Group (SHRG) in late 1978 and the adoption of a 'Declaration of Rights of Homosexual Men and Women', addressing a wide range of issues including employment, health and welfare, and espousing the pro-devolution campaign. After the 'No' vote on devolution in March 1979, the SHRG reverted to supporting a Bill to amend the 1976 Consolidation Act.[135] However, it also pursued what was then an innovative channel to force reform on the government, submitting a case to the European Court of Human Rights. Three Scottish gay activists testified that their rights under Article 25 of the European Convention of Human Rights had been breached because they suffered 'prejudice by reason of fear of prosecution for the commission of homosexual acts' and 'psychological harm and distress as a result . . .' as well as 'social stigma and loss of esteem', and that they were 'open to blackmail, intimidation and harassment'. They also claimed that they suffered discrimination as citizens of the United Kingdom, 'by reason of Scottish national minority status'.[136]

There is debate over whether the deployment of this new tactic, raising the prospect of a long, costly and possibly unsuccessful legal battle with Europe, forced the government's hand, or whether reform was driven by crusading parliamentarians, particularly Robin Cook.[137] Homosexual law reform for Scotland was finally achieved by means of an amendment to the Criminal Justice Bill, introduced by Cook and passed in October 1980. The opponents, who had delayed reform for so long, lobbied hard to defeat the amendment in the Lords, with a new organization, Parents Concern, propagating the myth that all homosexuals were child molesters. Many members of the SHRG viewed the amendment as unsatisfactory because Cook conceded that the age of consent should be 21, not 18, but the Bill scraped through the Lords. The law had changed, but reformers were keenly aware that attitudes among much of the media, the churches and the police in Scotland had not.[138]

Campaign and support groups were also active in Northern Ireland during the 1970s, including the Elmwood Association (which provided counselling), the Gay Liberation Society, the USFI and the Irish Gay Rights Association. All campaigned against the Rev Ian Paisley's 'Save Ulster from Sodomy' campaign.[139] The tactic of appealing to the European Court of Human Rights eventually proved successful in Northern Ireland, where reform had been held back by the opposition of both the Catholic and Protestant churches. Jeff Dudgeon's successful claim via the court that the criminalization of homosexuality violated his right to a private and family life led in 1982 to the application of the 1967 Act to Northern Ireland.

BACKLASH? THE IMPACT OF AIDS: 1980s TO 1990s

The political atmosphere of the 1980s was not conducive to extending what were now known as LGBT rights. Again, however, repression had the unintended consequence of encouraging self-organization.

The emergence of AIDS into public and political consciousness generated fear and panic that led to an explosion of homophobia.[140] The first Department of Health report on AIDS was produced in 1983, when three people were known to have died of the disease. Since the early 1980s, about 97,400 British people are known to have been infected with HIV, and more than 18,000 people have died.[141] Until about 1999, the majority affected were gay men and the disease was described in the media as a 'gay plague', known initially as 'Gay-Related Immune Deficiency'.

Fear and rumour outpaced fact and science, with the media constantly reporting new 'scares', revealing new groups of people who appeared to be at risk and behaviours perceived to heighten the risk of contracting the disease. This is illustrated in the following selection of headlines, from the relatively unsensational *Times*:

'Blood banks may spread Aids illness', 2 May 1983

'Gays told of festival Aids risk', 25 July 1983

'Aids fear halts autopsy', 2 November 1983

'Aids contracted by elderly couple', 7 January 1984

'AIDS cases may reach a million health chief says', 4 May 1984

'Call for gay blood donors ban', 17 November 1984

'Pathologist refused to handle Aids man's body', 16 January 1985

'Nurse caught Aids from needle jab', 25 February 1985

'How deadly Aids could sweep the world', 7 August 1985

'School bars Aids boy', 28 August 1985

Gay men became scapegoats, portrayed by the media not as innocent victims of AIDS, but as deviants who had 'brought it upon themselves', as the following editorial from *The Times* illustrates:

> Aids horrifies not only because of the prognosis for its victims. The infection's origins and means of propagation excites repugnance, moral and physical, at promiscuous male homosexuality – conduct which, tolerable in private circumstances, has with the advent of 'gay liberation' become advertised, even glorified as acceptable public conduct, even a proud badge for public men to wear. Many members of the public are tempted to see in Aids some sort of retribution for a questionable style of life but Aids of course is a danger not only to the promiscuous nor only to homosexuals.[142]

This atmosphere was all too evident to gay men, although, as one clerical worker recounted, sexual practices began to change once the routes of transmission for the disease became widely known:

> AIDS has affected me deeply. One friend has died recently and another is ill at the moment. I find it difficult not to get angry when I think about it because we [gay men] are both the main victims of the disease at the moment in the west and the people who get the least support in trying to combat the disease.
>
> I saw my partner (who I have lived with for the last 5 years) off at Heathrow last month. He kissed my cheek at the departure gate. As I walked away a man who passed me said 'Filthy AIDS queer'.[143]

After the splintering of the gay and lesbian movement in the 1970s, the AIDS crisis became a unifying force. The first self-help and support groups were set up by the gay community, including the Terence Higgins Trust (THT), founded in late 1982 in memory of the first Briton known to have died. As death rates rose among gay and bisexual men (as high as 1,000 per year by the early 1990s), their partners experienced the additional trauma caused by their lack of legal rights when it came to illness, death and inheritance.[144]

This fired calls for formal partnership rights and led some men to make living wills and pre-emptive funeral arrangements.[145]

In contrast, the government was slow to adopt a coordinated policy. While the Department of Health and the Chief Medical Officer, Sir Donald Acheson, saw the need for advice on safe sex via leaflets and advertising, the Prime Minister, Margaret Thatcher, was cautious. By late 1986, it was clear that HIV/AIDS was not just a 'gay plague' and that heterosexuals were being infected as well, contributing to a sense of panic in the media and the public. Mrs Thatcher was eventually persuaded to set up a Cabinet committee to deal with the crisis. An unprecedented health education campaign was launched, with press, radio and television advertising under the strapline 'Don't Die of Ignorance', a leaflet drop on 23 million homes, and a £20 million budget. There was intense wrangling over the wording of the campaign material, with Ministers keen to maintain a 'respectable' veneer and avoid embarrassing terminology.[146] The telephone number of the London Lesbian and Gay Switchboard was publicized during the campaign, but it received no additional funding and was overwhelmed by callers who were terrified of AIDs, as well as increased numbers of men and women wanting to discuss coming out.[147]

Thatcher was keen to wind down the campaign, quickly dissolving the Cabinet committee, vetoing funding for research into sexual behaviour to inform future policy and disbanding the Health Education Authority's AIDS division.[148] A heterosexual AIDS epidemic failed to materialize. It was suggested in the press and elsewhere that the reaction had been melodramatic, and even that it was part of a gay conspiracy to gain attention and prevent the unravelling of the previous decade's hard-won progress.[149] However, in several respects the government's handling of the campaign represented a brave departure, with its liberal rather than punitive stance and defence of individual rights, confidentiality, safe sex, and harm-minimisation for drug users, despite the government's moralistic public image.[150]

As the emphasis shifted to prevention, gay men were expected to take the lead in checking the spread of the disease, and, as a *Times* editorial suggested, society's toleration of their lifestyle might depend upon it:

> This disease is capable not only of physical harm, but also of dissolving the trust on which social life is built, the trust which allows us to separate and tolerate private conduct, even of an immoral or exotic kind, from the public business of society. Homosexuals thus have a double interest in impeding the disease.[151]

In fact, the rate of infection among heterosexuals was growing while among gay men it was falling.[152] While being castigated by politicians, the media and society for 'inviting' the disease with their 'deviant' behaviour, gay men had begun to adopt safe sex once the routes of transmission became clear, from about 1983. The gay activist Peter Tatchell highlighted how gay organizations had taken the lead in promoting safe sex, urging gay men not to donate blood and providing accurate public information. He also called for more government funding for research, education and a health service that was under strain from treating AIDS patients.[153] A clerical worker interviewed by Mass Observation was prescient:

> Gay men have got the message about AIDS but only because they have done the work themselves through organizations like the Terrence Higgins Trust. They are changing their sexual behaviour and, if Britain follows the pattern of places like San Francisco, AIDS amongst gay men will start to decrease dramatically. It is the heterosexual population that worry me. The attitudes that I have come across convince me that, for an awful lot of people, the Government campaign just hasn't made them understand the reality of AIDS.[154]

After the 1987 general election, family values and moral conservatism featured prominently in Thatcher's public statements.[155] The Labour Party's position concerning homosexuality was confused because the party was still deeply divided, on this as on many other issues. The attitudes of some of its accustomed voters were evident in Peter Tatchell's disastrous by-election campaign as Labour candidate in Bermondsey in 1983, when he was the subject of a homophobic onslaught incited by his opponents. On the other hand, in 1986, several Labour-controlled inner-London boroughs and the Inner London Education Authority began promoting more positive images of gay men and lesbians as part of sex education in schools, most controversially in Haringey. These were highly publicized and often caricatured in the media, prompting the formation of the Parents Rights Group in protest. A leaked letter from Patricia Hewitt, then-press secretary to Neil Kinnock, leader of the Labour Party, revealed concern that 'the gay and lesbians issue is costing us dear among the pensioners'.[156] When proposals began to come forward to ban the 'promotion' of homosexuality by local authorities, the party did not have a coherent position.[157]

The 1987 Conservative election manifesto made clear the party's intention to clamp down on 'sexual propaganda' in schools, and it was a significant issue during the election, explicitly supported by Thatcher.[158] The outcome was the passage of Section 28 of the 1987 Local Government Bill, introduced as a backbench amendment, which made it illegal for local authorities to 'intentionally promote homosexuality or publish material with the intention of promoting homosexuality' or to 'promote the teaching in any maintained school of the acceptability of homosexuality as a pretended family relationship'. The phrase '*pretended* family relationship' was inserted to replace 'acceptable family relationship', in order, it has been argued, to bolster traditional family structures and values, and to undermine gay and lesbian households.[159]

The amendment was largely unchallenged in the House of Commons and there was no vote on its adoption. It was only when the Local Government Bill moved to the Lords that extra-parliamentary opposition to Section 28 began to mobilize, but it was too late. The most radical response came in February 1988, when, the night before the Bill became law, three women abseiled into the House of Lords and then invaded the BBC Six O'Clock newsroom to protest against the Bill's passage. In the same month, 15,000 people demonstrated in Manchester and 40,000 joined a Gay Pride rally in June, compared with 15,000 in 1985.

The annual British Social Attitudes Survey, started in 1983, suggests that the supporters of Section 28 were in tune with public opinion. The 1987 survey showed that public opinion was marginally less discriminatory against homosexuality than in 1983, with more people opposed to the banning of homosexuals from certain professions, such as teaching.[160] But there was increased opposition to homosexual relationships: 74 per cent in 1987, compared with 69 per cent in 1985.[161] In 1987, 86 per cent supported banning lesbians from adopting children, compared with 93 per cent opposed to adoption by gay men.[162] A poll in the *Sunday Telegraph* in June 1988 found that 60 per cent thought that homosexuality should not be considered an acceptable lifestyle, compared with 34 per cent who believed it should.[163] The AIDS crisis is the probable reason for this hardening of opinion.[164]

Section 28 was never enforced in practice, but it had an impact on local government, where caution reigned on issues around homosexuality; no authority wanted to become the test case. One woman described how:

> Long after Section 28, I was at a secondary school fair in Stoke Newington which perhaps has the largest concentration of lesbian mothers and children of lesbians than any other place in London or England . . . There were a lot of really interesting looking books for teenagers and young people. . . . But there wasn't one on lesbians or gays or homosexuality in general . . . [I asked why and was told] well the librarian says we can't because of Clause 28 – it's too dangerous . . . the irony was that the librarian was a lesbian. Clause 28 has never been used but that story is just an illustration of its influence.[165]

However, Section 28 failed to halt the development of gay and lesbian lifestyles and identities.[166] The combination of the panic and homophobia in response to AIDS, followed by the campaign to overturn Section 28, galvanised gay and lesbian communities. Section 28 spurred the foundation in 1989 of Stonewall by 20 gay men and lesbians, including actors Michael Cashman and Ian McKellan. The founders created a tightly organized, professionally run body to lobby and engage with the government on issues affecting gay men and women, including Section 28, the age of consent, adoption and parenting and partnership recognition.[167] The GLF's tradition of direct action was continued by Outrage!, formed in 1990 by Peter Tatchell and others following the homophobic murder of the actor Michael Boothe. Tatchell and his colleagues revived the use of 'queer' to describe themselves, as 'gay' was now perceived as mainstream.[168]

The AIDS crisis had focused attention on bisexual people as well, as the medical profession explored how the disease might 'jump' from homosexuals to heterosexuals. Bisexuals did not fully identify with the gay or lesbian communities, from whom they had sometimes experienced discrimination:

Most bisexuals weren't out in the way that they are today . . . in the mid to late eighties many lesbian and gay groups explicitly banned bisexuals and even those that didn't . . . were quite hostile. For instance, at WFTVN [Women's Film and Television Video Network], my workplace we had an equal opportunities monitoring form which asked about your sexuality; and one woman had put bisexual. And one lesbian read this over my shoulder, and . . . said 'Yuk!'. Quite literally 'Yuk!'. And so I don't think that was really a context when one felt terribly happy about coming out.[169]

Some transgender people also experienced discrimination from members of the gay community, who believed that having surgery meant 'trying to conform to straight conventions'.[170] De La Grace Volcano articulated these divisions:

> To me, lesbian and gay community, is a utopian concept rather than a lived reality because . . . far too many people . . . are excluded . . . What I'm hoping is . . . people that are lesbian and gay will notice others that are transgendered intersex people and . . . stop campaigning in this very narrow way for the rights of gay men to cruise or the age of consent or lesbian mothers, these single issue politics have strictly to do with being lesbian and gay . . . There has been an extreme reaction in the last few years against transgender and against anything that rocks the boat of lesbian and gay politics, that nice stable world that now we've got Stonewall and we have the Equality Ball and we have gay MPs and everything seems to be really groovy. Well it isn't and yet we talk about it as if it is.[171]

By the late 1980s, there was still very little reliable information about sexual behaviour and attitudes, yet some government Ministers resisted research designed to help combat the spread of HIV/AIDS.[172] In 1988, researchers at the University of London piloted a survey to assess the success of health education campaigns and help plan future care. The Health Education Authority, Economic and Social Research Council and Department of Health were all supportive, but it appears that Margaret Thatcher intervened to block government funding.[173] There are differing accounts of the reasons for this, but Kenneth Baker's memoirs provide an insight:

> Early in 1989, the two Health ministers, David Mellor and Ken Clarke proposed that there should be a government-sponsored survey of the sexual behaviour of 20,000 British people in the year 1990 . . . George Younger, Douglas Hurd and I opposed this survey and stopped it. We believed that such a survey would become just another Kinsey Report, revealing that Britain had become a more promiscuous society – which we knew – and more experimental in the realm of bisexual relationships – which we also knew. A new survey therefore would neither increase the sum of human knowledge nor do anything actually to help AIDS sufferers.[174]

The research was rescued by funding from the Wellcome Trust, interviewing started in 1990, and the findings were published in 1994 as the *National Survey of Sexual Attitudes and Lifestyles* (NATSAL). They should be treated with caution because the number of gay men and, especially, women in the samples was small. The following table compares the results of the 1990 survey, with follow-up data from 2000. The researchers attributed the apparent rise in the reporting of homosexual partnerships to 'a combination of true change and greater willingness to report sensitive behaviours'.[175]

Table 6.1 Reported sexual partnerships: 1990 and 2000

Sexual partnerships	Men		Women	
	Natsal 2000	Natsal 1990	Natsal 2000	Natsal 1990
Ever had homosexual partners?				
Greater London	10.5%	8.4%	6.9%	3.0%
Rest of Britain	4.6%	2.9%	4.5%	1.6%
All	5.4%	3.6%	4.9%	1.8%
Homosexual partners in past 5 years				
Greater London	5.5%	4.8%	3.9%	1.4%
Rest of Britain	2.1%	1.0%	2.4%	0.7%
All	2.6%	1.5%	2.6%	0.8%

Source: Johnson *et al.*, 'Sexual behaviour in Britain: Partnerships, practices, and HIV risk behaviours'. (*The Lancet*, vol. 358, December 1, 2001, p. 1839.)

SEXUALITY AND THE BATTLE FOR LEGAL EQUALITY: 1990s TO 2000s

By the early 1990s, the battle to equalize the age of consent for gay sex was the most pressing issue. The Conservative government showed no inclination to reverse Section 28, but Prime Minister John Major was sympathetic to reviewing the homosexual age of consent, which had remained 21 since 1967.[176] He invited the 'out' gay actor, Ian McKellen, to Downing Street to discuss the issue, afterwards recalling:

> I [did not] see homosexuality as a social evil. Many people are gay, and I saw no reason to cast them into outer darkness for that reason . . . I was shocked at the attitude of mind that seemed to think I should not have spoken to Ian McKellen. [I] found him a courageous advocate for the cause of equal treatment of gays

before the law. I did not agree with him on every point – nor, I think, did he expect me to – but he had a case that deserved a hearing.[177]

In 1993, a new phase of campaigning began when teenagers Will Parry, Hugo Greenhalgh and Ralph Wilde, with the backing of Stonewall, brought a case to the European Court of Human Rights, claiming that British law breached their rights to privacy and family life. When Edwina Currie introduced a clause into the 1994 Criminal Justice Bill to lower the age of consent, Stonewall led an organized lobbying campaign to equalize the age of consent at 16 for homosexual as well as heterosexual sex, while the opposition was again dominated by religious leaders.[178] The crowds gathered in Parliament Square to await the result of the vote erupted in protest when the result came – MPs had voted to reduce the age of consent to 18, but not to equalize it.[179] Although draconian in many other respects, including its criminalization of travelling communities (see Chapter 4), the 1994 Criminal Justice and Public Order Act made male rape an offence for the first time, extended the provisions of the 1967 Act to the armed forces, and decriminalized anal sex between men and women.

New Labour's 1997 general election manifesto made no explicit mention of LGBT rights or the age of consent, but the party committed itself to 'end unjustifiable discrimination wherever it exists' and to incorporate the European Convention on Human Rights into British law, which was done in the Human Rights Act (HRA), 1998 (effective from 2000). Tony Blair's new government included the first openly gay Cabinet Minister, Culture Secretary Chris Smith, and in 1997 Labour MP Angela Eagle became the first lesbian MP to come out. The foreign partners of lesbians and gay men were soon given immigration rights on the same terms as straight couples. Campaigners were assured before the general election that in the first term there would be free votes on equalizing the age of consent and repealing Section 28.[180] Soon after New Labour came to power, the European Commission on Human Rights ruled in the case of *Euan Sutherland versus U.K.* that the unequal age of consent was in breach of the Convention, providing justification for the government to take action.

Labour MP Ann Keen introduced an amendment to the Crime and Disorder Bill, 1998, to equalize the age of consent, which passed the Commons but was defeated in the Lords after a campaign led by the Conservative Baroness Young. The clause was reintroduced in the government's Sexual Offences (Amendment) Bill 1998, which was eventually forced on the Lords, using the Parliament Act, on 30 November 2000. Even with the backing of a recently elected government with a large majority and the lobbying role played by Stonewall, an equal age of consent was hard fought. But, crucially, public opinion had changed since the fight began. A National Opinion Poll in 1994 found only 13 per cent of respondents supported 16 as the age of consent for gays, but, by February 1999, 66 per cent said the age of consent 'should be the same for everyone', and a slim majority – 54 per cent – thought this should be 16.[181] Stonewall and its political allies won support for 'sixteen' by using arguments for equalization, not for 'lowering' the age of consent for gay people.[182] As Shadow Home Secretary, Tony Blair had told the Commons in 1994 it was 'an issue not of age, but of equality'.[183] Fears about young men being 'seduced' by older, predatory homosexuals and 'homosexual spread' remained prevalent in the press and the parliamentary debates.[184]

Later parliamentary debates on the repeal of Section 28 and gay adoption revealed that homophobic prejudice was still very much alive. Ironically, given Scottish history in this respect, the new Scottish parliament was quicker to repeal Section 28 (in 2000) than Westminster (in 2003). The debate in early 2007 over measures to prevent discrimination in the provision of goods and services to lesbian and gay people demonstrated that the government could find itself trapped between competing interest groups. In this case, the Church of England and Roman Catholic Church claimed that their members' rights to practise their faith would be infringed if their adoption organizations were forced to provide services to gay and lesbian couples. The Conservative MP Anne Widdecombe claimed that the new regulations created 'a hierarchy of rights and whenever a homosexual right comes up against any other right the homosexual right prevails'.[185] A 21-month exemption for religious adoption agencies expired on 1 January 2009. It was reported that half of the Roman Catholic adoption agencies, which had threatened to close, would abide by the law.[186]

Research carried out for Stonewall revealed widespread public support for the equalities legislation in place and for a new law making incitement to homophobic hatred an offence. This received parliamentary assent in May 2008.

Table 6.2 Public attitudes to equalities legislation for gay and lesbian people

Law	Impact	Level of support
Employment Equality (Sexual Orientation) Regulations 2003	Protection from discrimination and harassment for gay employees	93%
Civil Partnership Act 2004	Partnership rights for same-sex couples, similar to civil marriages	68%
The Equality Act (Sexual Orientation) Regulations 2007	Makes it unlawful to refuse people services, such as health care, on the grounds of their sexual orientation	85%
Incitement to homophobic hatred (not a criminal offence when the survey was carried out, but came into law in May 2008)	Would make it unlawful to incite hatred on the grounds of sexual orientation, similar to existing laws for race	89%

Source: *Living Together: British Attitudes to Lesbian and Gay People* (Stonewall, 2007).

Despite the numbers of religious leaders and individuals among the opponents of extending legal rights for gay and lesbian people, Stonewall found that the majority of 'people of faith' supported the changes and 84 per cent disagreed with the statement that 'homosexuality is morally unacceptable in all circumstances'.[187] However, there were regional variations. The 2006 Scottish Social Attitudes Survey found that 30 per cent believed sexual relations between people of the same sex were 'always or mostly' wrong.[188] Fifty-one per cent believed that owners of bed and breakfast establishments should 'definitely or probably' be allowed to refuse a booking for a gay or lesbian couple, compared with 17 per cent in Wales.[189]

Stonewall's fifth annual Workplace Equality Index (WEI), for 2009, suggested that the organizational mindset had become more gay-friendly than ever before. Based on a survey of more than 7,000 gay and lesbian employees from 371 organizations across 23 sectors, it found that more organizations qualified for the index than before, headed by Lloyds TSB, Hampshire Constabulary and Brighton and Hove City Council. Seventeen police forces ranked in the top 1,000 organizations. Among the worst-performing sectors were the media (only one company made the list of 100), retail, construction and the National Health Service (NHS).[190] The method of compiling the index has been criticized[191] and homophobia persists, in workplaces and elsewhere, but there are signs of real change for gay and lesbian workers.

GENDER IDENTITY AND THE BATTLE FOR LEGAL EQUALITY: 1990s TO 2000s[192]

The 1990s also saw increased organization among trans people campaigning for legal change, and in particular the right to NHS gender reassignment treatment and legal recognition of their acquired gender. Press for Change (PfC) was founded in 1992 and proved especially effective in mobilizing the skills of its highly educated membership, a number of whom had acquired legal training as mature students.[193]

One of PfC's founding members was Stephen Whittle, who was involved in CHE while attempting to identify as a lesbian and the Beaumont Society after coming out as a trans man, and in 1990 founded the FTM (Female To Male) support group. Whittle and his long-term partner (now wife) Sarah, were instrumental in achieving change and inspiring others through a successful campaign of personal litigation. In the early 1990s, they established their right to artificial insemination treatment, then, through the European Court, their children's right to have Whittle legally recognized as their father. In June 2005, they could finally exercise their new-found right to marry.[194]

The legal changes from the late 1990s on were achieved through a combination of lobbying and well-informed use of the courts (including the European courts), assisted by equality moves promoted by the European Union. Following the successful referral of an employment tribunal case to the European Court of Justice by a British transsexual woman in 1994, the government introduced the 1999 Sex Discrimination (Gender Reassignment) Regulations. These made it clear that employment rights gained in Europe applied to those intending to undergo gender reassignment, as well as to those who had completed the process or were undergoing it.

In 1999, the Court of Appeal held that gender dysphoria (a feeling of being trapped within a body of the wrong sex) was an illness under the terms of NHS legislation, and so gender reassignment treatment could not, prima facie, be refused by the NHS. Although gender reassignment treatment had been provided on the NHS since its foundation in 1948, this case concerned the right of Primary Care Trusts to refuse treatment. The judgment held that gender reassignment treatments were not cosmetic, and therefore could not be downgraded by administrators to 'low priority' or subjected to a blanket ban, but must be based on the needs of the individual patient and clinical judgement.

However, trans people continued to face conflicts over whether they were assigned to male or female hospital wards or prisons, which toilet they were permitted to use in the workplace, and who searched them at airports. Male-to-female transsexual women were not allowed to draw their state pensions at the normal female age of 60 (see Chapter 1). Nor could most trans people marry, unless they happened to live in a gay or lesbian relationship according to their preferred gender role.

In 2002, the European Court of Human Rights found that the United Kingdom had breached the rights of transsexual people to marry and the right to respect for private life, and had a duty to rectify these breaches. In 2003, the House of Lords ruled that, as British law stood, a male-to-female transsexual could not marry a man. This was incompatible with the Human Rights Act. These rulings led directly to the UK Gender Recognition Act 2004. This established Gender Recognition panels and a process of application whereby a trans person could be afforded a gender recognition certificate, a new birth certificate in their acquired gender role (if their birth was registered in the United Kingdom) and recognition of their new gender for all legal purposes. Applicants had to demonstrate that they had lived permanently in their acquired gender for at least two years and intended to live in that gender until death. The application had to be backed by a medical diagnosis of gender dysphoria. However, genital reconstructive surgery was not a prerequisite for legal recognition in the new gender. This legislation was essential to comply with the decision of the European Court of Human Rights, but it retained a medical requirement that individuals must live in their new gender role for up to six years before obtaining access to genital surgery. Successful applicants were accorded all the rights of their lived gender, including the right to marry, to obtain pensions and other benefits appropriate for their legal gender, and to protection under anti-discrimination and equality legislation.

Problems remain with implementation of the law, and many trans people still face inequality of treatment and discrimination. Many cases alleging discrimination continue to be referred to tribunals and the courts, for example alleging demotion at work following gender reassignment surgery.[195] There is disappointment among trans people that all the legal gains of the last decade have come about due to court decisions forcing the government's hand, rather than through proactive government measures.[196]

CONCLUSION

Over the past 60 years, and especially since the 1960s, lesbian, gay, bisexual and trans people have made a transition from being defined by others to active self-definition, and from campaigning against prejudice and (in some groups more than others) unequal legal treatment, to demanding equality and full citizenship, for the right to lead uneventful, socially accepted lives.

While it should not be assumed that legal equality has always been matched by equality in practice, during the past decade many of the remaining barriers preventing LGBT people from living full and normal lives have been removed. The quiet but forceful lobbying of campaign groups, including Stonewall and Press for Change, has done much to achieve these changes. The stimulus to legal change has also often come from LGBT people choosing to live as equal citizens in defiance of the law.[197] Some changes were effected through backbench amendments to other legislation (although government support has sometimes proved crucial) and some were prompted by European Court rulings.[198] The creation of the Equality and Human Rights Commission in 2007, with a remit to protect the human rights of all, whatever their sexual orientation, presumably including trans people, is, it must be hoped, a further step forward by government.

The main drivers of change have been:

- campaigning by members of these groups, initially behind-the-scenes lobbying, more publicly since the 1970s. Campaigns have been effective despite the relatively small size of these populations, although (like most political campaigns) never achieving all that their supporters hoped. Trans people, in particular, have campaigned particularly effectively since the 1990s, aided by the high levels of education and legal qualifications of activists
- cultural change among the heterosexual population, as, from the 1970s, sexual mores and the range of relationships and household formations in the wider population shifted, and toleration of 'difference' increased. Gender roles and modes of self-representation in the wider population have become more flexible – for example, by the 1980s, it was acceptable for females to wear trousers in all social situations, as it was not even in the 1960s – blurring the everyday visibility of some lesbians, male-to-female transsexuals and transvestites
- the greater willingness of Labour than of Conservative governments to

promote equality, especially since 1997, when voter hostility seems to have been somewhat weaker than in the 1960s and 1970s
- the role of European institutions – for example, the use by trans and gay people of the European Court of Human Rights.

The main inhibitor of change towards greater equality, regardless of gender identity or sexuality, has been continuing, if diminishing, public prejudice (or perceptions of public prejudice among politicians and opinion-formers), frequently fuelled by the popular media, which also has a particularly poor record as an employer of LGBT people.

Chapter 7

Disability

Simon Millar

TIMELINE

1893	Elementary Education (Blind and Deaf Children) Act.
1899	Elementary Education (Defective and Epileptic Children) Act.
1920	Blind Pensions Act.
1944	Education Act states disabled children should receive mainstream education wherever possible. Disabled Persons' Employment Act requires employers of more than 20 employees to employ at least 3 per cent of workforce from Disabled Persons Register.
1946	Association of Parents of Backward Children (now MENCAP) formed by parents concerned about lack of support. National Association for Mental Health (now MIND) formed. Report of the Care of Children Committee published.
1948	National Health Service provides free healthcare to all, irrespective of disability. National Assistance Act obliges local authorities to make provision for disabled people within the community. Jack Archer, of radio programme *The Archers*, admitted to mental hospital with depression.
1957	Report of Royal Commission on the Law Relating to Mental Illness and Mental Deficiency.
1958	First television programme about a mental hospital, *The Hurt Mind*.
1959	Mental Health Act.
1965	Disablement Income Group formed.
1967–9	Allegations of misconduct at some mental hospitals.
1970	Chronically Sick and Disabled Persons Act leads to expansion of community-based provision. Education (Handicapped Children) Act gives Local Education Authorities responsibility for the education of all mentally handicapped children.

1972   National Schizophrenia Fellowship formed (name changed to
        Rethink in 2002). Scottish Union of Mental Patients formed.
        Establishment of Health Service Commissioner to investigate
        complaints of ill-treatment in hospitals.
1973   Publication of *Psychiatric Hospitals Viewed by their Patients*.
1974   Community Health Councils established. Disability Alliance
        formed.
1975   Chronically Sick and Disabled Persons Amendment Act.
        White Paper, *Better Services for the Mentally Ill*, indicates
        shift from institutional to community care.
1976   Jack Nicholson film, *One Flew Over the Cuckoo's Nest*, about
        mental illness.
1977   Beech Tree House, Hertfordshire, established by Spastics
        Society (later Scope) for severely mentally disabled
        children.
1978   Disability Information and Advice Line formed out of the
        Derbyshire Coalition of Disabled People.
1981   Education Act recognizes Special Educational Needs.
        Disabled Peoples International set up, leads to formation of
        British Council of Organisations of Disabled People.
        Care in the Community Green Paper recommends
        community care and hospital closures.
        Television documentary *Silent Minority* shown at peak
        viewing time.
1985   Voluntary Organisations for Anti-Discrimination Legislation
        formed.
1986   Disabled Persons (Services, Consultation and
        Representation) Act gives disabled people more involvement
        in local provision.
1990   National Health and Community Care Act.
1992   Report by BCODP on *Disabled People in Britain and
        Discrimination*.
        Jonathon Zito murdered by a paranoid schizophrenic
        outpatient.
1994   Zito Trust established. Publication of *Finding a Place:
        A Review of Mental Health Services for Adults*.
        Code of Practice for Special Educational Needs.
1995   Disability Discrimination Act focuses on direct
        discrimination in employment, services and sale of land.
        Carers (Recognition and Services) Act. Mental Health
        (Patients in the Community) Act.
1996   Community Care (Direct Payments) Act.
1997   Government agrees to amend Disability Discrimination Act
        and sets up a taskforce.
1998   Audit Commission Report, *Home Alone: The Housing Aspects
        of Community Care*.

1999	Audit Commission Report, *Children in Mind: Child and Adolescent Mental Health Services.*
	Disability Rights Commission Act amends Disability Discrimination Act, replaces National Disability Council with Disability Rights Commission.
2000	Audit Commission Report, *Forget Me Not: Mental Health Services for Older People.*
2001	Special Educational Needs and Disability Act.
	Valuing People: A New Strategy for Learning Disability for the 21st Century first White Paper on learning disabilities since 1971.
2002	Private Hire Vehicle Act.
	'Well?' Scottish Executive National Programme for Improving the Mental Health and Well-Being of Scotland's Population.
2003	Start of 3-year Royal College of Psychiatrists study of people who previously lived in mental hospitals.
2004	MENCAP launches 'Ask Mencap' website.
	Government launches New Deal for the Disabled, all businesses required to make 'reasonable changes' to their premises.
2005	Disability Discrimination Act.
2006	Disability Equality Duty.
2008	Disability Rights Commission merged into Equalities and Human Rights Commission.

INTRODUCTION

From at least medieval times in Britain and other countries, certain disabilities, in particular being blind, deaf or dumb, were regarded as 'natural' rather than medical conditions – 'God-given', as medieval Christians would have said. It was taken for granted that people with these and other conditions should participate as fully as possible in everyday life. For centuries, what training and support was available for disabled people in the United Kingdom was provided through voluntary, often religious, institutions, within families and through the Poor Relief system.

When the first steps were taken towards compulsory education for children in England and Wales in the Education Act 1870, increasing numbers of disabled children were in classrooms alongside other children, although the precise legal obligations of local education boards and parents remained vague. A clause in the 1870 Act required boards to provide sufficient accommodation in schools for all children who were resident in the district, but another clause exempted children from attending school if there was 'some reasonable cause'. From 1880, local authorities were required to provide education suited to the special needs of children whose disabilities were deemed to make it difficult for them to be educated in the same way as others, but the exemption clause remained. The 1893 Elementary Education (Blind and

Deaf Children) Act established that blind children were to receive compulsory education from the age of five to 16, and deaf children from age seven,
although local boards varied in the rigour with which they implemented the
law.[1] Throughout the nineteenth and early twentieth centuries, it was mainly
voluntary institutions that assisted blind, deaf or dumb adults to function
as independently as possible. From 1920, poorer blind people who were
'unable to perform work for which eyesight was essential' were eligible for
a means-tested pension at age 50, rather than at 70.

By contrast, people defined as 'feeble-minded' or 'lunatic', the conventional terms used for centuries, were traditionally regarded as untrainable
and uneducable, and given little more than basic care in institutions or in
the community. Views began to change from the late eighteenth century
on, when medical practitioners in France and Britain began to realize that,
with suitable support, people with some conditions could be 'cured', or at
least enabled to acquire skills and lead fuller lives than had previously been
thought possible – not necessarily by medical means, but with social support
and training. Some were recognized to require a combination of medical
and social support, although the boundary between the two has never been
clear cut. From 1899, the Elementary Education (Defective and Epileptic
Children) Act required local authorities to provide education to children
suffering from certain mental disabilities.[2]

Definitions of disability in both official and everyday discourse have
shifted and expanded markedly since 1945, and especially since the 1960s.
In 1945, disabled people were broadly defined as those suffering from visible conditions, such as blindness, deafness, multiple sclerosis or Down's
Syndrome, and those using wheelchairs or walking appliances. However, the
term was increasingly applied to a wider, sometimes idiosyncratic, range of
conditions. As recently as the 1960s, homosexuality was defined by medical
specialists and some in wider society as a disability, and its sufferers likened
to 'cripples' (see Chapter 6). In the recent past, mental illnesses, particularly
depression, have become recognized as disabilities to a far greater extent
than before. As awareness of, and sensitivity to, a wider range of forms
of disability has grown, there have been changes in the language associated with disability: words such as 'cripple', 'mentally deficient', 'backward'
'mongol' and 'spastic' have become far less commonly used over the past
20 years and are now deemed offensive. For example, the organization now
known as MENCAP was formed in 1946 as the Association of Parents of
Backward Children. However, an attempt in the 1990s to popularize the
term 'differently abled' as a more positive replacement for 'disabled' appears
not to have taken off. Changes in language have mainly been the outcome
of campaigning by and for disabled people for greater visibility, respect and
equal treatment.

In what follows, physical and mental disability are discussed separately
because the historical experience of these two broad categories of people
has differed, although some legislative changes have applied to all forms of
disability.

PHYSICAL DISABILITY

INTRODUCTION

Before World War II, disabled people were mainly the responsibility of their families or of the myriad charities devoted to specific needs, regardless of the cause of their disability. The only official provision was the very basic, stigmatizing, safety net for the destitute, Public Assistance (established in 1930 to replace the Poor Law, which had performed this role since 1601). The first state pensions for the blind were introduced in 1920 (see above). Historically, most disabilities were perceived as social as much as medical. Over the twentieth century, as medicine increased its capacity to diagnose and, less frequently, to cure, an increasing number of conditions were defined medically as disabilities, rather than as 'natural', if unfortunate, experiences.

Immediately after World War II, partly in response to the number of disabled ex-servicemen and civilian victims of bombing of all ages, new measures were introduced to address certain aspects of disability. The Education Act 1944 stated that disabled children should be educated wherever possible alongside their peers in mainstream education, although there were no strenuous efforts to implement this and separate education remained the norm. Eleven separate categories of children were identified as disabled: the blind, partially sighted, deaf, partially deaf, 'delicate', diabetic, educationally subnormal, epileptic, maladjusted, physically handicapped, and those with speech defects.

The Disabled Persons Employment Act 1944 stated that employers of more than 20 workers must employ at least 3 per cent of their workforce from the newly created national Disabled Persons Register. The National Health Service Act 1946 (implemented in 1948) provided free health care for all, irrespective of disability, for the first time. The National Assistance Act 1948, stipulated that local authorities should provide for disabled people within the community. Such measures sought to give disabled people similar opportunities to the rest of the population. The 1950s saw the expansion of services and institutions for disabled people, while the 1960s saw a shift from institutional to community care policies. Throughout this time, charities continued to provide services, supplementing the often very basic state provision.

THE 1960s – A HIGHER-PROFILE ISSUE

In the 1960s, disability, like other sources of inequality, became a more prominent public issue. There was growing awareness that the post-war welfare state had not removed poverty and inequality. Although the absolute, miserable poverty of the early twentieth century had largely vanished, it was becoming clear that, as society became more prosperous, many people were being left behind in what was defined as 'relative poverty' – unable to share the essential features of everyday living that most of the population now took for granted. This realization was prompted above all by the 'rediscovery of poverty' by researchers at the London School of Economics (see Chapter 1).[3] The groups they found to be suffering the most acute poverty were children, especially in single-parent households, and older and disabled people.

One outcome of the 'rediscovery of poverty' and of cultural changes becoming evident in the 1960s – including a more educated, prosperous, less deferential population and more assertive media – was the formation of activist groups, often more radical and outspoken in their demands for change than the charities that preceded them (see Chapters 1, 2, 4, 5 and 6).[4] One of these was the Disablement Income Group (DIG), formed in Surrey in 1965 by Megan du Boisson. Suffering the early stages of multiple sclerosis, she discovered there were no state benefits available for those such as herself – married women who were not in paid work and had not made adequate national insurance contributions – whom she referred to as 'the civilian disabled'. They could apply for the means-tested Supplementary Benefit if they had financial problems, but they had no rights to benefits to help meet the costs of their disability or chronic sickness. DIG campaigned for such benefits and sponsored research such as Mavis Hyman's *The Extra Costs of Disabled Living* (1977), Richard Stowell's *Disabled People on Supplementary Benefits* (1980) and Judith Buckle's *Mental Handicap Costs More* (1984).

DIG Scotland was formed in 1966 by another disabled woman, Margaret Blackwood, who was inspired by du Boisson's work. Once disability benefits had been achieved (see below), DIG Scotland introduced a free Welfare Benefits Information and Advisory Service for disabled people and carers. DIG Scotland continues to be active, but DIG has ceased to be active in England. The campaigners focused on the failure of society to recognize the specific needs of disabled people and the inadequacies of existing government policies and institutions.

With the help of sympathetic MPs, these activists played an important role in persuading the Labour government to introduce the Chronically Sick and Disabled Persons Act, 1970, which required all local authorities to register disabled people and publicize the services available to them. A full range of cash benefits was introduced for them and their carers, but they were under-resourced and means-tested. The Act also encouraged, but did not adequately fund, expanded community-based provision, such as home helps and day centres. This was reinforced by the Chronically Sick and Disabled Persons Amendment Act 1975 when Labour returned to power, having been out of office in 1970–4. But both Acts were advisory rather than compulsory and had only a limited impact on provision by local authorities.

In 1971, a long-term benefit, Invalidity Benefit (IVB), was introduced to replace earnings. This was available only to people who had paid sufficient National Insurance contributions, excluding, for example, women who were not in employment due to caring responsibilities, Gypsies and Travellers and many immigrants who did not have full contribution records, and those already incapacitated from regular work by disability. In 1975, such people became eligible for a means-tested Non-Contributory Invalidity Pension (NCIP), since 1990 named Severe Disablement Allowance (SDA). In 1970, 1973 and 1976 respectively, the higher- and lower-rate Attendance Allowance (AA) and Mobility Allowance (MA) were introduced to cover some impairment-induced expenses, such as transport costs. In 1975, Invalid Care Allowance became available for people of working age who acted as personal assistants (carers) to the disabled. However, it was not available to married women caring for close relatives, people over state pension age (who, together, were the great majority of assistants, very often of their partners or children), or to personal assistants of disabled people not receiving AA. The allowances were low in relation to average earnings. In 1986, a judgment by the European Court of Justice forced the government to extend eligibility to married women who were caring for relatives.

CAMPAIGNS AGAINST DISCRIMINATION

In 1974, the Disability Alliance was established, aimed principally at securing a national disability income as of right and improving the living standards of disabled people. It remains in existence and publishes an annual *Disability Rights Handbook*. The Disability Information and Advice Line (DIAL) emerged from the Derbyshire Coalition of Disabled People in 1978. DIAL UK is now a nationally organized network of approximately 130 local disability information and advice services, run by and for disabled people. The 1960s and 1970s saw a growth in activism by disabled people, as by other groups suffering inequality, focusing primarily on income support and services.

Through the 1970s and 1980s, activists were increasingly vocal about discrimination in everyday life and, in particular, about the need and capability of disabled people to control their own lives, and to live in the community rather than in residential institutions, in environments structured to support rather than obstruct independent living. They aimed to convince government and public opinion that disability in itself was not the sole cause of inequality. Among other things, they challenged the depersonalized everyday usage 'the disabled', substituting 'disabled people'. One researcher summed up the type of change needed in the public consciousness by recasting the questions used in a major government survey of disabled people.[5] Where the survey asked, 'Does your health problem/disability make it difficult for you to travel by bus?' he substituted, 'Do poorly designed buses make it difficult for someone with your impairment to use them?'[6]

In 1979, the Labour government was persuaded by disabled people and disability organizations to set up the Committee on Restrictions Against Disabled People (CORAD). Its aims were to establish the extent of discrimination and make proposals to prevent it. In 1982, it reported widespread discrimination against disabled people, such as in employment and access to buildings and transport, and recommended comprehensive anti-discrimination legislation. The Conservative government was unconvinced, and the 1980s saw cuts in community services for disabled people, as for older people, and increased pressure on charities rather than government to provide for their needs. However, charities lacked the resources and coordination to provide these services systematically.

The campaign for anti-discrimination legislation intensified nationally and internationally. In 1981, Disabled Peoples International (DPI) was established and led to the formation of the British Council of Organisations of Disabled People (BCODP). The first attempt to place anti-discrimination legislation on the statute book was made, unsuccessfully, in 1982, by Labour MP Jack Ashley, who was himself deaf. In 1985, Voluntary Organisations for Anti-Discrimination Legislation (VOADL) was formed, later and still known as Rights Now! At its heart were organizations set up and run by disabled people, but with the active support of the older disability charities. The Disabled Persons Representation (Services, Consultation and Representation) Act 1986, gave disabled people the potential for more input into the quality of local provision. It required local authority social service departments to assess the needs of all disabled people who requested services. This included providing, where need was identified, help in accessing telephone, television, radio and library facilities, holidays, recreation, education, transport to and from services, and occupational, social and cultural facilities. Disabled people were defined by the Act as being: 'Blind, deaf or dumb or who suffer from mental disorder of any description or who are substantially and permanently handicapped by their illness, injury or congenital deformity'.

Between 1982 and 1993, 15 Private Members' Bills were introduced by MPs and Peers, including Lord Morris of Manchester (Alf Morris, who as a Labour MP played an important role in guiding through the 1970 Chronically Sick and Disabled Persons Act) and Jack (now Lord) Ashley. Meanwhile, local and national organizations of disabled people worked to persuade local authorities and sometimes health authorities to provide funding that otherwise would have been spent on residential care or community services, to enable disabled people to employ personal assistants to meet their specific needs. Technically, this was illegal, but by 1992, about 40 per cent of authorities in England and eight out of ten London boroughs had introduced schemes of this kind.[7]

DISABILITY DISCRIMINATION LEGISLATION

From 1988, the Joseph Rowntree Foundation (JRF) funded research in which disabled people were directly involved, aimed at finding means to facilitate independent living for disabled, including older, people. This included research by BCODP into the evidence for and effects of discrimination, published in 1992 as *Disabled People in Britain and Discrimination*. The findings increased pressure on the government to act. Greatly influenced by the American Disabilities Act 1990, a prototype Civil Rights (Disabled Persons) Bill was introduced to parliament in 1991. Although defeated, it was reintroduced in 1992 and 1993. The Conservative government argued that it would place excessive burdens on businesses if they were required to take measures against discriminatory employment practices. However, it was aware of the growing strength of European anti-discrimination law. In addition, disabled people took to the streets to demonstrate against inaccessible transport and inadequate benefits. Plentiful media images of demonstrators in wheelchairs effectively shamed the government, which reluctantly introduced the Disability Discrimination Act (DDA) 1995.[8] The Centre for Disability Studies (CDS), an interdisciplinary centre for teaching and research in the field of disability studies at the University of Leeds, also played a major part in helping to achieve the DDA. Established in 1990 as a research unit for the BCODP, it continued the work of the former Disability Research Unit (DRU), much assisted by the JRF. It continues to be an important component of the disabled persons' movement, publishing research on disability.

The DDA focused on direct discrimination in employment, provision of services to the public and the selling of land; education was excluded. It established the National Disability Council (NDA), to advise government on disability issues, but it lacked the powers of the Equal Opportunities Commission (see Chapter 5) and the Commission for Racial Equality (see Chapter 2) to act against discrimination. The Act defined a 'disabled person' as 'someone who has a physical or mental impairment that has a substantial and long-term adverse effect on his or her ability to carry out normal day-to-day activities'. For the purposes of the Act, 'substantial' meant neither minor nor trivial; 'long-term' meant that the effect of the impairment had lasted, or was likely to last, for at least 12 months. 'Normal day-to-day activities' included eating, washing, walking and shopping. Ability to perform these must be affected by impairments to one of the 'capacities' listed in the Act, which include mobility, manual dexterity, speech, hearing, seeing and memory. Diverse conditions, including hay fever and a tendency to set fires, were specifically excluded. This definition remains in force, to assist adjudicating bodies in deciding whether a person is disabled for the purposes of the DDA. In 2005, the definition was amended, removing the requirement that a mental illness 'should be clinically well-recognized'. People with HIV, cancer and multiple sclerosis were now deemed to be covered by the DDA from the point of diagnosis, rather than from the point at which the condition had an adverse effect on their ability to carry out normal day-to-day activities.

The DDA brought substantially larger numbers of people within the official definition of disability, perhaps blurring the strict boundary some believed to exist between those who were or were not disabled. There is no clear evidence as to whether, or how, the legislation has affected public attitudes towards disabled people. Some activists fear that it may have diminished support for the campaigns they still think necessary for more effective guarantees of equality for all disabled people, due to a general belief that the legislation has already delivered equality. However, inequalities remain – for example, some people with learning difficulties are not covered by the Act.

As activism among disabled people grew, there was some friction between charities and organizations run *for* disabled people and those run *by* disabled people. The establishment of the NDA, with such limited powers, was strongly opposed by organizations of disabled people such as the BCODP, but six of Britain's older and largest charities for disabled people, including SCOPE, MENCAP and MIND, agreed to support it and were less outspoken on the need for anti-discrimination legislation.

The DDA was of major symbolic importance, but it lacked teeth. In 1997, the incoming Labour government agreed, under further activist pressure, to amend it, setting up a Disability Rights Task Force to monitor the legislation's implementation. Its recommendations led in 1999 to the establishment of the Disability Rights Commission (DRC), to replace the NDA, with a positive brief to monitor and promote equality for disabled people. At the same time, public service providers were required to make 'reasonable adjustments' to meet the needs of disabled people, such as providing information in alternative formats (for instance, large print or Braille) and equipment or support to use a service. In May 1998, an Audit Commission report, *Home Alone: The Housing Aspects of Community Care*, recommended considerable improvements in community care for disabled people, including housing provision, and provided case studies of good practice.

The JRF continued to support research designed to provide the government with evidence that independent living was possible for disabled people. In the late 1990s, it established a Task Force to investigate the disincentives to employment for disabled people due to means-tested benefits and charges for community care services: their incomes could fall if they moved into low-paid employment and ceased to be eligible for certain benefits. Research evidence combined with lobbying convinced the government in 2001 to discount earned income in means tests for direct payments or community care services for disabled people.

The Special Educational Needs and Disability Act 2001, extended the obligation to assist independent living and avoid all forms of discrimination to all educational institutions and the youth service. The Private Hire Vehicle Act 2002, extended anti-discrimination into this further sphere. From December 2006, all forms of public transport are required to make provision to enable disabled people to make full use of the service. Under Labour's New Deal for the Disabled, from 2004 all businesses were required to make reasonable changes to meet the needs of disabled people, for example by adapting premises and removing physical barriers such as steps that made buildings inaccessible in a wheelchair. These measures were consolidated in the Disability Discrimination Act 2005.

A number of law court decisions sponsored by the DRC from 2000, at British and European level, including on the definition of disability, pushed back the boundaries of inequality in employment, goods and services and education.[9] Research and action funded by the JRF influenced further developments in services. This included persuading the government in 2003 to commit to a national protocol on support services for mentally and physically disabled parents, to bring an end to the excessive and inappropriate burden of caring that had fallen on many children and young people. JRF continues to fund research into means to support independent living for disabled people.

In 2005, the Cabinet Office Strategy Unit published a detailed report and proposals for a 20-year programme designed to promote independent living, *Improving the Life Chances of Disabled People*.[10] It outlined a new approach, 'personalized according to individual need or circumstances', involving listening to disabled people and acknowledging their expertise concerning how their own needs might best be met, in order to maximize 'the choice and control that people have over how their additional requirements are met', and to provide 'people with security and certainty about what level of support is available'.

In 2006, the DRC confirmed these improvements regarding employment:

• 51 per cent of disabled people were in work in 2005, compared with 46.6 per cent in 2000
• in higher education, the total number of disabled students rose from 86,250 in 2000/1 to 121,080 in 2003/4
• the number of disabled people receiving direct payments rose from 5,500 in 2001 to nearly 20,000 by 2005
• by 2005, 2.9 per cent of employees in the Senior Civil Service were disabled people, compared with 1.5 per cent in 1998
• calls to the DRC Helpline – mainly from people requiring more information about their rights under the DDA – rose from 65,000 in 2000/1 to 124,000 in 2004/5.[11]

In October 2006, the commission also recommended that the government extend the legal definition of disability to enable more mentally and physically disabled people to make discrimination claims. Based on consultation in which four out of five respondents called for change, the commission argued that the definition within the Disability Discrimination Act should be extended to include everyone who has, or is perceived to have, an impairment, including impairments that affect people for periods of less than 12 months, such as depression.

In December 2006, the Disability Equality Duty (DED) placed a legal duty on all public sector organizations to promote equal opportunities for disabled people. Organizations including libraries, hospitals, schools and colleges, police forces and National Health Service (NHS) trusts were required to consider the impact of their work on disabled people and take action to counter inequality due to disability. The DED was intended to ensure that disabled people not only had improved employment opportunities, but that they would not encounter discrimination when using services, and to promote positive attitudes towards disabled people in everyday life.

In 2007, the Equality and Human Rights Commission took over responsibility for disability from the DRC.

BCODP played a major role in bringing about these changes. It now represented 70 groups run by disabled people in the United Kingdom, with a total membership of about 350,000. Through its membership of the DPI, it also worked at international level and was recognized by the United Nations.

CONCLUSION

The number of physically disabled people with high public profiles is probably greater now than at any time since 1945, and may have contributed to public acceptability of anti-discrimination legislation. The success of David Blunkett in overcoming blindness to attain high office in government may have provided a role model for other disabled people and helped to reduce popular stereotyping of the limited capacities of disabled people. The Cambridge University physicist and mathematician Stephen Hawking, who has Lou Gehrigs Disease and is confined to a wheelchair and speaks through a computer, may be a less equivocal role model of very high achievement by a severely disabled person. In the sporting world, increased television coverage and publicity involving the Paralympics has made a household name and role model of Dame Tanni Grey Thompson. This positive image of disabled people in sport has been reinforced by the publicity given to British successes in the 2008 Paralympics, and the award in 2009 of Member of the Order of the British Empire (MBE) to Eleanor Simmonds, double swimming gold medallist and the youngest person ever to receive an honour of this kind. However, these successes still have a lower profile than performances in the conventional Olympics.

The disabled artist Alison Lapper, who as a result of the medical condition phocomelia was born without arms and with shortened legs, has become a high-profile figure in a different field of activity. A sculpture of her naked body, eight months pregnant, was temporarily placed in Trafalgar Square in September 2005 as one of a succession of temporary art works, alongside more conventional statues of military men, something that was inconceivable until very recently. Lapper has commented:

> I regard it as a modern tribute to femininity, disability and motherhood. It is so rare to see disability in everyday life – let alone naked, pregnant and proud. The sculpture makes the ultimate statement about disability – that it can be as beautiful and valid a form of being as any other.[12]

MENTAL DISABILITY

INTRODUCTION: BREAKING THE SILENCE

Mental illness and impairment were sources of severe social stigma in the 1940s and earlier. In the early 1940s, one mother of a handicapped child who attempted to contact other parents of handicapped children to form a playgroup had her advertisement refused by her local newspaper, due to the 'shame and disgrace' associated with mental handicap. In 1946, the Association of Parents of Backward Children (renamed National Society for Mentally Handicapped Children in 1955, then MENCAP in 1969) was formed by Judy Fryd and other parents who were concerned about the lack of support available to them in caring for their children. In the same year, the National Association for Mental Health (later MIND) was formed.

From July 1948, the National Health Service took over responsibility for mental health from county councils and boroughs. It inherited more than one hundred therapeutic asylums, or 'mental hospitals', each with an average of 1,000 patients. By 1953, almost half of all NHS hospital beds were used for care of mental illness or mental impairment. In 1954, a Royal Commission on the Law Relating to Mental Illness and Mental Deficiency (the Percy Commission) was set up, out of concern about the numbers of patients in mental hospitals, fears that many were wrongly confined for long periods, and concern about quality of treatment. It was also the year in which Jack Archer, a character in the popular BBC Radio series *The Archers*, was admitted to a mental hospital with depression, then a rare admission in the popular media of the existence of such an illness. In May 1957, the Report of the Royal Commission made the innovative statement that mental disorder should be regarded and treated 'in much the same way as physical illness and disability'. In 1958, the BBC TV programme *The Hurt Mind* was shown, the first television programme to be made about a mental hospital.

By 1959, only 12 per cent of admissions to mental hospitals were compulsory, compared with much larger numbers before the NHS. The trend, following the recommendations of the Royal Commission, was towards shorter periods of in-patient treatment and more outpatient treatment and community care. Whereas in 1930 there had been almost no outpatients, by 1959 there were 144,100 attendances at outpatient clinics. The Mental Health Act 1959, building on the Percy Report, aimed 'to allow admissions for psychiatric reasons to be, wherever possible, as informal as those for physical reasons' and 'to make councils responsible for the social care of people who did not need in-patient medical treatment', in order to enable mentally ill people to live, as far as possible, in the community.[13] The 1960s saw further inroads into the silence about mental health in the media, through its treatment by television current affairs programmes such as *Man Alive*, and a newspaper feature by the *Observer* reporter John Gale about his own illness.

Between 1967 and 1969, there were allegations of misconduct at various hospitals, including Farleigh in Bristol and Whittingham in Preston, Lancashire, which resulted in 1972 in the establishment of a Health Service Commissioner (Ombudsman) to investigate complaints of individual ill-treatment. At the same time, the Guild of Teachers of Backward Children and others were pressing the government to improve educational provision for such children.[14] In 1970, the Conservative Government introduced the Education (Handicapped Children) Act, following the failure of a Labour Bill when the 1970 election brought an end to the parliamentary session. The 1970 Act gave Local Education Authorities (LEAs), from April 1971, responsibility for the education of all 'mentally handicapped' children, regardless of the severity of their condition. For the first time, all children, whatever their abilities, were defined as educable. This helps to explain why fewer children went into residential care in the 1970s.

In the late 1960s and 70s, as in other areas of inequality, campaigning groups grew in number, professionalism and public profile. David Ennals, a former Labour Minister, became MIND's first campaign director in 1971. In March 1972, 800 people met at Sidney Webb College in central London to discuss the threatened closure by the Regional Hospital Board of the thera-peutic centre Paddington Day Clinic, due to the opening of a psychiatric unit at a nearby general hospital. Users of the clinic believed that its methods increased their understanding of, and capacity to control, their problems, and they feared the new unit would seek to suppress and medicalize their symptoms. The meeting led to the formation of the Mental Patients Union in 1973. In 1972, the National Schizophrenia Fellowship was formed (changing its name in 2002 to Rethink). The Scottish Union of Mental Patients (SUMP) was also formed in 1972.

CARE AND INTEGRATION IN THE COMMUNITY

A White Paper proposing improved services for mentally handicapped peo-ple was published in 1971, but the economic crisis from 1973 led to major cuts in health and welfare capital expenditure both by the Conservative and the Labour governments, which followed in 1974–9. In 1973, surveys of the views of patients in seven mental hospitals were published as *Psychiatric Hospitals Viewed by their Patients*, despite doubts as to whether such surveys could usefully be conducted with the mentally ill.[15] The findings reinforced criticism of the hospitals, as did a further 11 surveys published in 1977.[16]

In 1975, the White Paper *Better Services for the Mentally Ill* was intro-duced in parliament by the Labour Minister of Health and Social Security, Barbara Castle. It was a long-term, strategic document, describing the direction the government wished services to take, prefaced by a statement that little progress could be made until the economic situation improved. It emphasized the need to provide a comprehensive range of community services in place of mental hospitals:

Our main aim is not the closure or rundown of mental illness hospitals as such; but rather to replace them with a local and better range of facilities. It will not normally be possible for a mental hospital to be closed until the full range of facilities described has been provided throughout its catchment area and has shown itself capable of providing for newly arising patients a comprehensive service independent of the mental hospital. Moreover, even then, it will not be possible to close the hospital until it is no longer required for the long stay patients admitted to its care before the local services came into operation.[17]

This signalled a further shift from hospital to community services. Between 1970 and 1975, the population of mental hospitals fell from 107,977 to 87,321; that of mental handicap hospitals, as they were then known, from 55,434 to 49,683.[18]

In 1977, Beech Tree House in Hertfordshire was established by the Spastics Society (founded 1953, renamed SCOPE in 1994, in view of the very negative popular connotations of the word 'spastic') to demonstrate that even the most severely disabled children could be successfully educated, given the appropriate resources and a supportive approach. Such revelations contributed to the establishment by the government of a committee, chaired by Dame Mary Warnock, to enquire into the education of 'handicapped children and young people'. This drew on research on the ill-effects on individuals of labelling and of special provision, and recommended that disability should be perceived as 'a continuum of special educational need rather than discrete categories of handicap', embracing 'children with significant learning difficulties and emotional or behavioural disorders as well as those with disabilities of mind or body'.[19] The result was a much broader definition of the needs of such children. The 1981 Education Act introduced the category of Special Educational Needs (SEN), which led to the identification of differing levels of need and support. These were set out in a 1994 Code of Practice following the 1993 Education Act.

In July 1981, the Conservative government issued its Care in the Community Green Paper. This built on the work since 1976 of a Conservative Party Policy Group, chaired by Cecil Parkinson MP, which reported in 1979, strongly recommending community care and further hospital closures, linked to financial incentives for councils to make community provision. An edited summary of the Parkinson Report was published in 1981 as *The Right Approach to Mental Health*. The 1983 Mental Health Act followed. This, the preamble stated, dealt with 'the reception, care and treatment of mentally disordered patients, the management of their property and other related matters'. It provided a legal definition of the types of mental health problem it was intended to cover, which fell into four categories: severe mental impairment, mental impairment, psychopathic disorder and mental illness. It made clear that people must not be deemed to have a form of mental disorder 'by reason only of promiscuity or other immoral conduct, sexual deviancy or dependency on alcohol and drugs', as had occurred earlier in the century, for example to some unmarried mothers and, more recently, to homosexuals (see Chapter 6). Campaigning by and on behalf of gay people and lone mothers helped to drive this change. The Act laid down regulations governing admission to and discharge from mental hospitals, consent to treatment, arrangements for aftercare and the circumstances in which close relatives or social workers could be allowed to control the affairs of a mentally ill person.

Also in 1981, the television documentary *Silent Minority* was shown at peak viewing time, a behind-the-scenes view of two hospitals for mentally handicapped people, St Lawrence's in Surrey and Borocourt in Reading, Berkshire. It contrasted the understaffed wards at St Lawrence's with conditions at Beechtree House (see above), suggesting that the intensive education of children in a small unit like Beechtree House prevented their becoming disturbed and frightened like those at Borocourt, who were kept in a wire-enclosed compound during daylight hours.

The 1986 Disabled Persons' (Services Consultation and Representation) Act (see above) continued the policy of encouraging community provision for mentally as well as for physically disabled people. The 1990 National Health and Community Care Act required social services departments to establish units to inspect services, establish complaints procedures and prepare Community Care Plans. From 1991, users became entitled to a Community Care assessment of needs. Nevertheless, in 1992, Jonathon Zito was murdered by a paranoid schizophrenic person who had been released from hospital with inadequate community care. The Zito Trust was established in 1994 to campaign for reform of mental health policy and law, and 'to provide advice and support to victims of mentally disordered offenders', as it continues to do.

In October 1994, *Finding a Place: A Review of Mental Health Services for Adults* was published by the Department of Health, followed in 1995 by the Carers (Recognition and Services) Act, which provided for assessment of the capacity of carers to provide suitable care. Also in 1995, the Mental Health (Patients in the Community) Act responded to growing public and media concern about the adequacy of community care for mentally ill people. It made provision for certain mentally ill patients to receive aftercare, under supervision, after leaving hospital, and tightened the law concerning patients who were absent without leave or on leave of absence from hospital. Most importantly, from 1995, the Disability Discrimination Act (see above) applied to mentally as well as to physically disabled people. The 1996 Community Care (Direct Payments) Act enabled local authorities to make payments to disabled people to help them buy community services.

The Audit Commission's 1998 report *Home Alone*, which recommended improved community care, referred to mentally as well as physically disabled people. It was followed in September 1999 by a further report, *Children in Mind: Child and Adolescent Mental Health Services*, which was again critical of existing services. In January 2000, another Audit Commission Report, *Forget Me Not: Mental Health Services for Older People*, again criticized the inadequacy of services for a large group experiencing mental health problems, a group that grows as the number of older people increases (see Chapter 1). The report recommended that local authority health and social services departments should work more closely and submit annual joint plans. It found wide variation in the provision of services, and often patchy and uncoordinated support for users and their assistants.

The JRF again funded pioneering training and support of people with learning difficulties to research and evaluate the experiences of people like themselves as they moved from institutional care to living in the community. This and other projects had a significant impact on the national strategy on learning disability the government was developing, in particular influencing the inclusion of children.[20] The document published in March 2001 as *Valuing People: A New Strategy for Learning Disability for the 21st Century* was the first White Paper concerning people with learning disabilities since *Better Services for the Mentally Handicapped* in June 1971. It emphasized the need for cooperation between public services to improve the life chances of people of all ages with learning disabilities, and their integration into the mainstream whenever possible. In October 2002, in a similar vein, the Scottish Executive introduced *Well? A National Programme for improving the Mental Health and Well-Being of Scotland's Population*.

MENTAL DISABILITY AMONG THE MINORITY ETHNIC POPULATION

An area of continuing concern is that of differences among ethnic groups in their experiences of mental disability and of treatment and care.[21] In England and Wales, ethnic origin has only recently been recorded in official statistics relating to this field. However, much existing research shows that certain groups, notably African Caribbean, African and Irish people, are disproportionately represented in psychiatric hospitals.[22] They are more than twice as likely to be hospitalised for mental distress as their White British counterparts.[23] Research carried out at two psychiatric hospitals in the 1990s found that Black people were over-represented among compulsorily detained patients, compared with their numbers in the local population. Of 224 patients admitted to one hospital, 106 (51 per cent) were Black, 16 (8 per cent) Asian and 86 (41 per cent) White. Census data from 1991 showed that 71 per cent of the population of the area studied was White (including the 5.2 per cent who were Irish), 17.2 per cent was Black, 9.2 per cent Asian, and 2.7 per cent classified themselves as 'other'.[24] One report stated that Afro-Caribbean men have 4.3 times and women 3.9 times the rate of White people for first admission with a diagnosis of schizophrenia.[25] Another study of more than one hundred Afro-Caribbean and African users of mental health services in Britain found that almost half had been diagnosed with schizophrenia.[26]

Research in the 1990s suggested that, although more people of Black Caribbean origin were treated for psychosis, this may not indicate that they are more likely to suffer from illness of this kind.[27] There are indications that Afro-Caribbean and other Black people with psychosis are being admitted to hospital for treatment because their initial referral to mental health services arises from contact with the police or other services. This occurs despite the fact that they are less likely than White people to show evidence of self-harm and are no more likely to be aggressive to others before admission to a mental health hospital.[28] Research also suggests that, despite the lack of evidence, staff in mental health hospitals are more likely to perceive them as potentially dangerous. It is possible that Afro-Caribbean people are more likely to be diagnosed with psychosis because of bias among those who treat them.[29]

Table 7.1 Estimated annual prevalence of psychosis by gender (percentage)[30]

	White	Irish	Caribbean	Bangladeshi	Indian	Pakistani
Men	1.0	1.0	1.6	0.6	0.9	1.4
Women	0.7	1.0	1.7	0.6	1.3	1.3
Total	0.8	1.0	1.6	0.6	1.1	1.3

Source: Fourth National Survey of Ethnic Minorities (FNS).

Psychotic illness affects a very small portion of the population – about one person in 200 in the United Kingdom.[31] Because of the small numbers, it is difficult to produce statistics that accurately reflect differences among ethnic groups.[32] The figures available show a higher rate of psychotic illness for Black Caribbean people than for White people, with Black Caribbean people twice as likely as White people to be diagnosed with psychosis. However, the difference shown in this 2002 study is much lower than previous studies have indicated. The study also showed that those from a poorer background were more likely to suffer from a psychotic illness. This was the case for both Black and White people. It also emerged that those living in inner cities seemed at higher risk.[33] These findings suggest that mental illness may be related to living conditions rather than ethnicity or race.

    Studies in the 1990s showed that Black people were more likely to receive 'physical' treatments (drugs and electro-convulsive therapy) than their White counterparts.[34] African people were likely to be given higher doses of medication in comparison with other groups, and stood a greater chance of receiving this by intramuscular means, which can be very painful.[35] Black people were less likely to be offered counselling, other talking treatments or non-medical interventions than White people, and were rarely offered counselling in any language but English.[36] There are no good statistics on the treatments most often given to Asian, South-east Asian or Irish people.

CONCLUSION

The continued inequalities experienced by those suffering from mental disability have been highlighted by high-profile figures such as Stephen Fry, Adam Ant and Terry Pratchett discussing their personal difficulties, suggesting how little public attitudes have changed, even towards relatively privileged people. Asked by an audience of psychiatric students and practitioners at a seminar on bipolar disorder at St Andrew's University why he had made a television programme about his experiences, Fry stated:

> I'm in a rare and privileged position of being able to help address the whole business of stigma, and why it is that the rest of society finds it so easy to wrinkle their noses, cross over, or block their ears when confronted with an illness of the mind and of the mood – especially when we reach out with such sympathy towards diseases of the liver or other organs that don't affect who we are and how we feel in quite such devastating complexity.[37]

Adam Ant's documentary about his experiences of bipolar disorder, *The Madness of Prince Charming*, appeared on Channel 4 TV in July 2003 and was one of the station's most-watched programmes that year.

In 2008, the author Terry Pratchett announced that he had been diagnosed with Alzheimer's disease, in a deliberate attempt to draw public attention to the extent of this disease among older people and the inadequacy of provision for it.

Research suggests that the NHS is still providing sub-standard treatment for people with learning disabilities and long-term mental health conditions. An 18-month investigation by the Disability Rights Commission, published in 2006 and the largest of its kind, based on examination of eight million medical records, found that people with learning difficulties and long-term mental health problems died five to ten years younger on average than other citizens. The commission reported that disabled people and those with severe mental problems were unlikely to receive health checks that were as thorough as those provided for other patients. The commission's chairman, Sir Bert Massie, stated:

> Tackling health inequalities is high on the government agenda, yet there has been a deeply inadequate response from health services and government to target these groups which, in some cases, is compounded by a dangerous complacent attitude and a lazy fatalism that they 'just do' die younger. This is completely unacceptable.[38]

In January 2009, Alan Johnson, the Health Secretary, set up a confidential inquiry into why at least six people with serious learning difficulties had died while under NHS care. These deaths were revealed by MENCAP in 2007, in a report called *Death by Indifference*, which accused the NHS of 'institutional discrimination' against such people. This was followed by a government-commissioned independent inquiry, which uncovered evidence of serious failings in care for people with learning difficulties. In January 2009, the Health Secretary also announced annual health checks for anyone with a mental disability, and personal health action plans for them.[39]

Since 1945, there has been progress towards equal treatment of disabled people with the rest of the population, although inequalities remain, particularly for those experiencing mental disability. The main drivers for change have been:

- campaigning on behalf of, and, increasingly from the 1960s, by disabled people, supported by research that has increased awareness of their capacities
- political support for equality, especially from Labour governments since 1997
- positive media representations of disabled people and prominent people with physical and mental disabilities providing public role models.

The main inhibitors of change have been:

- ignorance, sometimes technical (such as how to adapt machinery to the needs of disabled people), sometimes cultural (for example, of the capabilities of disabled people)
- cuts to public services that have periodically reduced essential sources of support.

STATISTICS

Table 7.2 Benefits for the sick and disabled: 1950–97/98a

	Recipients (000s)	Expenditure (£m) cash terms	Expenditure (£m) 1997 prices
1950[b]	908	69	1,294
1955[b]	921	100	1,416
1960[b]	896	135	1,697
1965/66[c]	900	248	2,614
1970/71	922	374	3,112
1975/76	998	873	3,829
1980/81	1,043	1,804	4,128
1985/86	1,137	2,625	4,318
1990/91	1,678	4,647	5,683
1995/96	2,406	7,906	8,293
1997/98	2,341	7,421	7,362

Notes:
(a) Figures relate to Sickness Benefit, Invalidity Benefit and Incapacity Benefit.
(b) For 1950–60, figures refer to average of monthly claims throughout the year, and financial years beginning in the stated year.
(c) For 1965 onwards, claimant figures refer to claimants incapacitated at the end of the statistical year (June, from 1965/6–80/1, and April from 1985/6 onwards) and expenditure figures relate to the financial year.

Table 7.3 Invalid Care Allowance: 1980–97

	Allowances current at end of year (000)			Expenditure (£m)	
	Men	Women	Total	Cash terms	1997 prices
1980	n/a	n/a	7	5	11
1985	6	4	10	13	21
1990	24	110	134	208	254
1995	74	242	316	617	647
1997	94	280	374	745	739

Table 7.4 Persons registered as substantially and permanently handicapped in England and Wales: 1950–97

		General classes[a] (000s)	Blind (000s)	Partially sighted (000s)	Deaf (000s)	Hard of hearing (000s)
England and Wales	1950	n/a	81.3	n/a	n/a	n/a
	1955	47.4	94.7	18.1	16.4	10.3
	1960	93.4	97.5	24.2	21.3	14.2
	1970	251.1	103.1	37.4	25.6	17.7
	1980	961.6	115.1	55.3	31.5	36.2
England only	1980	900.7	107.8	51.4	29.7	35.1
	1986	n/a	120.6	71.1	34.1	63.4
	1987	1,230.6	n/a	n/a	n/a	n/a
	1988	n/a	126.8	79.0	n/a	n/a
	1989	n/a	n/a	n/a	37.9	70.3
	1990	1,265.6	n/a	n/a	n/a	n/a
	1991	n/a	136.2	93.8	n/a	n/a
	1992	n/a	n/a	n/a	44.0	99.3
	1993	1,336.9	n/a	n/a	n/a	n/a
	1994	n/a	149.7	115.7	n/a	n/a
	1995	n/a	n/a	n/a	45.5	125.9
	1997	n/a	158.6	138.2	n/a	n/a

Notes:
(a) General classes include the very severely handicapped, the severely or appreciably handicapped, other classified persons and the unclassified.
(b) From 1981, returns from each register were required every three years, with a different register each year.

Table 7.5 Persons under 65 with physical or mental disabilities[a] in residential accommodation provided by or on behalf of local authorities in England: 1970–95

| | Type of accommodation | | | |
	Local authority[b]	Voluntary	Private and other	Total
1970	6,023	4,509		10,532
1975	5,840	4,414		10,254
1980[c]	4,962	4,074	285	9,321
1985	4,338	3,547	208	8,093
1990	3,406	2,784	356	6,546
1995	2,100	2,400	2,690	7,200

Notes:
(a) Includes blind, deaf, epileptic, physically handicapped, mentally ill, people with learning difficulties and people with other disabilities.
(b) Includes homes jointly used by local authorities and hospitals.
(c) From 1980, short-stay homes are included.

Sources for Tables 7.2 to 7.5: *Health and Personal Social Services Statistics for England*, 1986, Table 7.3; *Health and Personal Social Services Statistics for England*, 1991, Table 7.3; *Health and Personal Social Services Statistics for England*, 1993, Table 5.56; *Health and Personal Social Services Statistics for England*, 1996, Table 5.50.

Table 7.6 Local authority adult training centres and special care centres for people with learning disabilities in England and Wales:[a] 1930–90

	Local authority adult training centres[c]			
	Cases under local authority supervision (000s)	Numbers attending occupation centres,[b] all ages	Premises	Places (000s)
1930	46.7	n/a	10	n/a
1939	69.5	4,244	69	n/a
1950	70.4	5,340	n/a	n/a
1960	83.6	22,041[d]	n/a	n/a
1970	104.1	48,206	311	22.9
1975	n/a	n/a	415	36.3
1980	n/a	n/a	484	45.0
1985	n/a	n/a	541	52.0
1990	n/a	n/a	691	59.4

Notes:

(a) This series was discontinued for England after 1992.

(b) Includes both centres run by local authorities and those run by voluntary organizations.

(c) Training centres catering for both juniors and adults are excluded.

(d) Figure from 1961.

Sources: Board of Control *Annual Reports*, 1930, 1939; Ministry of Health *Annual Reports*, 1950, 1960; Department of Health and Social Security, *Digest of Health Statistics for England and Wales*, 1970; *Health and Personal Social Services Statistics for England*, selected years; *Health and Personal Social Services Statistics for Wales*, selected years.

Table 7.7 Local authority services for mentally ill adults[a] in England and Wales:[b] 1961–90

	Local authority day centres		
	No. under local authority supervision (000s)	Number attending	Places
1961	40.0	354	n/a
1970	100.5	3,644	2,736
1975	n/a	n/a	3,673
1980	n/a	n/a	5,339
1985	n/a	n/a	6,250
1990	n/a	n/a	7,811

Notes:
(a) Mentally ill and psychopathic aged over 16.
(b) This series was discontinued for England after 1992.

Sources: Department of Health and Social Security. *Digest of Health Statistics for England and Wales*, 1970; *Health and Personal Social Services Statistics for England*, selected years; *Health and Personal Social Services Statistics for Wales*, selected years.

Table 7.8 Grant-aided special schools for 'handicapped pupils' in England and Wales: 1900–50

Year	Schools	Pupils
1900/01	182	8,153
1910/11	336	22,791
1920/21	500	36,459
1930/31	607	48,934
1937/38	611	51,422
1950	601	47,119

Note: Includes day and boarding pupils; boarding includes hospital schools.

Source: *Education in 1950*, Historical Tables, England and Wales.

Table 7.9 Numbers of special schools and pupils in special schools in England: 1965–97

Year	Special schools	Pupils (full- and part-time)	Percentage of all pupils
1965	847	71,915	1.0
1970	951	84,304	1.0
1975	1,529	127,809	1.4
1980	1,597	129,724	1.5
1985	1,529	116,273	1.5
1990	1,398	99,295	1.3
1995	1,291	98,390	1.2
1997	1,239	98,249	1.2

Note: Includes maintained and non-maintained special schools.

Source: *Statistics of Education in England*, 1997, Department for Education and Employment.

Conclusion

Equalities in Britain

Pat Thane

Since 1945, there have been serious attempts in most of the areas considered in this volume to devise government policies and institutions to diminish inequalities. There have been fewest and least effective attempts in respect of Gypsies and Travellers, despite recognition of their difficulties throughout the period. That older people experience unjustified inequality for reasons of age alone has been recognized only recently, and it is too soon to tell how effective recent measures to diminish this inequality will be. Most serious policies and institutions have had some measurable success. None has succeeded in eradicating inequality.

The introduction of these policies and institutions was in all cases driven by organized activism by people who experienced inequality. Activism, when it is not driven by narrow, sectional self-interest among a minority with the loudest voices but seeks to represent the interests of a broader constituency, has been effective in achieving change. It can influence not only central government policy, but that of other institutions, such as businesses. Such activism has been increasingly evident over the period since 1945, especially since the 1960s, probably largely because of higher levels of education and confidence among members of social groups that experience inequality and the increasing receptiveness of the media to their activities and statements. However, the role of the media has been double-edged. There are all too many instances of sections of the press, in particular, reinforcing discriminatory attitudes. This is not historically new. Previous examples include critical press coverage of Jews at the beginning of the twentieth century and of the campaign for the extension of women's suffrage between the wars. However, its long survival is disappointing.

Despite such institutions as the CRE and EOC achieving some real changes, inequalities persist that may not best be tackled by measures targeted at specific groups in isolation. For instance, the relatively poor performance in the labour market of Bangladeshis compared with other ethnic groups suggests that socio-economic differences may be at the root of certain inequalities, as they are among the White British population. Further, effective government policies to narrow income and educational inequalities for the whole population could do much to assist specific disadvantaged groups. There should certainly be monitoring of existing policies to establish whether, for example, certain groups are less likely to take up

targeted benefits like the Working Family Tax Credit or Pension Credit, due
to linguistic problems or relative social isolation. All such measures have
take-up problems (about 20 per cent of eligible pensioners had not applied
for pension credit by 2008); we know all too little about the characteristics
of those who fail to apply for such benefits. Generally, there is a need to
mainstream equality issues in all areas of social policy.

Some inequalities seem to diminish with time, as certain groups become
part of British culture without necessarily losing their distinct identities, as
the experience of Jewish and Irish communities over the twentieth century
suggests. But much harm can be done during the long wait for history to
take its course, and for neither Jewish nor Irish people has inequality been
wholly eliminated.

Despite the many differences in their experiences since 1945, there are
striking similarities in the mechanisms used by the diverse groups considered here to achieve varying degrees of progress towards greater equality.
The chief drivers in common have been:

- activism by the groups concerned, with support from others. This has
  taken different forms but, especially since the 1960s, has clearly helped
  to shape government action
- the positive role of government institutions established to promote
  equality, such as the EOC, CRE and DRC and, since 2007, the
  Equalities and Human Rights Commission, which has amalgamated
  and replaced them while taking on responsibility also for the other
  forms of inequality discussed here. It is too soon to assess its
  impact
- Labour governments, which generally have done most to promote
  equality, sometimes, and especially in the late 1960s, contrary to the
  preferences of many of their potential voters
- the European Union and European Courts, which have been a resource
  for activists and a source of pressure on British governments
- research by independent groups, which has helped to make the case for
  equality in many instances
- cultural change, with a diffuse and amorphous set of influences, but
  generally higher living standards and standards of education, greater
  social confidence and diminished deference, more relaxed social and
  sexual attitudes helping to increase popular support for diminishing
  inequalities
- the media, which has played an ambiguous role, both as a resource
  increasingly used by campaigners since the 1960s to promote their
  causes, and in the case of the popular press in particular, in persistently
  reinforcing prejudice and stereotypes.

On most dimensions of inequality, there has been improvement since
1945, but it has been uneven across social groups and in all of them serious inequalities have yet to be eradicated. Major inhibitors of change have
been:

- the poverty, reinforcing cultural isolation, of some groups, especially Gypsies and Travellers and certain other ethnic minority groups
- hostility and prejudice, which survives in the majority population, more in, and against, some groups than others.

Endnotes

Notes to Introduction

1 For a useful survey of the research data, see Taylor, R. (2003), *Britain's World of Work – Myths and Realities*. Swindon: Economic and Social Research Council.

Notes to Chapter 1: Older people and equality

1 Thane, P. (2000), *Old Age in English History*. Oxford University Press, pp. 19–28.
2 Ibid., pp. 194–215, 308–32.
3 Thane, P. (2006), 'The "scandal" of women's pensions in Britain: How did it come about?' in H. Pemberton, P. Thane and N. Whiteside (eds), *Britain's Pensions Crisis: History and Policy*. Oxford University Press, pp. 77–90.
4 Thane, *Old Age*, pp. 333–52.
5 Groves, D., (1986), 'Women and Occupational Pensions, 1870–1983', Unpublished London University PhD.
6 Blaikie, A. (1990), 'The emerging political power of the elderly in Britain, 1908–1948', *Ageing and Society*, 10 (*1*): 30.
7 Ibberson, D. 'Special investigation into the condition of supplementary pensioners, 1942'. (Unpublished report, National Archives (TNA) ASR 7/589.)
8 Pedersen, S. (2004), *Eleanor Rathbone and the Politics of Conscience*. Yale University Press.
9 *Social Insurance and Allied Services*. Report by Sir William Beveridge. Cmd 6404, p. 92, para. 236.
10 UK Government Actuary's Department (1975, 1991), *Occupational Pensions Schemes*, Table 3.2; Table 2.1.
11 Thane, P., Ginn, J., and Hollis, P. (2006), 'Women and pensions in Britain' in Pemberton *et al.*, *Britain's Pensions Crisis*, pp. 77–124.
12 Steventon, A., and Sanchez, C. (2008), *The Under-Pensioned: Disabled People and People from Ethnic Minorities*. London: Equality and Human Rights Commission.
13 Sass, S. 'Anglo-Saxon occupational pensions in international perspective', in Steventon and Sanchez, *The Under-Pensioned*, pp. 191–255.
14 Pratt, H. (1986), *Gray Agendas: Campaigns by Older People in Britain and US*. Ann Arbor: University of Michigan Press.
15 Anderson, W. F., and Isaacs, B. (eds) (1964), *Current Achievements in Geriatrics*. London: Cassell, p. 2–4.
16 Hastings, Dr S. (1951), 'Blocked beds', *The Lancet*, November.
17 Richardson, I. M. (1953), 'Age and work: A study of 489 men in heavy industry', *British Journal of Industrial Medicine*, 10: 269–84.
18 Harper, S., and Thane, P. (1989), 'The "social construction" of old age 1945–1964' in M. Jefferys (ed.), *Growing Old in the Twentieth Century*. London: Routledge.

19 Townsend, P. (1957), *The Family Life of Old People*. London: Routledge; Townsend, P., and Wedderburn, D. (1965), *The Aged in the Welfare State*. Occasional Papers on Social Administration No.14. London: G. Bell and Sons.
20 Townsend, P. (1964), *The Last Refuge*. London: Routledge.
21 Pemberton *et al.*, *Britain's Pensions Crisis*.
22 Abel-Smith, B., and Townsend, P. (1965), *The Poor and the Poorest*. Occasional Papers in Social Administration No.17. London: G. Bell & Sons.
23 Hilton, M., Crowson, N., and McKay, J. (eds) (2009), *NGOs in Contemporary Britain: Non-state Actors in Society and Politics*. London: Palgrave.
24 Pratt, *Gray Agendas*.
25 Michel, S. (2008), 'Old age support in the land of stereotypes: Women, feminism and US pensions'. (University of Maryland unpublished paper to conference of American Historical Association, Washington, DC, January.)
26 Pratt, *Gray Agendas*, p. 136.
27 Berthoud R., and Blekesaune, M. (2006), 'Persistent employment disadvantage, 1974–2003', Institute for Social and Economic Research working paper 9, University of Essex, p. 10.
28 Salter, T., Bryans, A., Redman, C., and Hewitt, M. (2009), *100 Years of State Pensions: Learning from the Past*. London: Faculty of Actuaries and Institute of Actuaries, p. 223.
29 World Bank (1984), *Averting the Old Age Crisis: Policies to Protect the Old and Promote Growth*. Oxford University Press.
30 *Economist*, 18 February 2006.
31 See, for example, Bass, S. A. (ed.) (1995), *Older and Active*. Yale University Press.
32 UK Government (2004). *Pensions: Challenges and Choices: The First Report of the Pensions Commission*. London: The Stationery Office, p. 55.
33 Ibid., p. 3, www.statistics.gov.uk, 'Life expectations', 30 October 2008.
34 See www.gro-scotland.gov.uk/press/2008- News.
35 Ibid., pp. 95–122.
36 Home Office Citizenship Survey (2003), *People, Families and Communities*, http://www.homeoffice.gov.uk/rds/pdfs04/hors289.pdf. Accessed July 2009.
37 *Guardian*, 3 January 2009.
38 'Persistent employment disadvantage: Pensions challenges and choices: The first report', Institute for Social and Economic Research working paper, p. 55.
39 European Union Framework Directive for Equal Treatment in Employment, Brussels, 2000.
40 Age Concern (2006), *How Ageist is Britain?* London: Age Concern.
41 Thane, *Old Age*, pp. 119–46, 287–307, 407–35; Glaser, K., Tomassini, C., and Wolf, D. (2006), 'Family support for older people', special issue, *Ageing and Society*, 26 (5).
42 Grundy, E. (2005), 'Reciprocity in relationships: Socio-economic and health influences on intergenerational exchanges between Third Age parents and their adult children in Great Britain', *British Journal of Sociology*, 56: 233–55.
43 *Guardian*, 8 March 2005.
44 Steventon and Sanchez, *The Under-Pensioned*.
45 Ibid.
46 UK Government, *Pensions: Challenges and Choices*, pp. 66–7.
47 See www.equalityhumanrights.com. Accessed July 2009.

Notes to Chapter 2: Race and equality

1 Tabili, L. (1991), *We Ask for British Justice: Workers and Racial Difference in Late Imperial Britain*. Ithaca: Cornell University Press.

2   Dummett, A., and Nicol, A. (1990), *Subjects, Citizens, Aliens and Others: Nationality and Immigration Law*. London: Weidenfeld and Nicolson.
3   Panayi, P. (1999), *The Impact of Immigration*, Manchester University Press, p. 9.
4   Hansard (1914), House of Commons Debates, 4th series, vol. LXV, col. 1477, 13 May.
5   Sewell, T. (1993), *Black Tribunes: Black Political Participation in Britain*. London: Lawrence & Wishart. The MPs were Sir Mancherjee Bhowangree (Conservative), Dadabhaj Naoroji (Liberal) and Shapurji Saklatvala (Labour in 1922, Communist in 1924). Lord Sinha of Raijpur served in the Lords, 1863–1928.
6   Feldman, D. (1994), *Englishmen and Jews: Social Relations and Political Culture*. Yale University Press.
7   National Archive [TNA] HO 213/244, J. Murray *et al.* to Prime Minister, 22 June 1948.
8   Glass, R. (1960), *The Newcomers: The West Indians in London*. London: Allen and Unwin, p. 55.
9   Carter, T. (1986), *Shattering Illusions: West Indians in British Politics*. London: Lawrence & Wishart, p. 61.
10 Shukra, K. (1998), *The Changing Patterns of Black Politics in Britain*. London: Pluto Press, p. 21.
11 Hansard (1961), House of Commons Debates, 5th series, vol. 649, col. 799, 16 November.
12 Daniel, W. W. (1968), *Racial Discrimination in England: Based on the PEP Report*. London: Penguin.
13 Smith, D. J. (1977), *Racial Disadvantage in Britain*. London: Penguin.
14 Foot, P. (1968), *The Politics of Harold Wilson*. London: Penguin, p. 285.
15 Smith, *Racial Disadvantage*, pp. 73–4.
16 Modood, T., and Berthoud, R. (eds) (1997), *Ethnic Minorities in Britain: Diversity and Disadvantage*. London: Policy Studies Institute, p. 340.
17 Brown, C. (1984), *Black and White Britain*. Third PSI Survey. London: Heinemann, p. 138.
18 Layton-Henry, Z. (1992), *The Politics of Immigration*. Oxford: Blackwell, p. 102.
19 Renton, D. (2006), *We Touched the Sky: A History of the Anti-Nazi League, 1977–1981*. London: New Clarion Press.
20 Carter, *Shattering Illusions*.
21 Reid, A. (2005), *United We Stand: A History of Britain's Trade Unions*. London: Penguin, p. 354.
22 Whitfield, J. (2004), *Unhappy Dialogue: The Metropolitan Police and Black Londoners in Post-war Britain*. London: Willan; 'Policing the Windrush' (2006), *History and Policy*, www.historyandpolicy.org/archive/policy-paper-45.html, September; Stuart Hall, *et al.* (1978), *Policing the Crisis: Mugging, the State and Law and Order*. London: Macmillan.
23 'Multicultural Britain: An unlikely success story', *Independent*, 5 October 2005.
24 See the website of the Institute of Community Cohesion, led by Ted Cantle, http://www.cohesioninstitute.org.uk/home. Accessed July 2009.
25 Modood and Berthoud, *Ethnic Minorities*, p. 345.
26 Ibid., p. 343.
27 Pilkington, A. (2003), *Racial Disadvantage and Ethnic Diversity in Britain*. London: Palgrave, p. 68.
28 Li,Y., Devine., Heath,A (2008) *Equality Group Inequalities in Education, Employment and Earnings: Research Review and Analysis of Trends Over Time*. Research Report No. 10. UK Equality and Human Rights Commission, www.equalityhumanrights commission.com. Accessed July 2009.
29 Ibid.

30   *British Social Attitudes Survey, 1983–1991*. UK Data Archive, www.data-archive.ac.uk/
     findingData/bsaTitles.asp. Accessed July 2009.
31   Li *et al., Inequalities.*
32   *Guardian*, 26 October 2005.
33   *Observer*, 14 April 2006.
34   *Daily Telegraph*, 28 January 2006; *Guardian*, 6 February 2006.
35   Pilkington, *Racial Disadvantage*, p. 264.
36   *Guardian*, 9 November 2006.
37   Holmes, C. (1988), *John Bull's Island: Immigration and British Society, 1871–1971*.
     London: Macmillan.
38   *Guardian*, 8 January 2009.

Notes to Chapter 3: Religion and belief

1   The Liberty of Religious Worship Act of 1855 was the legislation that future faith
     groups in the twentieth century would draw on to build their own religious places of
     worship.
2   Feldman, D. (1994), *Englishmen and Jews: Social Relations and Political Culture*. Yale
     University Press; Gartner, L. (1973), *The Jewish Immigrant in England*. London: Allen
     & Unwin.
3   Robert Skidelsky (2004), 'Mosley, Sir Oswald Ewald, sixth baronet (1896–1980),
     Oxford Dictionary of National Biography. Oxford, Oxford University Press.
4   Bagon, P. (2003) 'The impact of the Jewish underground upon Anglo-Jewry 1945–7'.
     (University of Oxford MPhil thesis, p. 127.)
5   Ibid. p. 128–9, taken from *Manchester Guardian*, 5 August 1947, p. 4.
6   Ibid. p. 131, taken from *Manchester Guardian*, 6 August 1947, p. 5.
7   Runnymede Trust (1994), *A Very Light Sleeper: The Persistence and Dangers of
     Anti-Semitism*. Runnymede Trust: London. More recently, in 2006, an all-party
     group of MPs established an inquiry to investigate levels of anti-Semitism in Britain;
     see www.guardian.co.uk/comment/story/0,1732747,00.html (accessed 9 October
     2006).
8   Hornsby-Smith, M. (1989), 'The Roman Catholic Church in Britain since the
     Second World War', in P. Badham (ed.), *Religion, State and Society in Modern Britain*.
     Lampeter: Mellen Press, pp. 86–98.
9   *Scottish Daily Herald*, 3 September 1999.
10   Scottish Executive (2005), Edinburgh: Crown Office and Procurator Fiscal Service;
     The Guardian, 28 November 2006.
11   Weller, P., Feldman, A., and Purdam, K. (2001), *Religious Discrimination in England
     and Wales*, UK Home Office Research Study 220, p 41, February.
12   An-Nisa Society (1993), 'The need for reform: Muslims and the law in multi-faith
     Britain'. Memorandum submitted by the UK Action Committee on Islamic Affairs
     for consideration by the Second Review of the Race Relations Act, 1976. London:
     An-Nisa Society, Autumn, p. 49.
13   *Nyazi v Rymans Ltd Employment Appeals Tribunal 6/88.*
14   An-Nisa Society, 'The need for reform', p. 41.
15   *The Times*, 5 July 1989.
16   An-Nisa Society, 'The need for reform', p. 39.
17   See the Muslim Council of Britain website, www.mcb.org.uk. Accessed July 2009.
18   *Sunday Telegraph*, 3 February 1991.
19   Lewis, P. (1994), 'Introduction', in *Islamic Britain: Religion, Politics and Identity Among
     British Muslims: Bradford in the 1990s*. London: IB Tauris.
20   Weller *et al., Religious Discrimination*, p. 37.
21   Ibid., p. 15.

22 Speech by David Davies, then Shadow Home Secretary, www.telegraph.co.uk/news/ main.jhtml?xml=/news/2006/10/15/nveil15.xml (accessed 3 December 2006).

23 For full statistical evidence, see Beckford, J. A., Gale, R., Owen, D., Peach, C., and Weller, P. (2006), 'Review of the evidence base on faith communities'. London: Office of the Deputy Prime Minister, www.communities.gov.uk/publications/communities/ review (accessed 21 August 2008).

24 See http://news.bbc.co.uk/2/hi/uk_news/7232661.stm, accessed February 2008.

25 Department for Communities and Local Government (2008), *Face to Face and Side by Side: A Framework for Partnership in Our Multi-Faith Society*, www.communities. gov.uk, accessed July 2008.

26 An-Nisa Society (1993), *The Need for Reform: Muslims and the Law in Multi-faith Britain*. London: An-Nisa Society) p. 41.

Notes to Chapter 4: Gypsies and Travellers

1 Valentine, G., and McDonald, I. (2004), *Understanding Prejudice: Attitudes Towards Minorities*. London: Stonewall, p. 12.

2 For consideration of all the different travelling communities of Britain, see Clark, C. (2006), 'Who are the Gypsies and Travellers of Britain?', in C. Clark and M. Greenfields (eds), *Here to Stay: The Gypsies and Travellers of Britain*. University of Hertfordshire Press, pp. 10–27.

3 Commission for Racial Equality (2006), *Common Ground: Equality, Good Race Relations and Sites for Gypsies and Irish Travellers*. Summary report. London: Commission for Racial Equality, p. 2.

4 Ibid.

5 Department for Communities and Local Government (2007), *The Road Ahead: Final Report of the Independent Task Group on Site Provision and Enforcement for Gypsies and Travellers*. London: Department for Communities and Local Government, December, p. 50.

6 Ibid.

7 Department for Communities and Local Government (2008), *Count of Gypsy and Traveller Caravans on 21st January 2008: Last Five Counts*. London: Department of Communities and Local Government.

8 Mayall, D. (1998), *Gypsy Travellers in Nineteenth Century Society*. Cambridge University Press; Taylor, B. (2008), *A Minority and the State*. Manchester University Press.

9 Okely, J. (1983), *The Traveller-Gypsies*. Cambridge University Press.

10 Department of Health for Scotland (1936), *Health Report of the Departmental Committee on Vagrancy in Scotland*. London: HMSO, para. 94.

11 Steventon, A., and Sanchez, C. (2008), *The Under-pensioned: Disabled People and People from Ethnic Minorities*. London: Equality and Human Rights Commission.

12 Taylor, B. (2008), *A Minority and the State: Travellers in Britain in the Twentieth Century*. Manchester: Manchester University Press, p. 158.

13 TNA, AST 7/1480, Arbroath Area Office, 'Tinkers'.

14 Hill, M. J. (1969), 'The exercise of discretion in the National Assistance Board', *Public Administration* 47.

15 Taylor, *A Minority*, pp. 174–6.

16 TNA, ED11/234 HMI, Mr Smith to Board of Education, 6 November 1944.

17 'When Gypsies Squat', *Ipswich Evening Star*, 29 August 1946.

18 Taylor, *A Minority*, pp. 117–19.

19 For a detailed account of the key cases of this period, see Acton, T. (1974), *Gypsy Politics and Social Change. The Development of Ethnic Ideology and Pressure Politics*

among British Gypsies from Victorian Reformism to Romani Nationalism. London: Routledge and Kegan Paul, pp. 137–47.

20 Fraser, A. (1953), 'The Gypsy problem: A survey of post-war developments', *Journal of the Gypsy Lore Society* 3: 3–4; 87–8.

21 In fact, Gypsy Welfare Officers were never widespread. During the war, there was a very limited attempt to include Gypsies and Travellers in the war effort through Gypsy Welfare Officers, mainly on the part of the missionary Gypsy Williams.

22 Quoted in Acton, *Gypsy Politics*, pp. 138–9.

23 TNA, HLG 71/903, 'Camping places for Gypsies, findings from 1951 police questionnaire'.

24 TNA, HLG 71/1650, notes by Ministry of Housing and Local Government Parliamentary Secretary to prepare for Norman Dodds' question in the House of Commons, 7 May 1951.

25 See, for example, the practice of Hartley-Witney rural district council, Hampshire Record Office: 59M76/DDC207.

26 Taylor, *A Minority*, pp. 142–6.

27 Some of the ex-Darenth residents became tenants of a private site set up and run by Norman Dodds in Cobham, Kent. For his account of the process, see Dodds, N. (1966), *Gypsies, Didikois and Other Travellers*.

28 Taylor, *A Minority*, pp. 125–6.

29 Wilson, A. (1959), *Caravans as Homes*. CMND 872. London: HMSO, paras 59, 69.

30 Acton, *Gypsy Politics*, p. 134.

31 Connors, J. (1973), 'Seven weeks of childhood – An autobiography', quoted in Sandford, J. (1975), *Gypsies*. London: Sphere Books, pp. 166–7.

32 UNESCO (1977), *Ethnicity and the Media: An Analysis of Media Reporting in the United Kingdom, Canada and Ireland*. New York: United Nations, p. 151.

33 Acton, *Gypsy Politics*, p. 163.

34 Ibid.

35 Ibid. p. 167.

36 Religious observance among Gypsies and Travellers tends to be higher than among the general population, with the majority in the United Kingdom being Christian and many of them, particularly Irish Travellers, Roman Catholic. Priests and vicars often have longstanding knowledge of Gypsy and Traveller families in their area and can act as intermediaries in disputes over sites. See Greenfields, M., 'Family, community and identity', in Clark and Greenfields, *Here to Stay*, pp. 48–9.

37 Taylor, *A Minority*, p. 161.

38 Stockins, J. (2001), *On the Cobbles, The Life of a Bare-Knuckle Gypsy Warrior*. Edinburgh and London: Mainstream, pp. 46–7.

39 Adams, J. W. R. (1960), *Gypsies and other Travellers in Kent: Report on the Survey Carried Out in 1951/52 Gypsies and Other Travellers*. Kent County Council, p. 17.

40 Taylor, *A Minority*, p. 163.

41 Saunders, P., Clarke, J., and Kendall, S. (eds) (2000), *Gypsies and Travellers in their Own Words: Words and Pictures of Travelling Life*. Leeds County Council, pp. 10–11.

42 Reiss, C. (1971), 'Current trends in the education of Travelling children', in T. Acton (ed.), *Current Changes Among British Gypsies and Their Place in International Patterns of Development*. Proceedings of the Research and Policy Conference of the National Gypsy Education Council, St Peter's College, Oxford, 28 March, pp. 26–7.

43 Taylor, *A Minority*, pp. 146–52.

44 Stockins, *On the Cobbles*, pp. 46, 48.

45 Acton, *Gypsy Politics*, pp. 151–2.

46 Ibid, pp. 151–2.

47 Clark and Greenfields, *Here to Stay*, p. 72.

48 Taylor, *A Minority*, p. 113.

49 Acton, *Gypsy Politics*, pp. 179–82.
50 Clark and Greenfields, *Here to Stay*, p. 72.
51 Taylor, *A Minority*, p. 188.
52 Hawes, D., and Perez, B. (1996), *The Gypsy and the State: The Ethnic Cleansing of British Society*. Oxford: Polity Press, p. 29.
53 Ibid., p. 179.
54 Gypsies and Travellers without a permanent or Post Office-recognized address have struggled to join the electoral roll; see 'Voting Rights for the Homeless', an occasional discussion paper by the Traveller Law Research Unit, www.law.cf.ac.uk/tlru/Voting. pdf (accessed 18 November 2008).
55 Quoted in D. Hawes and B. Perez, *The Gypsy and the State*, p. 30.
56 Cripps, J. (1976), *Accommodation for Gypsies*. London: HMSO.
57 Ibid., para. 3.17.
58 Ibid.
59 Taylor, *A Minority*, p. 195.
60 Cripps *Accommodation*, 11.
61 Ibid.
62 Okely, *The Traveller-Gypsies*, p. 115.
63 Taylor, *A Minority*, p. 196.
64 Ibid.
65 Ibid. p. 199.
66 Open University, Association of Chief Police Officers Archive: Association of Chief Police Officers, Department of the Environment, 'The accommodation needs of long-distance and regional Travellers: A consultation paper', February 1982, Appendix 3, précis of a conversation with a long-distance Traveller in January 1982.
67 Also known as New Age Travellers.
68 Hawes and Perez, *The Gypsy and the State*, pp. 46–7.
69 *R v Secretary of State for Wales and West Glamorgan Council, ex parte Gilhaney*.
70 Hawes and Perez, *The Gypsy and the State*, p. 50.
71 Ibid., pp. 50–1.
72 Ibid. p. 117.
73 Ibid. pp. 118–19.
74 Quoted in Clark and Greenfields, *Here to Stay*, p. 79.
75 Ibid. p. 80.
76 ACERT was founded in 1973 by Lady Plowden (chair of the 1967 government study Children and their Primary Schools, which found that Gypsy children had the worst access to education of any group), Tom Lee, general secretary of the Romany Guild, and other representatives of the Gypsy and Traveller communities. ACERT has since expanded its remit to include equal access to safe and secure accommodation, education, health and other community services.
77 Hawes and Perez, *The Gypsy and the State*, p. 122.
78 Ibid. p. 120.
79 Ibid. p. 122.
80 Ibid. pp. 123–4.
81 Clark and Greenfields, *Here to Stay*, p. 87.
82 For further examples of inappropriate local criteria, see ODPM Circular 01/06 (2006), *Planning for Gypsy and Traveller Caravan Sites*. London: Office of the Deputy Prime Minister, pp. 21–2.
83 Greenfields, 'Family, community and identity', in Clark and Greenfields, *Here to Stay*, pp. 34, 46.
84 According to evidence introduced at later court cases, *South Bucks v Porter, Wrexham CBC v Berry* and *Chirchester DC v Keet and Searle*; see www.yourrights.org.uk/ yourrights/rights-of-gypsies-and-travellers/planning-permission-for-caravan-sites/ index.shtml (accessed 17 December 2008).

85   Home, R., 'The planning system and the accommodation needs of Gypsies', in Clark and Greenfields, *Here to Stay*, p. 97.
86   Quoted in Clark and Greenfields, *Here to Stay*, p. 87.
87   Ibid., pp. 85–6.
88   See www.gypsy-traveller.org/about-us/ (accessed 27 November 2008).
89   The unit's archived website is available at www.law.cf.ac.uk/tlru/WhatWeDo.html (accessed 18 November 2008).
90   See www.travellerstimes.org.uk/index.php (accessed 18 November 2008).
91   See www.law.cf.ac.uk/tlru/bill.html (accessed 18 November 2008).
92   For full details of the journey to publication of the Bill, see Clements, L., and Morris, R. (2001), 'The Traveller Law Reform Bill: A brief guide'. Traveller Law Reform Unit, Cardiff University Law School, November, www.law.cf.ac.uk/tlru/BriefGuide.pdf. Accessed July 2009.
93   Ibid, pp. 7–8.
94   See www.law.cf.ac.uk/tlru/bill.html (accessed 18 November 2008).
95   See www.liberty-human-rights.org.uk/news-and-events/3-human-rights-awards/2004-awards.shtml (accessed 20 November 2008).
96   See www.travellerslaw.org.uk/ (accessed 27 November 2008).
97   'Is there a gypsy camp near you?' *Daily Express*, 10 March 2005, p. 9.
98   Greenfields, 'Gypsies, Travellers and legal matters', pp. 137–9.
99   Clark, C., 'Who are the Gypsies and Travellers of Britain?', in Clark and Greenfields, *Here to Stay*, p. 19.
100 Greenfields, 'Gypsies, Travellers and legal matters', p. 154.
101 'Pikey' is a derogatory term for someone regarded as not being a 'pure-bred' Gypsy.
102 Clark and Greenfields, *Here to Stay*, p. 3.
103 Ibid., pp. 3–4.
104 Clark, C., 'Europe', in Clark and Greenfields, *Here to Stay*, p. 276.
105 Ibid. It is important to note that Mrs Buckley's planning case predated the abolition of the 1968 Caravan Sites Act in 1994.
106 Ibid., p. 275.
107 Ibid.
108 Ibid., p. 276.
109 *Clarke v The Secretary of State for the Environment, Transport and the Regions and Tunbridge Wells Borough Council (2001)*.
110 Quoted at www.yourrights.org.uk/yourrights/rights-of-gypsies-and-travellers/planning-permission-for-caravan-sites/conventional-housing.html (accessed 17 December 2008).
111 See *Implementing the Mobile Homes Act 1983 on Local Authority Gypsy and Traveller Sites: Consultation* (2008). London: Department of Communities and Local Government, September.
112 'Back Howard to end this human rights charade', *Daily Express*, 18 March 2005.
113 Porter, M. (2007) 'The ultimate folk devils? National newspaper representations of Gypsies and Travellers in 2005'. (University of Westminster unpublished MA thesis, pp. 85–92.)
114 *Gypsy and Traveller Sites: Thirteenth Report of Session 2003–4* (2004). London, House of Commons Office of the Deputy Prime Minister: Housing, Planning, Local Government and the Regions Committee, vol. 1, p. 123.
115 House of Commons Office of the Deputy Prime Minister (2004), *Planning for Gypsy and Traveller Sites: Consultation Paper*. London: Office of the Deputy Prime Minister, December.
116 'Cut council tax bill if gypsies can live near our houses', *Sunday Express*, 23 January 2005, p. 50.
117 Clark and Greenfields, *Here to Stay*, p. 7.
118 Stonewall (2005), *Profiles of Prejudice*. London: Stonewall, p. 1.

119   Valentine and McDonald, *Understanding Prejudice*, pp. 17–18.
120   Ibid. p. 18.
121   Recent research from Wales and Scotland has revealed similar prejudices. See Bromley, C., Curtice, J., and Given, L. (2007), *Attitudes to Discrimination in Scotland 2006: Scottish Social Attitudes Survey*. Edinburgh: Scottish Government Social Research; and Equality and Human Rights Commission (2008), *Who Do You See? Living Together in Wales*. London: Equality and Human Rights Commission.
122   Porter, 'Ultimate folk devils?' pp. 85–92.
123   'Rights, wrongs', *Sun*, 9 March 2005, p. 8.
124   Nuttall, E. (2006), 'Sun newspaper's stamp on the camps campaign', The Gypsy & Traveller Law Reform Coalition press statement, 13 April 2006.
125   Ibid.
126   Porter, 'Ultimate folk devils?' p. 7.
127   'Too tolerant of gypsies', *Daily Express*, 24 May 2005, p. 12.
128   'Wasted money', *Sun*, 13 August 2005, p. 6.
129   'Local councils are letting Gypsies down', *Independent*, 12 March 2005, p. 36.
130   Porter, 'Ultimate folk devils', pp. 93–8.
131   Department for Communities and Local Government (2007), *The Road Ahead: Final Report of the Independent Task Group on Site Provision and Enforcement for Gypsies and Travellers*. London: Department for Communities and Local Government, December, p. 11.
132   Ibid., p. 5.
133   Department of Communities and Local Government (2008), *Count of Gypsy and Traveller Caravans on 21st January 2008: Last Five Counts*. London: Department of Communities and Local Government.
134   Ibid.
135   Niner, P. (2003), *Local Authority Gypsy/Traveller Sites in England* London: Office of the Deputy Prime Minister, p. 25.
136   Ibid, p. 25.
137   Correspondence with Office of National Statistics, 10 November 2008.
138   Scottish Government Social Research (2007 and 2008), *Gypsies/Travellers in Scotland: The Twice-yearly Count*. No. 12: July 2007 and No.13: January 2008. Edinburgh: Scottish Government Social Research.
139   Welsh Assembly Government (2008), 'Gypsy and Traveller caravan count, July 2008', November, http://cymru.gov.uk/docs/statistics/2008/20081128sdr2002008en.pdf. Accessed July 2009.

Notes to Chapter 5: Gender equality

1   We are grateful to Esther Breitenbach, University of Edinburgh, for information on gender equality in Scotland.
2   Office of National Statistics (2006), *Census 1951: Key Population and Vital Statistics*. Series VS No. 33 PPI No 29. London, Office of National Statistics.
3   Hollis, P. (1987), *Ladies Elect: Women in English Local Government, 1865–1914*. Oxford: Clarendon Press.
4   Childs, S., Lovenduski, J., Campbell, R. (2005), *Women at the Top 2005: Changing Numbers, Changing Politics?* London: Hansard Society, p. 23.
5   Thane, P. (2001), 'What difference did the vote make?', in A. Vickery (ed.) *Women, Privilege and Power: British Politics, 1750 to the Present*. Berkeley: Stanford University Press, pp. 253–88.
6   Gallie, D. (2000), 'The labour force', in A. H. Halsey and J. Webb (eds) *Twentieth Century British Social Trends*. London: Macmillan, pp. 281–323.
7   Lewis, J. (2001), *The End of Marriage?* Cheltenham: Elgar, p. 30.

8   See, for example, Bowlby, J. (1953), *Child Care and the Growth of Love*. London: Penguin; and Winnicott, D. (1964), *The Child, the Family, and the Outside World*. London: Penguin.

9   Wilson, D., 'A new look at the affluent worker: The good working mother in post-war Britain' *Twentieth Century British History*, 17 (2): 210.

10   Freeguard, J. (2004), 'It's time for the women of the 1950s to stand up and be counted'. (University of Sussex unpublished D.Phil thesis); Potter, A. (1957), 'The equal pay campaign committee: A case-study of a pressure group', *Political Studies*, 5: 49–64.

11   Zweiniger-Bargielowska, I. (1996), 'Explaining the gender gap: The Conservative Party and the women's vote 1945–1964' in M. Francis and I. Zweiniger-Bargielowska (eds), *The Conservatives and British Society, 1880–1990*. Cardiff: University of Wales Press.

12   Sutherland, D. (2000), 'Peeresses, parliament and prejudice: The admission of women to the House of Lords'. (University of Cambridge, unpublished PhD thesis.)

13   Meehan, E. (1990), 'British feminism from the 1960s to the 1980s', in Harold Smith (ed), *British Feminism in the 20th Century*. Aldershot: Edward Elgar, pp. 189–204.

14   Centre for Contemporary British History (2001), 'The making of the 1967 Abortion Act'. Witness seminar, University of London, http://icbh.ac.uk. Accessed July 2009.

15   Gallie, 'The labour force'.

16   Perkins, A. (2003), *Red Queen: The Authorized Biography of Barbara Castle*. London: Macmillan.

17   Lovenduski, J. (1986), *Women and European Politics: Contemporary Feminism and Public Policy*. Brighton: Wheatsheaf, p. 77.

18   Perkins, *Red Queen*.

19   Fraser, K. M. (1999), *Same or Different: Gender Politics in the Workplace*. Aldershot: Ashgate.

20   Castle, C. (1993), *Fighting All the Way*. London: Macmillan.

21   Coote, A., and Campbell, B. (1987), *Sweet Freedom: The Struggle for Women's Liberation*. 2nd edn. Oxford: Basil Blackwell.

22   Hoskyns, C. (1996), *Integrating Gender: Women, Law and Politics in the European Union*. London: Verso.

23   Ibid.

24   Buckingham, G. L. (1973), *What to Do About Equal Pay for Women*. London: Gower Press.

25   Zabalza, A., and Tzannatos, Z. (1985), *Women and Equal Pay: The Effects of Legislation on Female Employment and Wages in Britain*. Cambridge University Press.

26   Coote and Campbell, *Sweet Freedom*.

27   From Adams, R. (1975; 2000), *A Woman's Place: 1910–1975*. First published 1975, London: Chatto & Windus; this edition 2000, London: Persephone Books, pp. 277–82. See also the ten techniques commonly used by employers in Lister, R., and Lowe, M. (1975), 'Equal pay and how to get it'. London: National Council for Civil Liberties, March.

28   Hoskyns, *Integrating Gender*; Meehan, E. (1985), *Women's Rights at Work: Campaigns and Policy in Britain and the United States*. London: Macmillan.

29   Sloane, P. J., and Sibert, W. S. (1980), 'Low pay amongst women – the facts', in P. Sloane (ed.), *Women and Low Pay*. London: Macmillan, p. 10.

30   Seear, N., Roberts, V., and Brick, J. (1964), *A Career for Women in Industry*. London and Edinburgh.

31   Lovenduski, (1195), 'An emerging advocate: The Equal Opportunities Commission in Great Britain', in A. Mazur and D. Stetson, *Comparative State Feminism*. London: Sage, pp. 114–32.

32   Rowbotham, S. (1999), *A Century of Women: The History of Women in Britain and the United States*. London: Penguin.

33   Lovenduski, *Women and European Politics*, p. 78.

34   Ibid, p. 78.

35   Ibid., p. 78.
36   Jackson, L. A. (2006), *Women Police: Gender, Welfare and Surveillance in the Twentieth Century*. Manchester University Press, pp. 185–93.
37   Ibid., p. 79.
38   Breitenbach, E., and Thane, P. (eds) (2009), *What Difference Did the Vote Make? Women and Citizenship in Britain and Ireland in the Twentieth Century*. London: Continuum.
39   Gelb, J. (1990), 'Feminism and political action', in R. J. Dalton and M. Kuechler (eds), *Challenging the Political Order: New Social and Political Movements in Western Democracies*. Oxford: Polity. For a more positive view of the Equal Opportunities Commission from the early 1980s, see Lovenduski, 'An emerging advocate'.
40   Crompton, R., and Le Feuvre, N. (1992), 'Gender and bureaucracy: Women in finance in Britain and France', in Savage and Witz, *Gender and Bureaucracy*. Oxford: Blackwell, pp. 334–48.
41   Mazey, S. (1989), *Women and the European Community*. London: PNL Press.
42   Barry, J. (1991), *The Women's Movement and Local Politics: The influence on councillors in London*. Aldershot: Avebury.
43   Watson, S. (1992), 'Femocratic feminisms', in M. Savage and A. Witz (eds), *Gender and Bureaucracy*. Oxford: Blackwell, pp. 186–207.
44   Gelb, 'Feminism and political action'.
45   Coote and Campbell, *Sweet Freedom*.
46   Office of National Statistics website, http://www.statistics.gov.uk/hub/index.html, 23 January 2006.
47   Cook, H. (2004), *The Long Sexual Revolution: English Women, Sex and Contraception, 1800-1975*. Oxford University Press.
48   Taylor, R. (2003), *Britain's World of Work, Myths and Realities*. Swindon: Economic and Social Research Council.
49   Lewis, *The End of Marriage?*
50   Cohen, M. (1998), '"A habit of healthy idleness": Boys' underachievement in historical perspective', in Epstein, D., Elwood, J., Hey, V., and Haw, J. (eds), *Failing Boys? Issues in Gender and Achievement*. Milton Keynes: Open University Press.
51   Douglas, J. W. B., Ross, J. M., and Simpson, H. R. (1971), *All Our Future*. London, Panther, p. 42.
52   Equality and Human Rights Commission (2008), *Sex and Power: Who Runs Britain, 2008?* London: Equality and Human Rights Commission, pp. 5–7.
53   'Stop gap' (2008). *The Fawcett Society Magazine*, Autumn, p. 10–11.
54   For a survey of lone parenthood from the Poor Law to the present, see Evans, T. (2006), 'Is it futile to try to get non-resident fathers to maintain their children?' History & Policy website, October, www.historyandpolicy.org/archive/policy-paper-48.html; Nutt, T. (2006), 'The Child Support Agency and the old Poor Law', History & Policy website, October, www.historyandpolicy.org/archive/policy-paper-47.html. Accessed July 2009.
55   British Social Attitudes (2007), www.britsocat.com/Body.aspx?control=BritSocAt19 Home. Accessed July 2009.
56   Henig, R., and Henig, S. (2000), *Women and Political Power: Europe since 1945*. London: Routledge.
57   Lovenduski, *Women and European Politics*.
58   Ibid. See also Perrigo, S. (1995), 'Gender struggles in the British Labour Party from 1979-1995'. *Party Politics*, 1(3): 407–17.
59   Rossilli, M. (ed.) (2000), *Gender Policies in the European Union*. Bern, New York, Oxford: Peter Lang.
60   Squires, J., and Wickham-Jones, M. (2002), 'Mainstreaming in Westminster and Whitehall: From Labour's Ministry for Women to the Women and Equality Unit', in Karen Ross (ed.), *Women, Politics, and Change*. Oxford University Press, pp. 57–71.

61   Butler, D., and Butler, G. (2000), *Twentieth-Century British Political Facts, 1900–2000.* London: Macmillan, p. 261.

62   Stephenson, M. (1998), *The Glass Trapdoor: Women, Politics and the Media during the 1997 General Election.* London: Fawcett Society.

63   Ibid.

64   MacDougall, L. (1998), *Westminster Women.* London: Vintage, ch. 8.

65   Childs, *et al., Women at the Top,* p. 16.

66   See, for example, Breitenbach, E., and MacKay, F. (2001), *Women and Contemporary Scottish Politics.* Edinburgh: Polygon.

67   Scottish Executive, *Equality Strategy: Working Together for Equality,* November 2000, www.scotland.gov.uk/library3/social/wtem-02.asp. Accessed July 2009.

68   Ibid.

69   Statistics relating to this chapter are incorporated within the text above.

Notes to Chapter 6: Gender identity and sexual orientation

1   We are grateful to Hera Cook, Roger Davidson, Matt Houlbrook, Jeffrey Weeks and Steve Whittle for their advice.

2   Weeks, J. (1981), *Sex, Politics and Society: The Regulation of Sexuality Since 1800.* Harlow: Longman, p. 103; McLaren, A. (1999), *Twentieth Century Sexuality: A History.* London: Blackwell, p. 100.

3   For the reasons behind this decision, see UK Office for National Statistics (2006), *Sexual Orientation and the 2011 Census – Background Information.* London: Office of National Statistics, March 2006.

4   Weeks, *Sex, Politics and Society,* p. 103; McLaren, *Twentieth Century Sexuality,* p. 98.

5   Weeks, *Sex, Politics and Society,* p. 112; McLaren, *Sexuality,* p. 94.

6   King, D. (1993), *The Transvestite and the Transsexual: Public Categories and Private Identities.* Aldershot: Avebury, p. 111.

7   Vicinus, M. (2004), *Intimate Friends. Women Who Loved Women.* University of Chicago Press.

8   Weeks, *Sex, Politics and Society,* p. 105.

9   Doan, L. (2001), *Fashioning Sapphism: The Origins of a Modern English Lesbian Culture.* Columbia University Press, p. 56.

10   Waites, M. (2005), *The Age of Consent: Young People, Sexuality and Citizenship.* London: Palgrave, pp. 91–5.

11   Weeks, J. (1990), *Coming Out: Homosexual Politics in Britain from the Nineteenth Century to the Present.* London: Quartet, pp. 138–42.

12   'Haire, Norman (1892–1952)', *Australian Dictionary of Biography – Online Edition,* www.adb.online.anu.edu.au/biogs/A140402b.htm, accessed 7 January 2009.

13   Doan, *Fashioning Sapphism,* p. 1.

14   Weeks, *Sex, Politics and Society,* p. 117.

15   Doan, *Fashioning Sapphism,* p. 10.

16   Weeks, *Sex, Politics and Society,* p. 117.

17   Cook, H. (2004), *The Long Sexual Revolution: English Women, Sex and Contraception 1800–1975.* Oxford: Oxford University Press, p. 184.

18   Jivani, A. (1997), *It's Not Unusual: A History of Gay and Lesbian Britain in the Twentieth Century.* London: Michael O'Mara/BBC, p. 55.

19   Titmuss, R. (1950), *History of the Second World War: Problems of Social Policy.* London: HMSO and Longmans, p. 211 n.2.

20   Ferguson, S. M., and Fitzgerald, H. (1954), *History of the Second World War: Studies in the Social Services.* London: HMSO and Longmans, pp. 13–16.

21   Quoted in Jivani, *It's Not Unusual,* p. 56.

22 Jivani, *It's Not Unusual*, p. 70.
23 Cook, M. (ed.) (2007), *A Gay History of Britain: Love and Sex Between Men Since the Middle Ages*. Westport, Connecticut: Greenwood, p. 149.
24 Jivani, *It's Not Unusual*, p. 72.
25 Cook, *Long Sexual Revolution*, p. 184.
26 Jivani, *It's Not Unusual*, pp. 89–91
27 McLaren, *Twentieth Century Sexuality*, p. 146.
28 Ibid., p. 147.
29 Weeks, *Coming Out*, pp. 152–3.
30 Quoted in ibid., pp. 154–5.
31 Quoted in King, *Transvestite and Transsexual*, p. 140.
32 Stanley, L. (1995), *Sex Surveyed, 1949–94: From Mass Observation's 'Little Kinsey' to the National Survey and the Hite Reports*. London: Taylor & Francis, p. 6.
33 Ibid. pp. 199–200.
34 England, L. (1950), 'A British sex survey'. *The International Journal of Sexology*, February iii (3): 153.
35 'Little Kinsey', in Stanley, *Sex Surveyed*, p. 82.
36 Ibid., pp. 200–3.
37 Ibid. p. 48.
38 Ibid. pp. 44–6.
39 Holden, A. (2005), *Makers and Manners: Politics and Morality in Post-war Britain*. London: Politico's, pp. 64–5.
40 Weeks, *Sex, Politics and Society*, pp. 239–40.
41 Cook, *Gay History of Britain*, p. 170.
42 Holden, *Makers and Manners*, p. 65.
43 Jivani, *It's Not Unusual*, p. 123.
44 Quoted in ibid., p. 106.
45 Ibid., p. 107.
46 Ibid. p. 109.
47 Quoted in Weeks, *Coming Out*, p. 162.
48 'The problem of homosexuality – Report by clergy and doctors', *The Times*, 26 February 1954, p. 5.
49 Ibid.
50 Holden, *Makers and Manners*, pp. 65–6.
51 Cook, *Gay History of Britain*, p. 172.
52 Self, H. (2003), *Prostitution, Women and the Misuse of the Law: The Fallen Daughters of Eve*. London: Routledge, p. 154.
53 Weeks, *Sex, Politics and Society*, pp. 242–3.
54 Waites, M. (2005), *The Age of Consent: Young Women, Sexuality and Citizenship*. London: Palgrave.
55 Weeks, *Coming Out*, p. 164.
56 Holden, *Makers and Manners*, p. 83.
57 Adrian, H. A., Albemarle, (Lady) D., Bagnold, E., Barnes, A., Bragg, A., Cohen, H., De Freitas, H., Hubback, J., Jay, P., Murdoch, I., Pakenham, E., Piper, M., Ridley, U., Rothschild, T., and Woodham-Smith, C. 'Homosexual Acts', *The Times*, 19 April 1958, p. 7.
58 'Lack of action on Wolfenden report', *The Times*, 3 September 1958, p. 9.
59 Cook, *Gay History of Britain*, p. 175.
60 Holden, *Makers and Manners*, p. 86; Cook, *Gay History of Britain*, p. 174.
61 'Vice', *The Times*, 26 November 1958, p. 11.
62 Holden, *Makers and Manners*, p. 87.
63 Ibid. pp. 89–90.
64 Cook, *Long Sexual Revolution*, p. 286.
65 Ibid., p. 339.

66   Weeks, *Coming Out*, p. 173.
67   Holden, *Makers and Manners*, pp. 119–20.
68   Ibid., pp. 122–5.
69   Cook, *Gay History of Britain*, p. 186.
70   Quoted in Holden, *Makers and Manners*, p. 128.
71   Ibid. p. 128; Cook, *Gay History of Britain*, p. 176.
72   Holden, *Makers and Manners*, pp. 129–30.
73   Weeks, *Sex, Politics and Society*, p. 275.
74   Quoted in Holden, *Makers and Manners*, p. 130.
75   Weeks, *Coming Out*, pp. 176–7.
76   Pearce (1973), 'Mass media and the homosexual', in Cohen and Young (eds), *The Manufacture of News: Social Problems, Deviance and the Mass Media*. London: Constable, p. 300.
77   Hall, L. A. (2005), 'Sexuality', in P. Addison and H. Jones (eds), *A Companion to Contemporary Britain, 1939–2000*. Oxford: Blackwell, pp. 150–1.
78   Davidson, R., and Davis, G. (2004), 'A field for private members: The Wolfenden Committee and Scottish homosexual law reform, 1950–67', in *Twentieth Century British History*, 5 (2): 177; 181–2.
79   Ibid., p. 186.
80   Ibid. p. 193.
81   Quoted in ibid., p. 192.
82   Ibid. p. 192.
83   Ibid. p. 191.
84   Quoted in ibid. pp. 193–5.
85   Ibid., pp. 195–9.
86   Ibid. pp. 195–9.
87   Hall, 'Sexuality', p. 151.
88   Oram, A. (2005), 'Cross-dressing and transgender', in H. Cocks and M. Houlbrook (eds), *Advances in the Modern History of Sexuality*. London: Palgrave, p. 279.
89   King, *Transvestite and Transsexual*, pp. 100–4.
90   Ibid.
91   Ibid. pp. 104–5.
92   Ibid., pp. 106–7.
93   Quoted in ibid. p. 112.
94   Quoted in ibid. p. 114.
95   Randell, J. (1959), 'Transvestitism and trans-sexualism – a study of 50 cases'. *British Medical Journal*, 26 December, pp. 1448–52.
96   King, *Transvestite and Transsexual*, p. 91.
97   Ibid., p. 91.
98   Weeks, *Coming Out*, pp. 186–90.
99   Cook, *Gay History of Britain*, p. 180.
100 Ibid., p. 179.
101 Ibid., pp. 179–81; Weeks, *Coming Out*, p. 191.
102 McLaren, *Twentieth Century Sexuality*, p. 191.
103 Waites, *Age of Consent*, p. 126.
104 Cook, *Gay History of Britain*, p. 187.
105 Quoted in Waites, *Age of Consent*, p. 128.
106 Quoted in Weeks, *Coming Out*, p. 236.
107 Cook, *Gay History of Britain*, p. 182.
108 Ibid., p. 183.
109 Ibid., p. 184.
110 Weeks, *Coming Out*, pp. 211–12.
111 Cook, *Gay History of Britain*, p. 184.
112 Weeks, *Coming Out*, p. 214.

113   Ibid. p. 216.
114   Ibid. p. 223.
115   Holden, *Makers and Manners*, p. 221.
116   Weeks, *Sex, Politics and Society*, pp. 280–1.
117   Cook, *Gay History of Britain*, p. 191.
118   Ibid., p. 192.
119   Ibid. p. 193.
120   Waites, *Age of Consent*, p. 136.
121   Ibid. p. 152.
122   King, *Transvestite and Transsexual*, pp. 145–6.
123   Ibid., p. 147.
124   Alice L100, 'Some of the history of the Beaumont Society', www.beaumontsociety.org. uk/history.html (accessed 9 January 2009).
125   King, *Transvestite and Transsexual*, p. 148.
126   Ibid., pp. 148–50.
127   Ibid., p. 150.
128   Davidson, R., and Davis, G. (2006), 'Sexuality and the state: The campaign for Scottish homosexual law reform, 1967–80', in *Contemporary British History*, December, 20 (4): 535.
129   Ibid., p. 541.
130   Ibid., p. 539.
131   Ibid., p. 541.
132   Holden, *Makers and Manners*, p. 222.
133   Davidson and Davis, 'Sexuality and the state', p. 542.
134   Quoted in ibid., p. 546.
135   Ibid. p. 546.
136   Ibid. p. 547.
137   Ibid. pp. 547–8.
138   Ibid. pp. 549–50.
139   Cook, *Gay History of Britain*, p. 185.
140   Weeks, *Coming Out*, p. 244.
141   Terence Higgins Trust, www.tht.org.uk/informationresources/factsandstatistics/uk/ (accessed 9 January 2009).
142   'Life blood, or death?', *The Times*, 21 November 1984, p. 19.
143   Quoted in *Mass Observation in the 1980s*, Spring Directive 1987, AIDS, University of Sussex: MO Archive, 1988, p. 1.
144   Cook, *Gay History of Britain*, pp. 198, 202.
145   Ibid., p. 202.
146   Berridge, V. (1996), 'Crisis what crisis?', in *Health Service Journal*, 8 August, 20–1.
147   Cook, *Gay History of Britain*, p. 198.
148   Berridge, 'Crisis what crisis?', p. 21.
149   Holden, *Makers and Manners*, p. 247.
150   Berridge, 'Crisis what crisis?', p. 21.
151   'Indiscipline over Aids', *The Times*, 19 February 1985, p. 13.
152   Weeks, *Coming Out*, p. 246.
153   Tatchell, 'Fear of Aids', *The Times*, 2 March 1985, p. 9.
154   Quoted in *Mass Observation in the 1980s*, p. 1.
155   Holden, *Makers and Manners*, p. 233.
156   Ibid., pp. 230–1; 250.
157   Ibid., pp. 253–5.
158   Quoted in Ibid. p. 252.
159   Weeks, *Coming Out*, p. 240; Cook, *Gay History of Britain*, pp. 206–7.
160   Weeks, *Coming Out*, p. 241
161   Ibid.

162   Ibid.
163   Ibid.
164   Ibid.
165   O'Sullivan, S., in V. Preston (ed.) (2001), 'Section 28 and the revival of gay, lesbian and queer politics in Britain.' Witness seminar held at University of London: Centre for Contemporary British History, Institute of Historical Research, pp. 32–3, www. ccbh.ac.uk/witness_section28_index.php. Accessed July 2009.
166   Weeks in ibid. p. 20.
167   Cook, *Gay History of Britain*, p. 208.
168   Ibid., p. 207.
169   George in *Section 28*, p. 29.
170   McLaren, *Twentieth Century Sexuality*, p. 200.
171   De La Grace Volcano in *Section 28*, pp. 41–2.
172   Holden, *Maker and Manners*, p. 247.
173   Ibid., pp. 247–8.
174   Quoted in ibid., p. 248.
175   Johnson, A. M., *et al.* (2001), 'Sexual behaviour in Britain: Partnerships, practices and HIV risk behaviours'. *The Lancet*, 1 December, 358: 1835–42.
176   Holden, *Makers and Manners*, p. 298.
177   Quoted in Holden, *Makers and Manners*, p. 298.
178   Waites, *Age of Consent*, p. 159.
179   David, *On Queer Street*, pp. 266–7.
180   Waites, *Age of Consent*, p. 161.
181   Ibid., p. 167.
182   Ibid., p. 168.
183   Ibid., p. 168.
184   Wharton, S. (1993), 'Glad to be gay? Journalistic portrayal of homosexuality in Britain and France'. Paper delivered to the Cambridge Social Stratification Seminar, 16 September.
185   Quoted in 'Archbishop warns of gay rights backlash', *Telegraph Online*, 29 November 2006, www.telegraph.co.uk/news/uknews/1535392/Archbishop-warns-of-gay-rights-backlash.html (accessed 13 January 2009).
186   news.bbc.co.uk/1/hi/uk/7806780.stm (accessed 13 January, 2009).
187   *Living Together: British Attitudes to Lesbian and Gay People* (2007). London: Stonewall, p. 18.
188   Bromley, C., *et al.* (2007), *Attitudes to Discrimination in Scotland: 2006*. Edinburgh: Scottish Government Social Research, p. 22.
189   Ibid., pp. 22, 47; Equality and Human Rights Commission (2008), *Who Do You See? Living Together in Wales*. London: Equality and Human Rights Commission, p. 16.
190   *Guardian*, 7 January 2009, p. 8.
191   *Society Guardian*, 10 January 2006, pp. 1–2.
192   This section is mainly, but not entirely, based on Whittle, S. (2006), 'Experiencing the law: From victim to defendant – the experience of transphobic victimhood'. A paper given to the conference Experiencing the Law, Institute of Advanced Legal Studies, University of London, 1 December.
193   Thirty-four per cent of trans people complete a degree – often later in life after leaving school early – compared with the British national average of 27 per cent. Whittle *et al.* (2007), *Engendered Penalties: Transgender and Transsexual People's Experiences of Inequality and Discrimination*. London: Department of Communities and Local Government, p. 17.
194   For a biography of Stephen Whittle, see www.pfc.org.uk/node/31 (accessed 13 January 2009).
195   *Guardian*, 20 December 2006, p. 12.
196   Whittle *et al.*, *Engendered Penalties*, p. 13.

197   Weeks, J. (2007), 'Wolfenden and beyond: The remaking of homosexual history', History & Policy website, February, www.historyandpolicy.org/papers/policy-paper-51.html.
198   Ibid.

Notes to Chapter 7: Disability

1   Hurt, J. S. (1988), *Outside the Mainstream: A History of Special Education*. London: Batsford, pp. 92–106.
2   Ibid., pp. 107–54.
3   Abel-Smith, B., and Townsend, P. (1965), *The Poor and the Poorest: A New Analysis of the Ministry of Labour's Family Expenditure Surveys of 1953–54 and 1960*. Occasional Papers on Social Administration, No.17. London: G Bell and Sons.
4   Hilton, M., Crowson, N., and McKay, J. (eds) (2009), *NGOs in Contemporary Britain: Non-state Actors in Society and Politics Since 1945*. London: Palgrave.
5   UK Office of Population, Censuses and Surveys (1988), *Disabled Adults Living in Private Households*. London: UK Office of Population, Censuses and Surveys.
6   Oliver, M., 'Changing the social relations of research production?' *Disability, Handicap and Society*, 7, (2): 101–13.
7   Zarb, G., and Nadash, P. (1994), *Cashing In On Independence: Comparing the Costs and Benefits of Cash and Services*. London: British Council of Organizations of Disabled People.
8   See www.bcodp.org.uk.
9   See http://83.137.212.42/sitearchive/drc/emailbulletin/bulletin_42.html#11.
10   Prime Minister's Strategy Unit (2004), *Improving the Life Chances of Disabled People: Final Report* London: Cabinet Office.
11   Ibid.
12   www.culture24/org.uk/art/sculpture/art30597 Accessed July 2009.
13   Alaszewski, A. (1983), 'The development of policy for the mentally handicapped since the Second World War: An overview', *Oxford Review of Education*, 9 (3): 227ff.
14   Hurt, *Outside the Mainstream*, pp. 182–3.
15   Raphael, W., and Peers, V. (1972), *Psychiatric Hospitals Viewed by Their Patients*. London: Kings Fund.
16   Raphael, W. (1977), *Psychiatric Hospitals Viewed by Their Patients*. 2nd edn. London: Kings Fund.
17   Department of Health and Social Services (1975), *Better Services for the Mentally Ill*. London: Department of Health and Social Services, para. 11.5.
18   Department of Health and Social Services (1975), *In-Patient Statistics*, London: Department of Health and Social Services, pp. 5, 7.
19   Warnock Report (1978), *Special Educational Needs: Report of the Committee of Enquiry into the Education of Handicapped Children and Young People*. London: HMSO, p. 327.
20   *Outside But Not Inside . . . Yet! Leaving Hospital and Living in the Community: An Evaluation by People with Learning Difficulties*. London: People First, 1994; Ward, L. (1997), 'Funding for change: Translating emancipatory disability research from theory to practice', in C. Barnes and G. Mercer (eds), *Doing Disability Research*. Leeds: The Disability Press, pp. 32–49.
21   Much of what follows is drawn from www.mind.org.uk/Information/Factsheets/#Black. Accessed July 2009.
22   Wilson, M., and Francis, J. (1997), *Raised Voices*. London: Mind; Bracken, P., 'Mental health and ethnicity: The Irish dimension', *British Journal of Psychiatry*, 172: 103–5.
23   Cochrane, R., and Bal, S. S., 'Mental Hospital Admission Rates for Immigrants to England', *Social Psychiatry*, 24: 2–11.

24 Browne, D. (1998), *Black People and Sectioning*. Little Rock Publishing; Dutt, R., and Ferns, P. (1998), *Letting Through the Light. A Training Pack on Black People and Mental Health*. London: Department of Health.

25 Cochrane, R., and Sashideran, S. (n.d.), *Mental Health and Ethnic Minorities: A Review of the Literature and Implications for Services*. University of Birmingham, School of Psychology.

26 Wilson and Francis, *Raised Voices*; Bracken, 'Irish dimension'.

27 Nazroo, J., and King, M. (1997), 'Psychosis-symptoms and estimated rates', in K. Sproston and J. Nazroo (eds), *Ethnic Minority Psychiatric Illness Rates in the Community*. London: National Centre for Social Research, TSO.

28 Nazroo, J. (2002), *Ethnicity, Class and Health*. London: Policy Studies Institute.

29 Nazroo and King, 'Psychosis-symptoms'.

30 Ibid.

31 Ibid.

32 Nazroo, *Ethnicity, Class and Health*.

33 Nazroo and King, 'Psychosis-symptoms'.

34 Smaje, C. (1995), *Race and Ethnicity: Making Sense of the Evidence*. London: King's Fund.

35 Moodley, P. (1993), 'Setting up services for ethnic minorities', in D. Bhugra and J. Leff (eds), *Principles of Social Psychiatry*. Oxford: Blackwell, pp. 490–501.

36 Willmot, J. (1996), 'Poor recognition, poorer services for Black women'. *Openmind*, September–October, 81: 8–9.

37 Fry, S., *The Secret Life of the Manic Depressive*, www.bbc.co.uk/health/tv_and_radio/secretlife_index.shtml. Accessed July 2009.

38 *Guardian*, 14 September 2006.

39 *Guardian*, 19 January 2009.

References

CHAPTER 1: OLDER PEOPLE AND EQUALITY

PUBLISHED SOURCES

Newspapers and periodicals

Economist, 18 February 2006.
Guardian, 8 March 2005.

Official publications

European Union (2000), *Framework Directive for Equal Treatment in Employment*, Brussels: European Union.
UK Government Actuary's Department (1975), *Occupational Pension Schemes*. London: HMSO.
UK Government (2004), *Pensions: Challenges and Choices: The First Report of the Pensions Commission*. London: HMSO
World Bank (1984), *Averting the Old Age Crisis: Policies to Protect the Old and Promote Growth*. Oxford: Oxford University Press.

Books, articles

Abel-Smith, B., and Townsend, P. (1965), *The Poor and the Poorest*, Occasional Papers in Social Administration No.17. London: G Bell and Sons.
Age Concern (2006), *How Ageist Is Britain?* London: Age Concern.
Anderson, W. F., and Isaacs, B. (eds) (1964), *Current Achievements in Geriatrics*. London: Cassell.
Bass, S. A. (ed.) (1995), *Older and Active*. New Haven: Yale University Press.
Blaikie, A. (1990), 'The emerging political power of the elderly in Britain, 1908–1948', *Ageing and Society*, 10 (*1*): 17–39.
Glaser, K., Tomassini, C., and Wolf, D. (2006), 'Family support for older people', special issue, *Ageing and Society*, 26, p. 5.
Grundy, E., (2005), 'Reciprocity in relationships: Socio-economic and health influences on intergenerational exchanges between third age parents and their adult children in Great Britain'. London: *British Journal of Sociology*, 55: 233–55.
Harper, S., and Thane, P. (1989), 'The "social construction" of old age 1945–1964' in M. Jeffreys (ed.), *Growing Old in the Twentieth Century*. London: Routledge.
Hastings, S. (1951), 'Blocked Beds', *The Lancet*, 10 November.
Hilton, M., Crowson, N., and McKay, J. (eds) (2009), *NGOs in Contemporary Britain: Non-state Actors in Society and Politics*. London: Palgrave.
Pedersen, S., and Rathbone, E. (2004), *And the Politics of Conscience*. New Haven: Yale University Press.

Pratt, H. (1986), *Gray Agendas: Campaigns by Older People in Britain and US*. Ann Arbor: University of Michigan Press.

Richardson, I. M. (1953), 'Age and work: A study of 489 men in heavy industry', *British Journal of Industrial Medicine*, 10: 269–84.

Sass, S. (2004), 'Anglo-Saxon occupational pensions in international perspective' in A. Steventon and C. Sanchez, *The Under-Pensioned: Disabled People and People from Ethnic Minorities*. London: Equality and Human Rights Commission.

Steventon, A., and Sanchez, C. (2004), *The Under-Pensioned: Disabled People and People from Ethnic Minorities*. London: Equality and Human Rights Commission.

Thane, P. (2005), 'The "scandal" of women's pensions in Britain: How did it come about?' in H. Pemberton, P. Thane, and N. Whiteside (eds), *Britain's Pensions Crisis, History and Policy*. Oxford: Oxford University Press, pp. 77–90.

Thane, P. (2000), *Old Age in English History*. Oxford: Oxford University Press.

Thane, P., Ginn, J., and Hollis, P. (2005), 'Women and pensions in Britain' in Pemberton *et al.* (eds), *Britain's Pensions Crisis*. Oxford: Oxford University Press, pp. 77–124.

Townsend, P. (1957), *The Family Life of Old People*. London: Routledge.

Townsend, P. (1964), *The Last Refuge*. London: Routledge.

Townsend, P., and Wedderburn, D. (1965), *The Aged in the Welfare State*, Occasional Papers on Social Administration No.14. London: G. Bell and Sons.

Salter, T., Bryans, A., Redman, C., and Hewitt, M. (2009), *100 Years of State Pensions: Learning from the Past*. London: Faculty of Actuaries and Institute of Actuaries.

UNPUBLISHED SOURCES

Berthoud R., and Blekesaune, M. (2006), 'Persistent employment disadvantage, 1974–2003'. Unpublished Institute for Economic and Social Research working paper, 2006–9, University of Essex.

Groves, D. (1986), 'Women and occupational pensions, 1870–1983'. Unpublished University of London PhD thesis.

Ibberson, D. (1942), 'Special investigation into the condition of supplementary pensioners, 1942'. Unpublished report, National Archives (TNA), ASR 7/589.

Berthoud R., and Blekesaune, M. (2007), 'Persistent employment disadvantage: Pensions: challenges and choices: The first report.' Unpublished Institute for Economic and Social Research working paper, University of Essex.

Michel, S. (2008), 'Old age support in the land of stereotypes: Women, feminism and US pensions'. Unpublished University of Maryland paper to conference of American Historical Association, Washington, DC, January.

ONLINE SOURCES

People, Families and Communities, 2003 Home Office Citizenship Survey, www.homeoffice.gov.uk/rds/pdfs04/hors289.pdf. Accessed July 2009.

Life Expectancies, 30 October 2008, www.statistics.gov.uk/hub/population/deaths/life-expectancies/index.html. Accessed July 2009.

Equality and Human Rights Commission, www.equalityhumanrights.com. Accessed July 2009.

CHAPTER 2: RACE AND EQUALITY

PUBLISHED SOURCES

Official publications

Hansard, House of Commons Debates, 4th Series, 1914, vol. LXV.
Hansard, House of Commons Debates, 5th Series, 1961, vol. 649.

Books and articles

Brown, C. (1984), *Black and White Britain*. The Third PSI Survey. London: Heinemann.
Carter, T. (1986), *Shattering Illusions: West Indians in British Politics*. London: Lawrence & Wishart.
Daniel, W. W. (1968), *Racial Discrimination in England: Based on the PEP Report*. London: Penguin.
Dummett, A., and Nicol, A. (1990), *Subjects, Citizens, Aliens and Others: Nationality and Immigration Law*. London: Weidenfeld and Nicolson.
Feldman, D. (1994), *Englishmen and Jews: Social Relations and Political Culture*. Yale University Press.
Foot, P. (1968), *The Policies of Harold Wilson*. London: Penguin.
Glass, R. (1960), *The Newcomers: The West Indians in London*. London: Allen and Unwin.
Hall, S. *et al.* (1978), *Policing the Crisis: Mugging, the State and Law and Order*. London: Macmillan.
Layton-Henry, Z. (1992), *The Politics of Immigration*. Oxford: Blackwell.
Modood, T., and Berthoud, R. (eds) (1997), *Ethnic Minorities in Britain: Diversity and Disadvantage*. London: Policy Studies Institute.
Panayi, P. (1999), *The Impact of Immigration*. Manchester University Press.
Reid, A. (2005), *United We Stand: A History of Britain's Trade Unions*. London: Penguin.
Renton, D. (2006), *We Touched the Sky: A History of the Anti-Nazi League, 1977–1981*. London: New Clarion Press.
Sewell, T. (1993), *Black Tribunes: Black Political Participation in Britain*. London: Lawrence & Wishart.
Shukra, K. (1998), *The Changing Patterns of Black Politics in Britain*. London: Pluto Press.
Smith, D. J. (1977), *Racial Discrimination in Britain*. London: Penguin.
Tabili, L. (1991), *We Ask For British Justice: Workers and Racial Difference in Late Imperial Britain*. Ithaca: Cornell University Press.
Whitfield, J. (2004), *Unhappy Dialogue: The Metropolitan Police and Black Londoners in Post-war Britain*. London: Willan.

UNPUBLISHED SOURCES

National Archive (TNA) HO 213/244, J. Murray *et al.* to Prime Minister, 22 June 1948.

ONLINE SOURCES

British Social Attitudes Survey, 1983–1991. UK Data Archive, www.data-archive.ac.uk/ findingData/bsaTitles.asp. Accessed July 2009.
Institute of Community Cohesion, http://www.cohesioninstitute.org.uk/home. Accessed July 2009.
Whitfield, J., 'Policing the Windrush' (2006). History & Policy website, www. historyandpolicy.org/archive/policy-paper-45.html. Accessed July 2009.

CHAPTER 3: RELIGION AND BELIEF

PUBLISHED SOURCES

Newspapers and periodicals
Guardian, 28 November 2006.
Scottish Daily Herald, 3 September, 1999.
Sunday Telegraph, 3 February 1991.
The Times, 5 July 1989.

Official publications
Appeals Tribunal 6/88 *Nyazi v Rymans Ltd Employment.*

Books, journals, pamphlets
An-Nisa Society (1993), *The Need for Reform: Muslims and the Law in Multi-faith Britain*. Memorandum submitted by the UK Action Committee on Islamic Affairs for consideration by the Second Review of the Race Relations Act 1976. London: An-Nisa Society, Autumn.
Feldman, D. (1994), *Englishmen and Jews: Social Relations and Political Culture*. New Haven: Yale University Press.
Gartner, L. (1973), *The Jewish Immigrant in London*. London: Allen & Unwin.
Hornsby-Smith, M. (1989), 'The Roman Catholic Church in Britain since the Second World War' in P. Badham (ed.), *Religion, State and Society in Modern Britain*. Lampeter: Mellen Press.
Lewis, P. (1994), *Islamic Britain: Religion, Politics and Identity Among British Muslims: Bradford in the 1990s*. London: IB Tauris.
Runnymede Trust (1994), *A Very Light Sleeper: The Persistence and Dangers of Anti-Semitism*. London: Runnymede Trust.
Weller, P., Feldman, A. and Purdam, K. (2001), *Religious Discrimination in England and Wales*. UK Home Office Research Study 220, February. London: HMSO.

UNPUBLISHED SOURCES

Bagon, P. (2003), 'The impact of the Jewish underground upon Anglo-Jewry 1945–7'. University of Oxford MPhil thesis.

ONLINE SOURCES

Muslim Council of Britain, www.mcb.org.uk. Accessed July 2009.
Department for Communities and Local Government (2008), *Face to Face and Side by Side: A Framework for Partnership in our Multi-Faith Society*, www.communities.gov.uk/corporate/publications. Accessed July 2009.
Beckford, J. A., Gale, R., Owen, D., Peach, C. and Weller, P. (2006), 'Review of the evidence base of faith communities'. London: Office of the Deputy Prime Minister. www.communities.gov.uk/corporate. Accessed July 2009.

CHAPTER 4: GYPSIES AND TRAVELLERS

PUBLISHED SOURCES

Newspapers and periodicals
'Back Howard to end this human rights charade', *Daily Express*, 18 March 2005.
'Cut council tax bill if gypsies can live near our houses', *Sunday Express*, 23 January 2005.
'Is there a gypsy camp near you?', *Daily Express*, 10 March 2005.
'Local councils are letting gypsies down', *Independent*, 12 March 2005.
'Rights, wrongs', *Sun*, 9 March 2005.
'Too tolerant of gypsies' *Daily Express*, 24 May 2005.
'Wasted money', *Sun*, 13 August 2005.
'When gypsies squat', *Ipswich Evening Star*, 29 August 1946.

Official publications

Commission for Racial Equality (2006), *Common Ground: Equality, Good Race Relations and Sites for Gypsies and Irish Travellers*, summary report. London: CRE.
Communities and Local Government (2007), *The Road Ahead: Final Report of the Independent Task Group on Site Provision and Enforcement for Gypsies and Travellers*. London: Department for Communities and Local Government, December.
Count of Gypsy and Traveller Caravans on 21st January 2008: Last Five Counts (2008). London: Department of Communities and Local Government.
Gypsies/Travellers in Scotland: The Twice-Yearly Count – No. 12 (2007). Edinburgh: Scottish Government Social Research, July.
Gypsies/Travellers in Scotland: The Twice-Yearly Count – No. 13. (2008). Edinburgh: Scottish Government Social Research, January.
Implementing the Mobile Homes Act 1983 on Local Authority Gypsy and Traveller Sites: Consultation (2008). London: Department of Communities and Local Government, September.
Niner, P. (2003), *Local Authority Gypsy/Traveller Sites in England*. London: Office of the Deputy Prime Minister.
Office of the Deputy Prime Minister: Housing, Planning, Local Government and the Regions Committee (2004), *Gypsy and Traveller Sites*, Thirteenth Report of the Session 2003–4, vol. 1.
Office of the Deputy Prime Minister (2004), *Planning for Gypsy and Traveller Sites: Consultation Paper*. London: ODPM, December.
Planning for Gypsy and Traveller Caravan Sites (2006). London: Office of the Deputy Prime Minister
Department of Health for Scotland (1936), *Report of the Departmental Committee on Vagrancy in Scotland*. London: HMSO.
Saunders, P., Clarke, J., and Kendall, S. (eds) (2000), *Gypsies and Travellers in their Own Words: Words and Pictures of Travelling Life*. Leeds: Leeds City Council.
Steventon, A., and Sanchez, C. (2008), *The Under-Pensioned: Disabled People and People from Ethnic Minorities*. London: Equality and Human Rights Commission.
The Road Ahead: The Final Report of the Independent Task Group on Site Provision and Enforcement for Gypsies and Travellers (2007). London: Department for Communities and Local Government, December.
UNESCO (1977), *Ethnicity and the Media: An Analysis of Media Reporting in the United Kingdom, Canada and Ireland*. New York: United Nations.
Who Do You See? Living Together in Wales (2008). London: Equality and Human Rights Commission.
Wilson, A. (1959), *Caravans as Homes*, CMND 872. London: HMSO.

Books and articles

Acton, T. (1974), *Gypsy Politics and Social Change: The Development of Ethnic Ideology and Pressure Politics among British Gypsies from Victorian Reformism to Romani Nationalism*. London: Routledge and Kegan Paul.

Adams, J. W. R. (2000), *Gypsies and Other Travellers in Kent: Report on the Survey Carried Out in 1951/52 Gypsies and Other Travellers*. Maidstone: Kent County Council.

Bromley, C., Curtice, J., and Given, L. (2007), *Attitudes to Discrimination in Scotland 2006: Scottish Social Attitudes Survey*. Edinburgh: Scottish Government Social Research.

Clark, C. (2006), 'Europe', in C. Clark and M. Greenfields (eds), *Here To Stay: The Gypsies and Travellers of Britain*. Hatfield: University of Hertfordshire Press.

Clark, C. (2006), 'Who are the Gypsies and Travellers of Britain?', in C. Clark and M. Greenfields (eds), *Here To Stay: The Gypsies and Travellers of Britain*. Hatfield: University of Hertfordshire Press.

Clark, C., and Greenfields, M. (eds) (2006), *Here To Stay: The Gypsies and Travellers of Britain*. University of Hertfordshire Press.

Connors, J. (1973), 'Seven weeks of childhood – an autobiography' in J. Sandford, *Gypsies*. London: Sphere Books.

Cripps, J. (1976), *Accommodation for Gypsies*. London: HMSO.

Dodds, N. (1966), *Gypsies, Didikois and Other Travellers*. London: Johnson Publications.

Fraser, A. (1953), 'The Gypsy problem: A survey of post-war developments', *Journal of the Gypsy Lore Society*, 3: 3–4, 82–100.

Greenfields, M. (2006), 'Family, community and identity', in C. Clark and M. Greenfields (eds), *Here To Stay: The Gypsies and Travellers of Britain*. Hatfield: University of Hertfordshire Press.

Greenfields, M. (2006), 'Gypsies, travellers and legal matters', in C. Clark and M. Greenfields (eds), *Here To Stay: The Gypsies and Travellers of Britain*. Hatfield: University of Hertfordshire Press.

Hawes, D., and Perez, B. (1996), *The Gypsy and the State: The Ethnic Cleansing of British Society*. Oxford: Polity Press.

Hill, M. J. (1969), 'The exercise of discretion in the National Assistance Board', *Public Administration*, vol. 47.

Home, R. (2006), 'The planning system and the accommodation needs of Gypsies', in Clark and Greenfields (eds), *Here To Stay: The Gypsies and Travellers of Britain*. Hatfield: University of Hertfordshire Press.

Mayall. D. (1988), *Gypsy Travellers in Nineteenth Century Society*. Cambridge: Cambridge University Press.

Okely, J. (1983), *The Traveller-Gypsies*. Cambridge: Cambridge University Press.

Reiss, C. (1971), 'Current trends in the education of travelling children'. in T. Acton (ed), *Current Changes among British Gypsies and their Place in International Patterns of Development*. Proceedings of the Research and Policy Conference of the National Gypsy Education Council, St Peter's College, Oxford, 26–28 March.

Stockins, J. (2001), *On the Cobbles: The Life of a Bare-Knuckle Gypsy Warrior*. Edinburgh and London: Mainstream.

Stonewall (2005), *Profiles of Prejudice*. London: Stonewall.

Taylor, B. (2008), *A Minority and the State: Travellers in Britain in the Twentieth Century*. Manchester: Manchester University Press.

Valentine, G., and McDonald, I. (2004), *Understanding Prejudice: Attitudes Towards Minorities*. London: Stonewall.

UNPUBLISHED SOURCES

Hampshire Record office: 59M76/DDC207.

Open University, Association of Chief Police Officers Archive: ACPO, Department of the

Environment, 'The accommodation needs of long-distance and regional Travellers: A consultation paper', February 1982, Appendix 3, précis of a conversation with a long-distance Traveller in January 1982.

Porter, M. (2007), 'The ultimate folk devils? National newspaper representations of Gypsies and Travellers in 2005'. University of Westminster unpublished MA thesis.

TNA, AST 7/1480, Arbroath Area Office, 'Tinkers'.

TNA, ED11/234, HMI Mr Smith to Board of Education, 6 November 1944.

TNA, HLG 71/903, 'Camping Places for Gypsies, findings from 1951 police questionnaire'.

TNA, HLG 71/1650, notes by MHLG Parliamentary Secretary to prepare for Norman Dodds' question in the House of Commons, 7 May 1951.

ONLINE SOURCES

Clements, L., and Morris, R., 'The Traveller Law Reform Bill: A brief guide'. Traveller law Reform Unit, Cardiff University Law School, www.law.cf.ac.uk/tlru/BriefGuide.pdf. Accessed July 2009.

'Conventional housing', Liberty, www.yourrights.org.uk/yourrights/rights-of-gypsies-and-travellers/planning-permission-for-caravan-sites/conventional-housing.html. Accessed July 2009.

Friends, Families, and Travellers, www.gypsy-traveller.org/about-us. Accessed July 2009.

'Gypsy and Traveller caravan count, July 2008' (2008) Welsh Assembly Government, November, http://cymru.gov.uk/docs/statistics/2008/20081128sdr2002008en.pdf. Accessed July 2009.

Liberty, www.liberty-human-rights.org.uk/news-and-events/3-human-rights-awards/2004-awards.shtml. Accessed July 2009.

'Planning permission for caravan sites', Liberty, www.yourrights.org.uk/yourrights/rights-of-gypsies-and-travellers/planning-permission-for-caravan-sites/index.shtml. Accessed July 2009.

Traveller Law Reform Project, www.travellerslaw.org.uk. Accessed July 2009.

Traveller Law Research Unit, www.law.cf.ac.uk/tlru/WhatWeDo.html. Accessed July 2009.

'Voting rights for the homeless', occasional discussion paper, Traveller Law Research Unit, www.law.cf.ac.uk/tlru/Voting.pdf. Accessed July 2009.

www.travellerstimes.org.uk. Accessed July 2009.

CHAPTER 5: GENDER EQUALITY

PUBLISHED SOURCES

Official publications

Census 1951: Key Population and Vital Statistics (2006), series VS no.33, PPI no.29. London: Office of National Statistics.

Sex and Power, Who Runs Britain, 2008? (2008). London: Equality and Human Rights Commission.

Newspapers and periodicals

'Stop Gap' (2008), *The Fawcett Society Magazine*, Autumn.

Books and articles

Adams, R. (2000), *A Woman's Place: 1910–1975*. London: Persephone Books.

Barry, J. (1991), *The Women's Movement and Local Politics: The Influence on Councillors in London*. Aldershot: Avebury.

Bowlby, J. (1953), *Child Care and the Growth of Love*. London: Penguin.

Breitenbach E., and MacKay, F. (2001), *Women and Contemporary Scottish Politics*. Edinburgh: Polygon.

Breitenbach, E., and Thane, P. (eds) (2010), *What Difference Did the Vote Make? Women and Citizenship in Britain and Ireland in the Twentieth Century*. London: Continuum.

Buckingham, G. L. (1973), *What To Do About Equal Pay For Women*. London: Gower Press.

Butler, D., and Butler, G. (2000), *Twentieth-Century British Political Facts, 1900–2000*. London: Macmillan.

Castle, B. (1993), *Fighting All the Way*. London: Macmillan.

Childs, S., Lovenduski, J., and Campbell, R. (2005), 'Women at the top, 2005', *Changing Numbers, Changing Politics?* London: Hansard Society.

Cohen, M. (1998), '"A habit of healthy idleness": Boys' underachievement in historical perspective', in D. Epstein, J. Elwood, V. Hey and J.Haw, (eds), *Failing Boys? Issues in Gender and Achievement*. Milton Keynes: Open University Press.

Cook, H. (2004), *The Long Sexual Revolution: English Women, Sex and Contraception, 1800–1975*, Oxford: Oxford University Press.

Coote, A, and Campbell, B. (1987), *Sweet Freedom: The Struggle for Women's Liberation*, 2nd edn. Oxford: Basil Blackwell.

Crompton, R., and Le Feuvre, N. (1992), 'Gender and bureaucracy: Women in finance in Britain and France' in M. Savage and A. Witz, *Gender and Bureaucracy*. Oxford: Blackwell, pp. 334–48.

Douglas, J. W. B., Ross, J. M., and Simpson, H. R. (1971), *All Our Future*. London: Panther.

Fraser, K. M. (1999), *Same or Different: Gender Politcs in the Workplace*. Aldershot: Ashgate.

Gallie, D. (2000), 'The labour force' in A. H. Halsey and J. Webb (eds), *Twentieth Century British Social Trends*. London: Macmillan, pp. 281–323.

Gelb, J. (1990), 'Feminism and political action'. in R. J. Dalton and M. Kuechler (eds), *Challenging the Political Order: New Social and Political Movements in Western Democracies*. Oxford: Polity.

Henig, R., and Henig, S. (1995), *Women and Political Power: Europe Since 1945*. London: Routledge.

Hollis, P. (1987), *Ladies Elect: Women in English Local Government, 1869–1914*. Oxford: Clarendon Press.

Hoskyns, C. (1996), *Integrating Gender: Women, Law and Politics in the European Union*. London: Verso.

Jackson, L. A. (2006), *Women Police. Gender, Welfare and Surveillance in the Twentieth Century*. Manchester: Manchester University Press.

Lewis, J. (2001), *The End of Marriage?* Cheltenham: Elgar.

Lister, R., and Lowe, M. (1975), *Equal Pay and How to Get It*. London: National Council for Civil Liberties, March.

Lovenduski, J. (1986), *Women and European Politics: Contemporary Feminism and Public Policy*. Brighton: Wheatsheaf.

Lovenduski, J. (1995), 'An emerging advocate: The Equal Opportunities Commission in Great Britain' in A. Mazur and D. Stetson, *Comparative State Feminism*. London: Sage.

MacDougall, L. (1998), *Westminster Women*. London: Vintage.

Mazey, S. (1989), *Women and the European Community*. London: PNL Press.

Meehan, E. (1985), *Women's Rights at Work: Campaigns and Policy in Britain and the United States*. London: Macmillan.

Meehan, E. (1990), 'British feminism from the 1960s to the 1980s' in H. Smith (ed.), *British Feminism in the 20th Century*. Aldershot: Edward Elgar, pp. 189–204.

Perkins, A. (2003), *Red Queen: The Authorized Biography of Barbara Castle*. London: Macmillan.

Perrigo, S. (1995), 'Gender struggles in the British Labour Party from 1979–1995', *Party Politics*, 1 (3): 407–17.

Potter, A. (1957), 'The equal pay campaign committee: A case-study of a pressure group', *Political Studies*, 5: 49–64.

Rossilli, M. (ed.) (2000), *Gender policies in the European Union*. Bern, New York, Oxford: Peter Lang.

Rowbotham, S. (1999), *A Century of Women: The History of Women in Britain and the United States*. London: Penguin.

Seear, N., Roberts, V., and Brick, J. (1964), *A Career for Women in Industry*. London and Edinburgh: Oliver and Boyd.

Sloane, P. J., and Sibert, W. S. (1980), 'Low pay amongst women – The facts' in Peter Sloane (ed), *Women and Low Pay*, London: Macmillan.

Squires, J., and Wickham-Jones, M. (2002), 'Mainstreaming in Westminster and Whitehall: From Labour's Ministry for Women to the Women and Equality Unit', in K. Ross (ed.), *Women, Politics, and Change*. Oxford: Oxford University Press, pp. 57–71.

Stephenson, M. (1998), *The Glass Trapdoor: Women, Politics and the Media during the 1997 General Election*. London: Fawcett Society.

Taylor, R. (2003), *Britain's World of Work: Myths and Realities*. Swindon: Economic and Social Research Council.

Thane, P. (2001), 'What difference did the vote make?', in A. Vickery (ed.), *Women, Privilege and Power: British Politics, 1750 to the Present*. Berkeley: Stanford University Press.

Watson, S. (1992), 'Femocractic feminisms', in M. Savage and A. Witz (eds), *Gender and Bureaucracy*. Oxford: Blackwell, pp. 186–207.

Wilson, D. (2005), 'A new look at the affluent worker: The good working mother in post-war Britain', *Twentieth Century British History*. Oxford: Oxford University Press, 17 (2).

Winnicott, D. (1964), *The Child, the Family, and the Outside World*. London: Penguin.

Zabalza, A., and Tzannatos Z. (1985), *Women and Equal Pay: The Effects of Legislation on Female Employment and Wages in Britain*. Cambridge: Cambridge University Press.

Zweiniger-Bargielowska, I. (1996), 'Explaining the gender gap: the Conservative Party and the women's vote 1945–1964', in M. Francis and I. Zweiniger-Bargielowska (eds), *The Conservatives and British Society, 1880–1990*. Cardiff: University of Wales Press.

UNPUBLISHED SOURCES

Freeguard, J. (2004), 'It's time for the women of the 1950s to stand up and be counted'. University of Sussex unpublished D.Phil thesis.

Sutherland, D. (2000), 'Peeresses, parliament and prejudice: The admission of women to the House of Lords'. University of Cambridge unpublished PhD thesis.

ONLINE SOURCES

British Social Attitudes online, www.britsocat.com/Body.aspx?control=BritSocAt19Home. Accessed July 2009.

Centre for Contemporary British History (2001), 'The making of the 1967 Abortion Act', witness seminar, University of London, http://icbh.ac.uk. Accessed July 2009.

Evans, T., 'Is it futile to try to get non-resident fathers to maintain their children?', History & Policy, www.historyandpolicy.org/archive/policy-paper-48.html. Accessed July 2009.

Nutt, T., 'The Child Support Agency and the Old Poor Law', History & Policy, www. historyandpolicy.org/archive/policy-paper-47.html. Accessed July 2009.

Scottish Executive, *Equality Strategy: Working Together For Equality*, www.scotland.gov.uk/library3/social/wtem-02.asp. Accessed July 2009.

CHAPTER 6: GENDER IDENTITY AND SEXUAL ORIENTATION

PUBLISHED SOURCES

Newspapers and periodicals

Adrian, Hester A., Diana (Lady) Albemarle, Enid Bagnold, Anne Barnes, Alice Bragg, Helen Cohen, Helen De Freitas, Judith Hubback, Peggy Jay, Iris Murdoch, Elizabeth Pakenham, Myfanwy Piper, Ursula Ridley, Teresa Rothschild, Cecil Woodham-Smith, 'Homosexual Acts', *The Times*, 19 April 1958.

Berridge, V. (1996), 'Crisis what crisis?', *Health Service Journal*, 8 August, 20–1.

Guardian, 20 December 2006.

Guardian, 7 January 2009.

'Indiscipline over Aids', *The Times*, 19 February 1985.

'Lack of action on Wolfenden Report', *The Times*, 3 September 1958.

'Life blood, or death?', *The Times*, 21 November 1984.

'The Problem of homosexuality – Report by clergy and doctors', *The Times*, 26 February 1954.

Society Guardian, 10 January 2006.

Tatchell, 'Fear of Aids', *The Times*, 2 March 1985.

'Vice', *The Times*, 26 November 1958.

Official publications

Bromley, C. *et al.* (2007), *Attitudes to Discrimination in Scotland: 2006*, Edinburgh: Scottish Government Social Research.

Equality and Human Rights Commission *(2008), Who Do You See? Living Together in Wales*. London: Equality and Human Rights Commission.

UK Office for National Statistics (2006), *Sexual Orientation and the 2011 Census – Background Information*. London: ONS.

Whittle, S., *et al.* (2007), *Engendered Penalties: Transgender and Transsexual People's Experiences of Inequality and Discrimination*, London: Department of Communities and Local Government.

Books, articles, reports

Cook, H. (2004), *The Long Sexual Revolution: English Women, Sex and Contraception 1800–1975*. Oxford: Oxford University Press.

Cook, M. (ed.) (2007), *A Gay History of Britain: Love and Sex Between Men since the Middle Ages*. Westport, Connecticut; Greenwood.

Davidson R., and Davis, G. (2004), 'A field for private members: The Wolfenden Committee and Scottish homosexual law reform, 1950–67', *Twentieth Century British History*, 5 (2).

Davidson R., and Davis, G. (2006), 'Sexuality and the state: The campaign for Scottish homosexual law reform, 1967–80', *Contemporary British History*, 20 (4), December.

Doan, L. (2001), *Fashioning Sapphism: The Origins of a Modern English Lesbian Culture*. New York: Columbia University Press.

England, L. (1950), 'A British sex survey', *The International Journal of Sexology*, iii, (3), February.

Ferguson, S. M., and Fitzgerald, H. (1954), *History of the Second World War: Studies in the Social Services*. London: HMSO and Longmans.

Hall. L. A. (2005), 'Sexuality', in P. Addison and H. Jones (eds), *A Companion to Contemporary Britain, 1939–2000*. Oxford: Blackwell.

Holden, A. (2005), *Makers and Manners: Politics and Morality in Post-war Britain*. London: Politico's.

Jivan, A. (1997), *It's Not Unusual: A History of Gay and Lesbian Britain in the Twentieth Century*. London: Michael O'Mara/BBC.

Johnson, A. M., *et al.* (2001), 'Sexual behaviour in Britain: Partnerships, practices and HIV risk behaviours', *The Lancet*, 1 December, 358.
King, D. (1993), *The Transvestite and the Transsexual: Public Categories and Private Identities*, Aldershot: Avebury.
Stonewall (2007), *Living Together: British Attitudes to Lesbian and Gay People*. London: Stonewall.
University of Essex Library (1988), *Mass Observation in the 1980s, Spring Directive 1987, AIDS*. Brighton: University of Sussex, Mass Observation Archive.
McLaren, A. (1999), *Twentieth Century Sexuality: A History*. London: Blackwell.
Oram, A. (2005), 'Cross-dressing and transgender', in H. Cocks and M. Houlbrook (eds), *Advances in the Modern History of Sexuality*. London: Palgrave.
Pearce, J. (1973), 'Mass media and the homosexual', in Cohen and Young (eds), *The Manufacture of News: Social Problems, Deviance, and the Mass Media*. London: Constable.
Randell, J. (1959), 'Transvestitism and trans-sexualism – a study of 50 cases', *British Medical Journal*, 26 December, 148–52.
Self, H. (2003), *Prostitution, Women and the Misuse of the Law: The Fallen Daughters of Eve*. London: Routledge.
Stanley, L. (1995), *Sex Surveyed, 1949–94: From Mass Observation's 'Little Kinsey' to the National Survey and the Hite Reports*. London: Taylor and Francis.
Titmuss, R. (1950), *History of the Second World War, Problems of Social Policy*. London: HMSO and Longmans.
Vicinus, M. (2004), *Intimate Friends: Women Who Loved Women*. Chicago: University of Chicago Press.
Waites, M. (2005), *The Age of Consent: Young People, Sexuality and Citizenship*. London: Palgrave.
Weeks, J. (1981), *Sex, Politics and Society: The Regulation of Sexuality since 1800*. Harlow: Longman.
Weeks, J. (1990), *Coming Out: Homosexual Politics in Britain from the Nineteenth Century to the Present*. London: Quartet.

UNPUBLISHED SOURCES

Wharton, S. (1993), 'Glad to be gay? Journalistic portrayal of homosexuality in Britain and France'. Paper delivered to the Cambridge Social Stratification Seminar, 16 September.
Whittle, S. (2006), 'Experiencing the law: From victim to dependent – the experience of transphobic victimhood'. Paper given to the conference Experiencing the Law, Institute of Advanced Legal Studies, University of London, 1 December.

ONLINE SOURCES

Alice L100, 'Some of the History of the Beaumont Society', www.beaumontsociety.org.uk/history.html. Accessed July 2009.
'Archbishop warns of gay rights backlash', Telegraph online, 29 November 2006, www.telegraph.co.uk/news/uknews/1535392/Archbishop-warns-of-gay-rights-backlash.html. Accessed July 2009.
'Haire, Norman (1892–1952)', in *Australian Dictionary of Biography – Online Edition*, www.adb.online.anu.edu.au/biogs/A140402b.htm. Accessed July 2009.
O'Sullivan, S. (2001), in V. Preston (ed.), 'Section 28 and the revival of gay, lesbian and queer politics in Britain', witness seminar at University of London: Centre for Contemporary British History, Institute of Historical Research, www.ccbh.ac.uk/witness_section28_index.php. Accessed July 2009.
'Stephen Whittle – PFC campaigner', Press for Change, www.pfc.org.uk/node/31. Accessed July 2009.

Terence Higgins Trust, www.tht.org.uk/informationresources/factsandstatistics. Accessed
    July 2009-07-10.
Weeks, J. (2007), 'Wolfenden and beyond: The remaking of homosexual history',
    February, www.historyandpolicy.org/papers/policy-paper-51.html. Accessed July
    2009.

CHAPTER 7: DISABILITY

PUBLISHED SOURCES

Newspapers and periodicals

Guardian, 14 September 2006.
Guardian, 19 January 2009.

Official publications

Better Services for the Mentally Ill (1975), London: Department of Health and Social
    Services.
Disabled Adults Living in Private Households (1988), London: UK Office of Population,
    Censuses and Surveys.
Dutt, R., and Ferns, P. (1998), *Letting Through the Light. A Training Pack of Black People and
    Mental Health*. London: Department of Health.
In-patient Statistics (1975), London: Department of Health and Social Security.
Prime Minister's Strategy Unit (2004), *Improving the Life Chances of Disabled People: Final
    Report*. London: Cabinet Office.
Warnock Report (1978), *Special Educational Needs: Report of the Committee of Enquiry into
    the Education of Handicapped Children and Young People*. London: HMSO.

Books, periodicals, reports

Abel-Smith, B., and Townsend, P. (1965), *'The Poor and the Poorest. A New Analysis of the
    Ministry of Labour's Family Surveys of 1953–54 and 1960*, Occasional Papers on Social
    Administration, No. 17. London: G Bell and Sons.
Alaszewski, A. (1983), 'The development of policy for the mentally handicapped since the
    Second World War: An overview', *Oxford Review of Education*, 9 (3).
Barnes, C. (1991), *Disabled People in Britain and Discrimination: A Case for
    Anti-discrimination Legislation*. London: Hurst and Co.
Bracken, P. (1986), 'Mental health and ethnicity: The Irish dimension', *British Journal of
    Psychiatry*, 172.
Browne, D. (1997), *Black People and Sectioning*. London: Little Rock Publishing.
Cochrane, R., and Bal, S. S. 'Mental health admission rates for immigrants to England', *Social
    Psychiatry*. London: Sage, 24: 2–11.
Cochrane, R., and Sashideran, S. (n.d.), *Mental Health and Ethnic Minorities: A Review of the
    Literature and Implications for Services*. Birmingham: University of Birmingham, School
    of Psychology.
Hilton, M., Crowson, N., and McKay, J. (eds) (2009), *NGOs in Contemporary Britain:
    Non-state Actors in Society and Politics since 1945*. London: Palgrave.
Hurt, J. S. (1988), *Outside the Mainstream: A History of Special Education*. London: Batsford.
Moodley, P. (1993), 'Setting up services for ethnic minorities', in D. Bhugra and J. Leff (eds),
    Principles of Social Psychiatry. Oxford: Blackwell, pp.490–501.
Nazroo, J. (2002), *Ethnicity, Class and Health*. London: Policy Studies Institute.
Nazroo, J., and King, M. (1997), 'Psychosis-symptoms and estimated rates', in K. Sproston
    and J. Nazroo (eds), *Ethnic Minority Psychiatric Illness Rates in the Community*. London:
    National Centre for Social Research, TSO.

Oliver, M. (1990), 'Changing the social relations of research production?', *Disability, Handicap and Society*, 7 (2): 101–13.

Outside But Not Inside . . . Yet! Leaving Hospital and Living in the Community: An Evaluation by People with Learning Difficulties (1994). London: People First.

Raphael, W., and Peers, V. (1972), *Psychiatric Hospitals Viewed by their Patients*. London: Kings Fund.

Smaje, C. (1995), *Race and Ethnicity: Making Sense of the Evidence*. London: King's Fund.

Ward, L. (1997), 'Funding for change: Translating emancipatory disability research from theory to practice', in C. Barnes and G. Mercer (eds), *Doing Disability Research*. Leeds: The Disability Press.

Willmot, J. (1996), 'Poor recognition, poorer services for Black women', *Openmind*, September–October. London: National Association for Mental Health, p. 81.

Wilson, M., and Francis, J. (1997), *Raised Voices*. London: Mind.

Zarb, G., and Nadash, P. (1994), *Cashing In on Independence: Comparing the Costs and Benefits of Cash and Services*. London: British Council of Organizations of Disabled People.

ONLINE SOURCES

Fry, S., *The Secret Life of the Manic Depressive*, www.bbc.co.uk/health/tv_and_radio/secretlife_index.shtml. Accessed July 2009.

'Alison Lapper pregnant takes plinth position in Trafalgar Square' www.culture24.org.uk/art/sculpture/art30597 Accessed July 2009.

'Statistics 3: Race, culture and mental health', Mind, www.mind.org.uk/Information/Factsheets/Statistics/Statistics+3.htm. Accessed July 2009.

Index

Page numbers in **bold** refer to figures and tables.